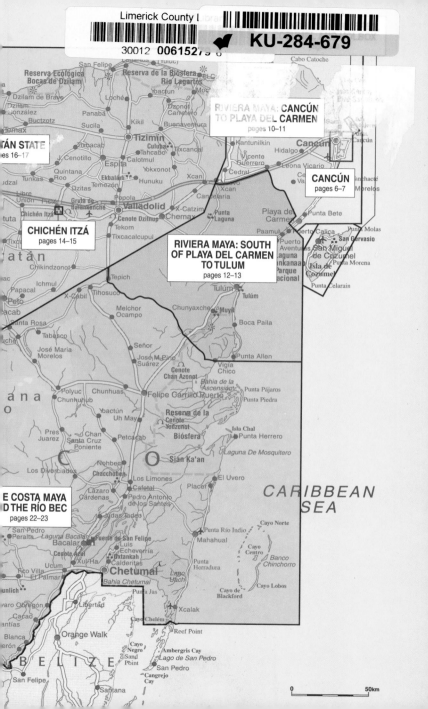

Cabo Catoche

San Felipe

Reserva Ecológica
Bocas de Dzilam

Reserva de la Biósfera
Río Lagartos

Yoactun

Dzilam de Bravo

Loché

Dzonot
Carretero

Dzilam
González

Panabá

Buctzotz

Sucila

Kikil

Buenaventura

Tizimín

**RIVIERA MAYA: CANCÚN
TO PLAYA DEL CARMEN**
pages 10–11

ÁN STATE
es 16–17

Ixcacab

Culuba

Tixcancal

Kantunilkin

Tahcabo

Cancún

J. Cenotillo

Espita

Calotmul

Yokxonot

Vicente
Guerrero

Hidalgo

Quintana
Roo

Tunkas

Ekbalam

Hunuku

Xcan

Cedral

Leona Vicario

CANCÚN
pages 6–7

anchaces

dzal

Temozón

Popola

Xcan

Candelaria

Morelos

Libre
Union

Pisté

Dzitas

Gruta de
Balankanché

Valladolid

X-Catzim

Chemax

Playa del
Carmen

Punta Bete

Punta Molas

Chichén Itzá

Cenote Dzitnup

Tekom

Punta
Laguna

Paamul

Puerto Calica

San Gervasio

tuta

CHICHÉN ITZÁ
pages 14–15

Tixcacalcupul

**RIVIERA MAYA: SOUTH
OF PLAYA DEL CARMEN
TO TULUM**
pages 12–13

Puerto
Aventuras

San Miguel
de Cozumel

Tix

atán

Chikindzonot

Tepich

Laguna
Yalahau
Parque
Nacional

Isla de
Cozumel

Punta Morena

ac

Ichmul

Tulúm

Punta Celarain

Papacal

X-Cabil

Tihosuco

Chunyaxche

Muyil

Peto

Melchor
Ocampo

Tulúm

acab

Santa Rosa

Boca Paila

che

Tabasco

José Maria
Morelos

Señor

José M. Pino
Suárez

Punta Allen

Cenote
Chan Azonot

Vigía
Chico

ána

Polyuc

Chunhuas

Felipe Carrillo Puerto

Bahía de la
Ascensión

Punta Pájaros

o

Chunhunub

Ybactún

Punta Piedra

Pres
Juarez

Chan
Santa Cruz
Poniente

Uh May

Petcacab

Reserva de la

Cenote
Vozuzonot

Isla Chal

Los Divorciados

Nohbec

Biósfera

Punta Herrero

Chacchoben

Sián Ka'an

Laguna de Mosquitero

Los Limones

C O

Lázaro
Cárdenas

Cafetal

Placer

El Uvero

**CARIBBEAN
SEA**

**E COSTA MAYA
D THE RÍO BEC**
pages 22–23

Pedro Antonio
de los Santos

Judas Tadeo

San Pedro

Peralta

Laguna Bacalar

Puente de San Felipe

Punta Río Indio

Cayo Norte

Bacalar

Luis
Echeverría

Mahahual

Cayo
Centro

Cenote Azul

Ixtankah

Banco
Chinchorro

co Villa

Ucum

Xul-Ha

Calderitas

Punta
Herradura

El Palmar

Chetumal

Lago
Uach

unlich

Bahía Chetumal

Cayo Lobos

aro Obregón

Libertad

Punta Jas

Cayo de
Blackford

Cacao

antías

Xcalak

Blanca
erón

Orange Walk

Cayo
Negro

Cayo Chelém

Reef Point

San Felipe

Sand
Point

Ambergris Cay
Lago de San Pedro

Santana

Cangrejo
Cay

San Pedro

B E L I Z E

0   50km

INSIGHT GUIDES

CANCÚN
& THE YUCATÁN
smart guide

Discovery
CHANNEL

APA PUBLICATIONS
Part of the Langenscheidt Publishing Group

Areas

Contents

A–Z

Below: easygoing warmth is
a Yucatecan trademark.

Left: one of the world's most dazzling beachscapes, at Tulum.

Atlas

Below: traditional handicrafts in Izamal's Centro Cultural.

Cancún and the Yucatán

This is a place that conjures up contradictory images: Cancún and the Riviera Maya, one of the great, good-time tourist hubs, and a much older Yucatán of Mayan relics, Spanish colonial towns and sleepy villages. The two actually intersect, which is part of the Yucatán's fascination.

Cancún and the Yucatán Facts and Figures

Population: **3.7 million**
Population by state: **Yucatán 1.82 million;**
Quintana Roo 1.13 million; Campeche 0.75 million
Area: **139,426 sq km**
Area by state: **Campeche 50,812 sq km; Quintana**
Roo 50,212 sq km; Yucatán 38,402 sq km
Average number of visitors to Cancún,
Cozumel, Isla Mujeres and the Riviera Maya:
5.7 million per year
Number of hotel rooms in Cancún, Cozumel,
Isla Mujeres and the Riviera Maya: **59,000**
Percentage of Mayan-speakers: **Yucatán 43 percent;**
Quintana Roo 29 percent; Campeche 15 percent

A Unique Setting

It's not always obvious just how special a place the Yucatán is. Most of it is very flat, and seen from a car window it can look to a new arrival just like an endless expanse of scrub jungle – *selva baja*. Then, people who like maps might notice that it doesn't have a single river above Champotón on the west coast and the Belize border on the east. This unusual phenomenon is due to the fact that the whole peninsula is made up of one huge slab of limestone, which does not retain surface water. Instead, water is below ground – sometimes far below – in a vast web of caves and holes in the rock called *cenotes*, amongst which are the largest underwater caverns on earth.

There is no other landscape like this in the world, and it hosts a special mix of wildlife – elusive, often nocturnal animals, millions of birds, breeding sea turtles drawn by spectacularly soft beaches. The Yucatán's underground labyrinth is also inseparable from the rich undersea environment around its coasts, in an intricate demonstration of ecological interdependence. Nutrients from the caves are filtered out through mangrove lagoons to feed the stunning coral reefs that line the entire Caribbean coast.

From the Maya to Colonial Yucatán

This harsh landscape was an unlikely location for an ancient civilization, and yet this was where the Maya developed the most sophisticated culture in pre-Hispanic America. It went far beyond a few very famous cities like Chichén Itzá or Uxmal: Mayan sites – which are anything but uniform – are found all over the peninsula, with strings of ancient cities even in now-remote areas like the Río Bec *(see p.88)*. Classic Maya civilization had a catastrophic "collapse" in AD 800–950, but city-building revived in northern Yucatán from about 1200.

Then the Spaniards arrived, bringing Catholicism, and building Franciscan monasteries and elegant cities such as Mérida and Campeche. This new aristocratic colonial society did not eliminate the Maya; in fact the complaint was made that instead of the natives learning Spanish, in the countryside Spaniards were obliged to learn Maya to get along.

Below: the great Franciscan monastery at Izamal.

Yucatecan Essence

A distinct character and a sense of separateness – in food, music, dress, the blend of Maya and Hispanic cultures, the tone of village life – are essential to the Yucatán. After independence – as one entity, before its split into three states – it only grudgingly became part of Mexico. There was no real road link with the rest of the country until the 1940s, and politicians from Mexico City came by boat. The peninsula – above Yucatán state – has kept a feeling of being an island, in its own special world.

Cancún and its New Ways

Into this world there came a brash newcomer in 1970, when Mexico's government launched its all-new Caribbean resort, Cancún, to take advantage of the area's fabulous reefs and beaches. From small beginnings Cancún and the Riviera Maya, the 130km stretch down to Tulum, have burst forth beyond all expectations. They have provided a whole new economic outlet for the Yucatán's country people. The options for visitors along the beaches run from giant, multi-bed resorts to luxury retreats and palm-roofed *cabañas* beneath the trees.

Cancún is now both a glittering fun-capital and a modern city, while Riviera development goes on at an unstoppable pace. The Yucatán has become a world destination – but, even next to the biggest resort, its unique, stubborn charms are never far away.

Highlights

▲ The **Caribbean beaches** of the Riviera Maya are among the world's best, with tranquil waters and deliciously soft sand that's always cool underfoot even when the sun is at its hottest.

▲ Superb **diving and snorkeling**, at sea or in caves and caverns.
▶ **Yucatecan food** is succulent, distinctive, and enormously varied.

▲ **Mérida** and the Yucatán's other Spanish colonial cities and towns have a special charm and flavor.

▲ **Mayan ruins**, spread across the whole peninsula, let us see inside a complex civilization.
▶ The **natural world**: from the flamingos of the mangrove lagoons to jaguars in the rainforest.

Cancún

It's a wonder nobody discovered it earlier: Cancún Island has one of the most dazzling beaches anywhere in the world, a spectacular strip of soft white sand stretching for over 23km. And yet, before 1970 there was nothing here except a few lonely fishing lodges. Since then, Cancún has mushroomed and mushroomed again to become the biggest resort on the Caribbean. People tend to divide into Cancún-haters and Cancún-lovers: some find its size, glitz, whoop-and-holler nightlife and all-round newness just too much, and get through the airport as fast as they can on their way to other parts of the Yucatán; others just think it's fabulous.

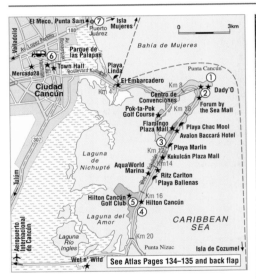

See Atlas Pages 134–135 and back flap

Above: El Rey.

An All-New City

As the story goes, in the late 1960s Mexican politicians and financiers were casting around for a location in which to create a Caribbean resort, and came upon Cancún. It's not clear they knew quite what they were starting. Cancún has proved unstoppable: even faced with disasters – above all Hurricane Wilma in 2005 – it has developed a habit of bouncing back, and just rebuilds bigger than ever.

To go with its huge beach, Cancún meets the needs of tourism on a big scale, with extra-sized hotels, malls, nightclubs, and restaurants. This scale gives the city its energy and character.

The Hotel Zone

Cancún has two sides. Cancún Island – better known as the **Hotel Zone**, or just the beach – is a long sandbar, in the form of a seven on the map. Its north and east sides have the beaches and the

The First Cancún

Cancún may seem completely new, but it is the successor to a Mayan community that flourished from around 1200 AD up to the Spanish Conquest, one of a string of coastal towns along a rich trade route between Honduras and central Mexico. Its ruins are at **El Rey**, at km 17 on Boulevard Kukulcán. Modest by comparison with the great Mayan cities, it still gives a vivid impression of a small Mayan town, with its main street and plaza that once served as a market. When explorer John Lloyd Stephens sailed here in 1842, however, the island was empty except for a few fishermen stopping over from the mainland.

Left: a Palapa provides chade on Cancún Beach.

The Hotel Zone (Cancún Island) has one main avenue for the whole of its length, **Boulevard Kukulcán**. Addresses along it are identified by kilometer markers, like km 4, km 9.5.

town'). From a dormitory for the Hotel Zone's workers it has developed into a real city, and now even has its own soccer team.

It doesn't have the quiet graciousness of Mérida or Campeche, but it has nice mid-price hotels, great restaurants and relaxing corners. The center of town is the main stretch of **Avenida Tulum** ⑥, with the town hall and the bus station. Just off it is **Parque de las Palapas**, a charming square. Nearby are **Avenida Yaxchilán**, for local restaurants and nightlife, and **Mercado 28**, the main market.

To the north are **Puerto Juárez** ⑦, which as the Isla Mujeres ferry dock existed before the rest of Cancún, the Isla car ferry at **Punta Sam**, and a Mayan ruin at **El Meco**. This area is also a new tourism target, with huge schemes under way at **Playa Mujeres**.
SEE ALSO MAYAN RUINS AND RELICS, P.88; SHOPPING, P.114.

Caribbean; to the west is the Nichupté lagoon. Cancún's beaches underwent massive restoration after Wilma, which, if not without problems, has been remarkably effective.

Hotels and attractions are spread along the beach, with various clusters of activity. Hub of the Cancún strip is the bend of the seven, near **Punta Cancún** ① and the **Convention Center**, with a vista dominated by the Vegas-meets-Versailles creations of the Riu hotel corporation. Here, too, are big nightclubs like **Dady'O** and the **Coco Bongo** ②, at their most booming for that Cancún institution, Spring Break. Getting up and down the strip often involves using taxis and the (excellent) buses, but here clubs and bars are within walking distance.

Near km 12 is shopping central, with massive malls in **Flamingo Plaza**, **Kukulcán**

Plaza and **La Isla** ③. Further south is one of Cancún's most popular beaches at **Playa Delfines** ④, very near the Mayan ruins of **El Rey** ⑤.
SEE ALSO BARS AND NIGHTLIFE, P.30; BEACHES, P.36; CHILDREN, P.44; HOTELS, P.76; MAYAN RUINS AND RELICS, P.88; SHOPPING, P.114.

Ciudad Cancún

For a change of style, head for the ever-expanding city on the mainland (or 'Down-

Below: quiet it ain't: the Cancún strip at night.

Islands: Isla Mujeres, Cozumel, and Holbox

The three islands off Mexico's Caribbean coast offer a complete contrast in atmosphere. Despite its closeness to Cancún, Isla Mujeres retains a laid-back, beach-bum feel, and offers great diving offshore. Cozumel, discovered for tourism long before the mainland, has the most famous diving reefs of all, and is a favorite with families and an ever-growing cruise destination. Tiny, remote Holbox, meanwhile, at the end of a long forest road, can give you a total escape from the everyday world.

Isla Mujeres

Bahía de Mujeres — Faro Lighthouse — Punta Sam, Punta Juárez, Cancún — Sac Bajo — Salina Grande — Laguna Makax — Turtle Sanctuary — Playa Pescador — Playa Lancheros — Playa Indios — Playa Garrafón — Punta Sur — 0 1km

Isla Mujeres

This was the site of the first Spanish landfall in Mexico in 1517, when Hernández de Córdoba's men found Mayan figures of the goddess Ixchel, which led them to call it 'Island of Women.' They didn't stay, and for 350 years the island was scarcely inhabited except for the odd pirate (*see right*). It was finally settled by a mixed bunch from Yucatán, Cuba, and around the Caribbean. They built a very Caribbean little town, with clapboard houses in candy-box colors that are an Isla characteristic.

Development has gained pace, but **Isla Town** ① has kept its tiny, sandy streets, full of dive shops and souvenir stands, and its small-town air. Hotels run from luxury retreats to backpacker hostels. The place to spend much of the day is **Playa Norte** ②, even if lately it has been hit by (hopefully temporary) beach erosion.

Isla's main road runs down to its one crossroads, by a park on the one-time estate of an ex-slave trader, **Hacienda**

Pirate Days
Isla Mujeres's sheltered lagoon made it a favorite hiding place for pirates, from Henry Morgan in the 1660s to the Louisiana brothers Jean and Pierre Lafitte in the 1820s. In the 1840s Cozumel's only residents were an ex-pirate and his family, before refugees arrived from the mainland, fleeing Yucatán's Caste War (*see also History, p.75*).

Mundaca ③. A turn right takes you up beside the inlet of **Laguna Makax**. The main road runs south to **Garrafón** snorkel park and **Punta Sur** ④, with superb views.

Isla's sheltered west side, facing Cancún, has the best beaches; the ocean side is far more rugged and windblown. Isla is a first-rate diving center, for beginners and experienced divers, with a main reef at **Manchones** that's especially rich in wrecks.

SEE ALSO DIVING, SNORKELING, AND WATERSPORTS, P.52.

Below: keeping track of what's going on in Isla town.

Left: the Holbox view.

Cozumel's real jewels are not on shore but in the sea around it, in renowned coral reefs such as **Palancar** ④. Even non-divers can see a spectacular range of marine life, armed only with a snorkel.
SEE ALSO DIVING, SNORKELING, AND WATERSPORTS, P.53; MAYAN RUINS AND RELICS, P.88

Holbox

At the meeting point of the Gulf of Mexico and the Caribbean, Holbox is a tiny strip of an island with just one **village** ① – where golf carts are the main traffic – and utterly seductive little hotels.

It's a magical place for total relaxation, and for fishing, birdwatching or snorkeling at **Isla de Pájaros** ②. A unique draw is the gathering of **whale sharks** at **Cabo Catoche** ③ from June to September.
SEE ALSO DIVING, SNORKELING, AND WATERSPORTS, P.54; TOURS AND GUIDES, P.120; WILDLIFE AND NATURE, P.127

Below: snorkeling off Cozumel is addictive.

Cozumel

Mexico's largest island was a divers' secret until 1961, when Jacques Cousteau filmed the glories of the Cozumel reefs. More and more divers came in his wake, and other tourists soon followed.

For details of island ferries, *see also Transportation, p.125.*

Cozumel and its capital **San Miguel** ① are far less hectic than Cancún, with a safe, cozy feel. San Miguel is also one of the world's busiest cruise ports, and its waterfront **Malecón** (Avenida R. Melgar) is lined with handicraft and jewelry stores, where cruise passengers can buy tax-free.

Cozumel was once a Mayan pilgrimage center, with a shrine to Ixchel, goddess of fertility and weaving. The ruins of **San Gervasio** ② are half-way across the island.

Cozumel's east shore is rocky and impressively empty. Coziness returns on the west coast, with beach clubs and **Chankanaab** ③ snorkel park leading back to San Miguel.

9

Riviera Maya: Cancún to Playa del Carmen

Not long ago Cancún and Cozumel had northeast Yucatán to themselves, and anyone who wandered down this coast found miles of empty, palm-lined beaches. Since around 1998, though, when the name 'Riviera Maya' was dreamed up, it has taken off with a pace that leaves even Cancún behind, as resorts large and small lay claim to those same beaches. Interrupting them are two very contrasting towns: remarkably low-key Puerto Morelos, and the fastest-growing, hippest spot on the coast, Playa del Carmen.

Above: Puerto Morelos has its own special style.

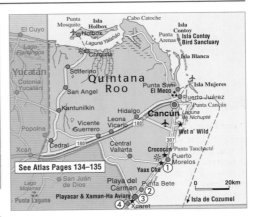

See Atlas Pages 134–135

On the Road

Highway 307 – now a four-lane highway all the way from Cancún to Akumal, 2–3km inland – leads down to the Riviera Maya. Elaborate fantasy gateways announce the entrances to big resorts. Some turnings, though, lead to discreet condo developments, and there are still a few quiet, rustic spots – left behind, so far, in the rush to build.

Puerto Morelos ①

It can be hard to credit Puerto Morelos still exists. Turn off the highway (where the buses stop; local taxis will take you from there) and after 2km you emerge onto an unfussy small-town plaza by the beach, often with kids playing. It still looks like a fishing village, with real fishermen. It has kept its friendly tranquility thanks to an alliance of locals and the many foreign residents, who have resisted pressures for big-scale development here, despite the giants gathering around them.

Around the plaza are **Alma Libre** English-language bookstore, and great restaurants like **Los Pelícanos**, with an irresistible beach terrace. Puerto Morelos – which pre-1970 was actually the biggest town on this coast – also has a working harbor. Offshore is one of the richest coral reefs

Around Puerto Morelos are more natural attractions. The **Crococún** 'crocodile zoo' is to the north, while to the south is a botanical garden, the **Yaax Ché**. Inland there are **cenotes** that have recently been opened to visitors. *See also Caves and Cenotes, p.40; Children, p.46; Wildlife and Nature, p.127.*

on this side of the Cozumel channel, now protected as a national park. It's close to the beach, and so is wonderful for snorkelling as well as diving. SEE ALSO BEACHES, P.37; DIVING, SNORKELING, AND WATERSPORTS, P.54; RESTAURANTS, CAFÉS, AND CANTINAS, P.108; SHOPPING, P.116

Left: the beachfront at Playa del Carmen.

hotels and hip clubs. If Cancún is the capital of the loud good time, Playa has a far greater sense of cool. In its rocket-growth, though, traces of its former selves have been left behind, so you can find boho little cafés and cabañas – and excellent diving operators – in among the style dens.

Guests at hotels not right on the beach mainly head for **Mamita's Beach**, on the north side of town. South of the main plaza and Cozumel ferry is the **Playacar** development, with 12 all-inclusives, a golf course, and **Xaman-Ha** aviary.
SEE ALSO ALL INCLUSIVES, P.29; BARS AND NIGHTLIFE, P.33–5; BEACHES, P.38; DIVING, SNORKELING, AND WATERSPORTS, P.54; HOTELS, P.79; RESTAURANTS, CAFÉS, CANTINAS, P.107; WILDLIFE AND NATURE, P.127.

Punta Bete ②

Some 24km further south, a turn leads to an arc of exquisite beaches. They're enjoyed by resorts like **Tides Riviera Maya** luxury spa (now seen first on road signs), but also here are some simple restaurants and beach cabañas.
SEE ALSO BEACHES, P.37; PAMPERING, P.103.

Playa del Carmen ③

Playa del Carmen is a phenomenon. A tiny village in the early 1980s, its population has grown by at least 500 percent, and now passes 100,000. So fast is the pace of growth here, it can change identity every couple of years. A backpacker hangout not long ago, it's now exploding with luxury condos.

Playa (as it's often called) long sold itself as the laid-back alternative to Cancún; today it's more a case of a different style. Cancún has its car-sized strip, but Playa's main artery is 5th Avenue (**Quinta Avenida** or **la Quinta**), a long pedestrian promenade, making it easier to meet people. Among the restaurants and shops strung along it are some very sleek boutique

Xcaret ④

Just south of Playa is one of the Riviera's all-time favourite attractions, the 'eco-theme park' of Xcaret. With a snorkel river, zoo, beach, live show, the remains of the Mayan city of **Polé**, and extraordinary butterfly garden, this very well-arranged immersion in tropical nature is a huge hit with kids, and never fails to impress.
SEE ALSO CHILDREN, P.46; MAYAN RUINS AND RELICS, P.89

There are frequent bus services up and down Highway 307, and taxis from Cancún, Puerto Morelos, Playa or Tulum will also take you anywhere on the Riviera – but agree the fare first. *See also Transportation, p.124.*

Below: strolling the Quinta Avenida at night.

Riviera Maya: South of Playa del Carmen to Tulum

The beaches of the Riviera's southern stretch are even finer than those to the north: longer, whiter, more arching, with broader skyscapes. They are breeding-places for turtles, and face superb coral reefs – as well as hosting an ever-growing squad of all-inclusive resorts. Nearby are the ancient Mayan city of Cobá, and the world's best cave-diving locations. The Riviera ends spectacularly at Tulum, with a Mayan ruin on a cliff, and captivating beach cabañas leading down to the vast empty spaces of the Sian Ka'an reserve.

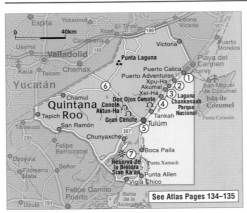

See Atlas Pages 134–135

Xpu-Ha and Akumal

The bays of **Xpu-Ha** are some of the Riviera's great beauties. All-inclusives have now taken over most of them, but three of the access roads still lead to low-key bars and hotels.

Akumal ③ is (mostly) another new-minted holiday town, but feels more relaxed, more like a real community, than Puerto Aventuras, with modest-sized condos set along enchanting bays like the famed **Media Luna** (Half-Moon), which leads to a great snorkeling lagoon, **Yal-Ku**. Akumal – 'place of the turtles' in Mayan – has important turtle-breeding beaches, and is another prime diving spot.
SEE ALSO BEACHES, P.38; DIVING, SNORKELING, AND WATERSPORTS, P.54; WILDLIFE AND NATURE, P.127

Puerto Calica and Paamul

Below Xcaret is this coast's one industrial installation, **Puerto Calica** ①, a small port first created for shipping stone from a nearby quarry. It now has a car ferry service to Cozumel, and receives occasional cruise-ship visits.

Paamul, 8km south, is a fine bay with the Riviera's largest RV park, and cabañas.

Puerto Aventuras ②

Resort gateways cluster more closely around this purpose-built, Mediterranean-style holiday village, created around an equally all-new yacht marina. As well as resort hotels, Puerto Aventuras has vacation homes, golf, a choice of waterside restaurants, and good diving and fishing facilities, and regularly hosts sport fishing competitions.

Below: space to breathe on Akumal's beaches.

Left: Tulum's superb Castillo.

Tulum's other jewels are its fabulous 11km **beach**, prime home of the palm-roofed beach cabaña (basic to luxurious) and the chance to dive in open sea or explore the cenotes between here and Cobá. Tulum and its still ragged little town are growing fast, but for the most part retain their mellow, laid-back style, a great place for total relaxation.

SEE ALSO CAVES AND CENOTES, P.41; DIVING, SNORKELING, AND WATERSPORTS, P.55; HOTELS, P.80; MAYAN RUINS AND RELICS, P.89

Cobá ⑥

Mayan Tulum was far smaller than Grijalva thought, but 45km inland are the remains of one of the great Mayan cities, at Cobá. Temples and pyramids are scattered through a dense forest, full of birds.

SEE ALSO MAYAN RUINS AND RELICS, P.88

Sian Ka'an ⑦

The Riviera has to end at the **Sian Ka'an Biosphere Reserve**, an immense swathe of mangrove, lagoon and jungle. Tours, run from Tulum, are a must. The beach road runs on, as a dirt track, to the lost-world village of **Punta Allen**.

SEE ALSO TOURS AND GUIDES, P.120; WILDLIFE AND NATURE, P.128

Xel-Ha ④

Signs promising 'snorkel heaven' lead to another major family attraction, Xel-Ha park. Centered on a natural lagoon, it's an enjoyable, kid-friendly introduction to snorkeling. Across the highway are the **Mayan ruins** of Xel-Ha.

The Akumal-Tulum area is the finest in the world for cave-diving, and 3km south is the **Dos Ojos** cave, best visited from **Hidden Worlds** center. Beach-seekers have two fine stops before Tulum, at **Tankah** and **Punta Solimán**.

SEE ALSO BEACHES, P.39; CAVES AND CENOTES, P.41; CHILDREN, P.47; MAYAN RUINS AND RELICS, P.89

Tulum ⑤

The majestic **Castillo** or main pyramid of Mayan Tulum is set on a crag above the beach. In 1518 Spanish explorer Juan de Grijalva reported seeing 'a burg so large Seville would not have appeared larger or better.'

Below: Tulum shopping.

Tulum Layout
Tulum has three parts. The **ruins** are to the north of the town, **Tulum Pueblo**, which runs south from the main cross-roads *(El Crucero)*. From the Crucero a road inland leads to Cobá, another (signposted Boca Paila) runs off 2km to a T-junction with the **beach road**, which begins at the ruins. Cabañas are spread all along the 11km down to Sian Ka'an.

Chichén Itzá

Extraordinary scale is the first thing that hits you as you enter Chichén Itzá, recently declared one of the world's 'new seven wonders' in a global Internet poll. Its temples, ball court and great pyramid, the Castillo de Kukulcán, seem like the creations of a science fiction fantasy movie – plenty of which have taken visual references from Chichén – rising up out of the flat Yucatán. It's a little odd that this should be the best-known Mayan city, for the square-cut style of its most famous buildings is very untypical of Mayan architecture. But, as a first contact with the power and ambition of the ancient Maya, Chichén Itzá is truly awe-inspiring.

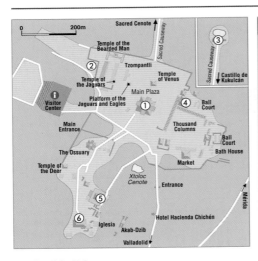

Above: from Las Monjas.

The Chichén Enigma

The origins of Chichén Itzá have been endlessly debated. The severe, flat-walled style of its Castillo and other large buildings seem more like those of central Mexico than other Mayan cities, which prompted the idea they were not Mayan at all, but were built by a migrant people from central Mexico, the Toltecs.

It's now fairly clear that Chichén was a mixed community, of Yucatán Maya and 'Mexicans' like the Toltecs and the Itzaes. It grew to splendor late in the Classic Maya era,

after AD 700. After defeating its older rival Cobá it dominated northern Yucatán from 850–950, before becoming the last great city hit by the collapse of Mayan civilization, around 1000. At its peak, its population was about 40,000.

Castillo and Ball Court

Chichén's 'sacred mountain,' the **Castillo de Kukulcán** ①, is a magnetic presence on the huge plaza. It is a massive representation of the Maya calendar, with 365 steps, and other calculations reflected in the number of panels and

levels. It is also aligned – with amazing precision – with the sun and stars, to create the 'Descent of Kukulcán' on the equinoxes *(see right)*. The feathered monsters lining the stairways represent vision serpents, conduits between this world and that of the gods.

Across the plaza is the great **Ball Court** ②. Again, it is

The site opens daily, 8am–5pm, with a nightly sound and light show, Nov–Mar 7pm, Apr–Oct 8pm. Entry costs around $9 (free for over-60s, under-13s), plus $1 to park. The show is included, but headphones with English commentary are $2.50. Guides can be hired for $50.

Left: stairway to heaven: the Castillo de Kukulcán.

To make the most of Chichén, stay the night before in one of the hotels nearby or in the little town of **Pisté**, and get to the site early. You are no longer allowed to climb the Castillo or any other major structures.

columns in front carved with images of over 200 warriors, priests, and other figures, each an individual portrait. Behind it, the **Thousand Columns** group, row on row of pillars that once supported arched roofs, form a huge quadrangle that was the main market and business space of the city.

The Observatory and Las Monjas

The south part of Chichén is far more Mayan in style than the 'Toltec-Maya' plaza, but was built around the same time. Attention focuses on the fascinating **Observatory** ⑤, with a drum tower with slots for tracking the sun and moon.

The buildings known to the Spaniards as **Las Monjas** ⑥ (the Nunnery) have wildly elaborate Mayan carving, featuring the long-nosed rain god Chac and a riot of other gods, spirits, and animals.

The Equinox

On the spring equinox (March 20 and 21) the afternoon sun picks out the tail of the great serpent flanking the Castillo's main stairway, and gradually moves down to its head, 'bringing it alive.' A similar but fainter effect occurs on the fall equinox, September 22–23. Thousands gather at Chichén on these days, above all in March. *See also Festivals, p.64.*

played – to Chichén Itzá's awesome great well, 60m in diameter. Offerings were thrown into it, as a gateway to *Xibalba*, the underworld, but no solid evidence has ever been found that virgin sacrifices were cast down here too.

The Warriors and the Thousand Columns

On the east side of the plaza, the **Temple of the Warriors** ④ gets its name from the

vastly bigger than the courts of older Mayan cities, and it's thought games were between teams of seven, rather than just two or four players. Reliefs around the court show fearsome images of sacrifice and rebirth, indicating the immense ritual significance of the game.

The Sacred Cenote ③

From the plaza a path leads past the **Tzompantli** or skull platform – where the heads of sacrificial victims were dis-

Below: a walk among the Thousand Columns.

15

Yucatán State

Head west from the newborn Riviera and you find a different world, one with a very clear sense of its own history and culture. Venerable churches preside over the well-shaded squares of gracious Spanish colonial towns. In the countryside there are green lagoons with flamingos and many other kinds of wildlife, placid Mayan villages, and an extraordinary wealth of remains of their ancient ancestors, while below ground lies a magical web of caves and cenote pools. What seduces most, though, is simply the atmosphere: a blend of vibrant tropical colors, easygoing pace, and people with a marvellous mix of friendliness and gentle courtesy.

Valladolid ① and Eastern Yucatán

Founded 425 years before Cancún, in 1545, Valladolid offers an instant immersion in Yucatecan charm. It's the main place to meet up, buy and sell, and generally do business for the east of the state, and centered, in the way of Spanish colonial towns, on its main square or **Parque Principal**, with **San Servacio** cathedral. It's also known for fine embroidery, which is always on sale in the square.

Built on top of an older Mayan town called Zací, Valladolid still has its town cenote (**Cenote Zací**), as well as one of the most imposing early Franciscan monasteries, **San Bernardino Sisal**.

Above: keeping up with local affairs at a market stall.

Just west of town is the village of **Dzitnup**, with two of the Yucatán's absolute mustsees: **Cenotes Dzitnup** and **Samula**, soaring underground caverns that are exquisite for swimming. Valladolid also makes a fine base for visiting

Chichén Itzá *(see p.14–15)*, 42km to the west, and the caves at **Balankanché**.

A road runs straight north from Valladolid to the coast via **Tizimín**, center of Yucatán's cattle country. Some 18km from Valladolid it passes the Mayan ruins of **Ek-Balam**, where excavations carried out only in the last 10 years have revealed remarkable treasures.

The road ends at **Río Lagartos** ②, and a 20km mangrove lagoon that is a breeding ground for flamingos and a host of other birds. Local fishermen provide tours, and there are empty beaches nearby and at the neighboring village of **San Felipe**.

SEE ALSO CAVES AND CENOTES, P.41; CHURCHES, P.48; MAYAN RUINS AND RELICS, P.90; WILDLIFE AND NATURE, P.128

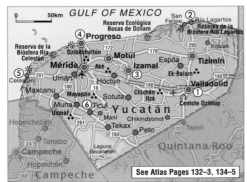

See Atlas Pages 132–3, 134–5

Left: Izamal, the golden city.

restaurants serving up delicious, bargain seafood. On the way back to Mérida is another fascinating Mayan city, **Dzibilchaltún**.

Celestún ⑤ is the state's most-visited natural attraction. The mangrove lagoon broadens into channels that host a huge range of birds – most famously, flamingos. Celestún is also a very laid-back little beach town: stay over after a tour to enjoy fabulous sunsets.
SEE ALSO BEACHES, P.39; WILDLIFE AND NATURE, P.129

Southern Yucatán

The south of the state, leading down to the great Mayan sites around **Uxmal** *(see p.20)*, is a kind of Yucatecan heartland. The road south past the last great Mayan city at **Mayapán** and the first of all the Spanish monasteries at **Maní** has been labelled *Ruta de los Conventos* because of its many colonial churches, but there are fine churches all over the area, as well as caves, swimmable cenotes and charming country towns like **Ticul** ⑥, with their irresistible tricycle-taxi pace.
SEE ALSO CHURCHES, P.49; MAYAN RUINS AND RELICS, P.91

Below: a fine *terno* for a fiesta.

Izamal ③

Dubbed the *ciudad dorada* or 'golden city' for the rich ochre-yellow of its buildings, Izamal is also the gold standard for Yucatán colonial towns. The Franciscans built their headquarters here in the midst of a Mayan town, and nowhere else are Mayan and Hispanic Yucatán so clearly intertwined: three lovely central squares are dominated by the giant monastery of **San Antonio de Padua**, a few streets from the **Kinich Kakmó**, one of several pyramids spread around town. Izamal also produces fascinating handicrafts. Horse-drawn *calesas* (buggies) clip-clop around, and it's great to stop off here for a few days, to soak up a very amiable way of life.

In deep countryside west of Izamal are the ruins of **Aké**, one of the Mayan sites with an entirely unique style.
SEE ALSO CHURCHES, P.48; MAYAN RUINS AND RELICS, P.90; SHOPPING, P.116

Huípiles and Ternos

The embroidered *huípil* dress, in spotless white with vivid flowers around yoke and skirt, is an unmistakable symbol of the Yucatán. The everyday *huípil* is a one-piece garment; a variation for special occasions– such as dancing the *jarana* – is the three-piece *terno*, trimmed with lace and much more gorgeous embroidery. Perfect for a tropical climate, the *huípil* also seems ideally adapted to the Mayan-Yucatecan body shape. For non-locals, traditional embroidery can now be found applied to more international styles.

The Gulf Coast

The northwest coast is a long sandbar, with beaches facing the opal-green Gulf of Mexico backed by hushed lagoons, and dotted with villages and beach homes. **Progreso** ④, Mérida's port, is also its favorite beach town, with a line of waterfront

17

Mérida

Yucatán's historic capital, like the state, is a charmer. The long, straight streets the Spaniards laid out for the *ciudad blanca*, the white city, are interrupted by tranquil squares shaded by laurel trees, where old men chew the fat and couples exchange sweet nothings into the night on s-shaped love seats or *confidenciales*. Mérida's favorite music, the lilting boleros of its guitar trios, is unmistakably tropical, and unreservedly romantic. It has fine food and fine museums, and a market that can satisfy every human need. The traffic density can seem to get out of hand at times, but every weekend the center of the city is closed to traffic for all-day free fiestas.

Above: from the portico of the Casa de Montejo.

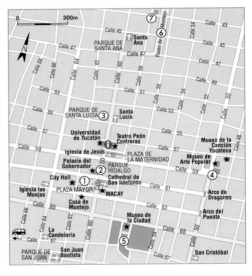

A Colonial City

Mérida was built among the ruins of Mayan *Ti'ho*, founded around 300 BC. It was already abandoned when Spanish soldiers took refuge among the ruins in 1540, led by two Francisco de Montejos, *el mozo* (the boy) and *el sobrino* (the nephew). They were besieged here by the Maya for over a year, until one final, savage battle. The Spaniards won, and founded Mérida as their capital in January 1542.

In 1545 Franciscan friars began the first of many churches. In 1546 Francisco de Montejo *el adelantado* (father of *el mozo*, uncle of *el sobrino*) took over as governor of the new colony. Under Spain – and long after independence – Mérida ruled over the whole Yucatán peninsula.

Plaza Mayor and Calle 60

As a classic Spanish colonial city, Mérida is firmly centered on its great square, the **Plaza Mayor** ① (or Plaza Grande, or Zócalo). On its north side is the governor's palace or **Palacio del Gobernador**, with dramatic murals by Fernando Castro Pacheco. On the west is the colonnaded **City Hall**.

The east side is filled by the massive **Cathedral de San Ildefonso**, oldest on the American mainland, completed in 1598 (only Santo Domingo in the Dominican Republic is older in the continent). The first Spanish stone building here, though, was the house the Montejos built for

A special attraction of Mérida as a base is its charming small hotels, many around colonial patios. *See also Hotels, p.83.*

Left: a city that leaves time to think: on Parque Hidalgo.

Deciphering Addresses
Streets going north–south have even numbers, east–west odd. As the streets of Mérida's grid are so long, it's usual to give cross-streets as an extra locator in addresses, ie. *Calle 55 no. 533, x 64 & 66* (Calle 55, between Calles 64 and 66). Campeche and other colonial towns use the same system.

---

available in this vast, fascinating bazaar, from superb fruit to hats or images of saints. There is also the **Museo de la Ciudad**, the city history museum.
SEE ALSO MUSEUMS, P.98; SHOPPING, P.117

Paseo de Montejo ⑥

For a radical change, go north. In 1904 Mérida, newly rich from sales of *henequen* (sisal rope), built its broad 'Champs-Elysées', Paseo de Montejo. Wealthy families lined the avenue with opulent mansions. The grandest is now the **Museo de Antropología** ⑦, an essential call for anyone interested in the Maya. Modern sculpture is on show on the paseo, and the smart districts nearby have some of Mérida's best restaurants.
SEE ALSO MUSEUMS, P.97

themselves in 1549, the **Casa de Montejo** on the south side. Most of it is now a bank, but it retains its astonishing portico, with giant figures of Spanish warriors standing on the heads of beaten Maya.

Calle 60 ② north of Plaza Mayor is the prime avenue for people-watching and street life, with languid squares like **Parque Hidalgo**. The plaza and Calle 60 are the venues

Below: the Portal de Granos (grain gate) market, from 1790.

for Mérida's weekly street parties, **Corazón de Mérida** on Saturday nights and **Mérida en Domingo** on Sundays. A few blocks up 60, one of the loveliest squares, **Parque de Santa Lucía** ③, hosts the **Serenatas Yucatecas** of traditional music every Thursday.

Colonial churches appear all around the old city. East of 60 **La Mejorada** ④ sits on a square by two stand-out museums, the **Museo de la Canción Yucateca**, of 'Yucatecan song', and the colorful **Museo de Arte Popular**.
SEE ALSO CHURCHES, P.50; FESTIVALS, P.62–3; MUSEUMS, P.97

The Market District ⑤

South of the Plaza Mayor are Mérida's giant markets. It's hard to imagine anything *not*

Walking around Mérida, look out for glimpses of patios, often lofty, lush and ornate behind plain facades.

Below: Paseo de Montejo.

Uxmal and the Puuc Cities

There is no greater demonstration of the refinement and sophistication of Mayan builders than Uxmal. In the 1840s John Lloyd Stephens recognized it as matching the grandest creations of ancient Greece or Rome. At the same time, the emphatic visual rhythm and sense of design of its greatest buildings, the subtle interplay of plain walls and extravagantly intricate carvings and reliefs, can make them seem strangely modern, with touches of Art Deco. Uxmal was the largest of a series of connected Mayan cities and settlements in the same style across the dry Puuc Hills of Yucatán, a spectacular late flourish of Mayan civilization.

The Puuc Style

Puuc is Mayan for hill, and is used to refer to a range of low hills that stand out against the flatness of Yucatán. In the hills, the usual problems the Maya had finding water were magnified: there are no accessible cenotes, water is far underground, and rainwater often had be garnered in artificial cisterns. This was a bizarre place to create ancient cities. The Puuc towns grew late in Maya history, around AD 700, thrived for just 200 years, then – maybe because their resources were so fragile – declined soon after about 920.

Uxmal and the smaller Puuc cities developed a very distinctive architectural style, with plain walls topped by exuberant friezes, and obsessive, rhythmic repetition of visual motifs such as flowers, symbols of magic, or the long-nosed Chac, god of rain.

Uxmal is open daily, 8am–5pm, with a nightly sound and light show, Nov–Mar 7pm, Apr–Oct 8pm. Admission is around $9 (free for over-60s, under-13s), plus $1 to park. Headphones with English commentary are an additional $2.50. Guides can be hired for $50.

Pyramid of the Magician ①

This majestic pyramid is the first sight to greet all visitors to Uxmal (even though you're no longer allowed to climb it). Completely different from the Castillo at Chichén Itzá, it's a very Mayan pyramid, with rounded ends. The 'Magician' was an *alux*, a Mayan leprechaun-like spirit, who in legend built the pyramid in one night to be his home, after driving out a previous king of Uxmal by cunning.

Below: the Governor's Palace, as seen by Catherwood in 1842.

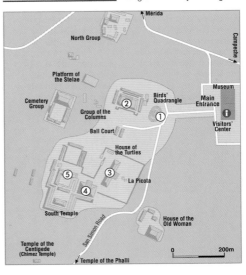

Left: the Magician's Pyramid.

Some of the most enjoyable places to stay in the Puuc region are in the Mayan village of **Santa Elena**, between Uxmal and Kabah. *See also Hotels, p.84.*

pieces, representing the calendar and movements of the sun, stars and the rains.

Nearby is the beautifully proportioned little **House of the Turtles**. Turtles, evocative of rain, are a frequent symbol at dry Uxmal. Rising up beside the palace platform is the older **Great Pyramid** ④, with beyond it the complex, only part-excavated, called **House of the Pigeons** ⑤ as its roof-combs suggested dovecotes.

SEE ALSO MAYAN RUINS AND RELICS, P.92

Nunnery Quadrangle ②

The four sides of Uxmal's massive masterpiece are each different, and at different levels, but combine to form a remarkable ensemble.

The Nunnery – one of the names given arbitrarily to Uxmal's buildings by a Spanish priest, Diego López de Cogolludo, in 1658 – was a venue for politics and the rituals of rebirth that were an essential part of the life of a Mayan city. Its imagery of Vision Serpents, latticework and more represents the divine origins of Uxmal, and its contacts with the heavens.

The Governor's Palace ③

Father Cogolludo had more luck with his naming here, for it seems this was the palace of the rulers of Uxmal, especially one known as Lord Chac, who reigned around 890–910. Over 100m long, the palace sits on an artificial platform. Its frieze is made up of over 20,000

The Puuc Route

Just as much a part of a visit to Uxmal is an exploration of the 'Puuc Route' sites nearby. **Kabah** has some of the most extravagant Puuc carving; **Sayil** has one of the finest Mayan palaces; **Labná** has a true gem of Mayan architecture, its famous arch. **Xlapak** is a small, peaceful forest site, while also on the route are the mysterious caves at **Loltún**.

SEE ALSO CAVES AND CENOTES, P.43; MAYAN RUINS AND RELICS, P.91–2.

Below: Chac-masks and Vision Serpents from Kabah (left) and the Nunnery Quadrangle at Uxmal.

The Costa Maya
and the Río Bec

South of Tulum the scale of development, so far, slims down drastically. Many villages are solidly Mayan-speaking. Getting around has the feel of exploration: a turn seawards leads to the still semi-discovered beaches and reefs of the Costa Maya, while further south there is a delicious lake at Bacalar, and the Yucatán's most quirkily likeable state capital, Chetumal. Continue west on the long Río Bec road and you will find an astonishing richness of Mayan sites, and Mexico's largest rainforest reserve.

The Zona Maya

Around 100km from Tulum is an abrupt contrast from the tourist world of the Riviera. This is the area into which the rebel Maya retreated after Yucatán's Caste War of 1847–50, rallied around a 'Talking Cross' said to transmit messages from God, and maintained their own independent state until 1901. Some villages have a testy relationship with Mexico to this day.

The capital of the *Cruzob* (people of the Cross) Chan Santa Cruz, renamed **Felipe Carrillo Puerto** ①, is a rough-and-ready little town. Local villages resist conventional tourism, but some can now be visited with **Xiimbal**'s individual tours from Felipe Carrillo. SEE ALSO TOURS AND GUIDES, P.121.

Above: roads can be wonderfully empty.

The Costa Maya

It long went unnoticed that, as well as the Riviera, Mexico has a Caribbean coastline south of the Sian Ka'an reserve. Efforts to develop it, now labelled the Costa Maya and with a black-top road, have gained pace, but were knocked back by Hurricane Dean in 2007. The small hotels dotted along the

beaches have an ability to bounce back, though, and, with superb diving offshore, make ideal hideaways for beach-lovers who now find even Tulum just too busy.

Mahahual ② has been the focus of development, with a dock for cruise ships as well as cabaña hotels, but sadly received a full hit from Dean.

Below: any day, in Xcalak.

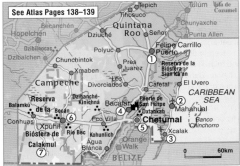

See Atlas Pages 138–139

Left: exquisite Laguna Bacalar.

you can join locals in catching the breeze. To the north is a Mayan site, **Oxtankah**.

SEE ALSO MAYAN RUINS AND RELICS, P.92; MUSEUMS, P.98.

The Río Bec

West of Chetumal, Highway 186 heads for Campeche past a stunning wealth of Mayan sites, in astonishing locations. For anyone interested in the Maya beyond familiar images of Chichén Itzá, exploring the Río Bec is a must.

First, closer to Chetumal, come **Dzibanché-Kinichná** and spectacular **Kohunlich**, with giant stucco masks of its rulers. The real Río Bec area is in Campeche state, around **Xpuhil** ⑥, its only town. The walled city of **Becán** is one of the nearby; most important of all is **Calakmul** ⑦, recently excavated but one of the largest Mayan cities. It is deep inside a rainforest reserve, home to jaguars, monkeys, and a profusion of other wildlife. Local guides provide tours.

SEE ALSO MAYAN RUINS AND RELICS, P.93; TOURS AND GUIDES, P.121; WILDLIFE AND NATURE, P.129.

Some conventional facilities are scarce in south Quintana Roo. Gas/petrol stations are found only in a few main towns. There are no banks or ATMs on the Costa Maya or the Río Bec, so take enough cash – in **pesos**, not dollars – for your stay. Internet cafés are easier to find.

Reconstruction could bring big changes, with a bigger cruise dock. To the north and south are secluded hotels, now all picking themselves up.

Xcalak ③, 60km south on the Belize frontier, is a sand-street-and-palm-trees village that's still more out of the way, and missed Dean's full force. Offshore, **Banco Chinchorro** is one of the richest of all the Yucatán reefs, and there's great fishing, and seductive little beach hotels that invite you to kick back and settle in.

SEE ALSO BEACHES, P.39; DIVING, SNORKELING, AND WATERSPORTS, P.55

Bacalar ④

Tagged 'lake of seven colors' for its ever-changing shades, Laguna Bacalar is a giant cenote, fed not by rivers but underground streams; almost like mineral water, this is an unforgettable place to swim.

Bacalar town, with places to stay and simple restaurants enjoying fabulous views from its *Costera* or lakeshore road, is one of the Yucatán's special towns. It has its only castle, **Fuerte de San Felipe**, now a museum, built in 1725 as a defence against Belize pirates.

Chetumal ⑤

The state capital of Quintana Roo is a sultry, tropical little city, facing Belize across the Río Hondo. It has an unusual museum, the **Museo de la Cultura Maya**, and an amazing range of discount stores and markets. Handy as a service center, Chetumal also has great open-air restaurants on its long bay boulevard, where

Below: Calakmul's great pyramids loom up in the forest.

23

Campeche

Facing the Gulf of Mexico is one of the most complete walled cities in the Americas, once a trading fortress of the Spanish Main. Old Campeche sits within a ring of massive stone bastions, built by Spanish governors to hold back pirates. Inside the walls there are cobbled streets of ornate churches and gracious colonial houses painted in delicate pastel colors, with plant-filled patios glimpsed through lofty iron window-grills. Compared to equally colonial Mérida, Campeche seems to have its head more firmly in the past, but this helps keep up its distinctive, airy charm. The state around it, too, often has a feel of quiet remoteness.

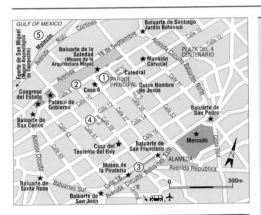

Campeche City

Campeche was the first city founded by the Spaniards in the Yucatán, in 1540, after they had overcome the 20-year resistance of the local Maya led by a redoubtable lord called Moch-Cuouh. It was the sole port of colonial Yucatán, and – despite being plagued by pirates – became one of the wealthiest trading cities of the Spanish Empire.

After the Yucatán grudgingly became part of an independent Mexico in 1821, Campeche resented being governed from Mérida, and lobbied hard to be made a separate state, which it achieved in 1863. Left to itself, Campeche has never

Above: the Cathedral and the colonnades of Parque Principal.

again boasted the status it enjoyed under Spanish rule. In the 1990s, though, its old city was beautifully restored, and later declared a World Heritage Site by UNESCO.

AROUND THE OLD CITY

An obvious place to start is the **Parque Principal** ①, the main square, with the lofty **Cathedral de La Immaculada**. Opposite is **Casa 6**, a fine old townhouse that has been carefully restored in the style of a wealthy merchant family's home of the early 19th century, and now is also a cultural center, hosting concerts and other events.

Left: old Campeche is a city of subtle colors.

A sound and light show evoking Campeche's history is presented at the Puerta de Tierra every Tue, Fri and Sat at 8pm.

Museo Arqueológico de Campeche, is, again, its location: **Fuerte San Miguel**, one of two mighty Spanish forts built on hilltops either side of the city. Its display of Mayan artifacts is superb, above all the astonishing jade tomb-masks from Calakmul.
SEE ALSO MUSEUMS, P.99.

Campeche State

INLAND

Rural Campeche can look as if it has fewer people now than 1,500 years ago, given the number of Mayan ruins around the state. Best-known, 55km from the city, is **Edzná**, with its unique temple-palace of the Five Stories.

Further east is the Chenes region. *Chen* is Mayan for well, and many villages here were sited next to deep, well-like caves, like the celebrated **Grutas de Xtacumbilxunaan**. The ancient Chenes cities also had their own style of architecture, with temple entrances like giant monsters. This is a region for explorers, especially the remote but spectacular ruins of **Santa Rosa Xtampak**.
SEE ALSO MAYAN RUINS AND RELICS, P.93

THE GULF COAST

Campeche's coast is almost as far off the standard tourist routes. South of the city the road follows the Gulf, past clutches of beachside restaurants at towns like **Champotón**, an opal sea, and one landmark hotel, at **Sihoplaya**.
SEE ALSO HOTELS, P.85

The next thing to do is take a walk around the surviving walls, starting at the 'sea gate' or **Puerta de Mar** ②. Campeche has many museums, several housed in old bastions, like the **Museo de la Arquitectura Maya** in **Baluarte de la Soledad**. On the opposite side from Puerta de Mar, the **Puerta de Tierra** ③ ('land gate') has beside it a **Museo de la Piratería**, to tell you all about pirates.

Museums aside, old Campeche is a place for directionless wandering, calling in at old cantinas or churches like **San Francisquito** ④, and watching the locals chatting through the window-grills.
SEE ALSO CHURCHES, P.51; MUSEUMS, P.99.

One of Campeche's special draws is its distinctive cuisine. *See also Food and Drink, p.66–71, and Restaurants, Cafés, and Cantinas, p.113.*

OUTSIDE THE WALLS

Beyond the Puerta de Mar, and businesslike 1970s streets and hotels, is another of Campeche's joys, kilometers of waterfront **Malecón** ⑤ facing the vast, flat Gulf. Strollers and joggers head up and down it all day, before numbers increase around the often gorgeous sunsets.

An added attraction of the city's finest museum, the

Below: Edzná's Five Stories.

A–Z

In the following section, attractions and services in Cancún and the Yucatán are organized by theme, under alphabetical headings. Items that link to another theme are cross-referenced. All sights covered by the atlas at the end of the book are given a page number and grid reference.

All-Inclusives

The convenience stores of modern travel are the pacemakers of development on the Riviera Maya, as bay after bay is enclosed by giant resort complexes with rooms, restaurants, spas, kids' clubs, and more all in one spot, linked up by neat landscaped gardens. Some are vast 3,000-bed vacation-factories, some (which are generally more expensive) offer an intimate charm; some treat the Yucatán landscape like a strip-mine, others show more concern. All-inclusive resorts cater to a range of tastes, from ultra-luxurious retreats or 'adults-only' getaways to fun-in-the-sun-and-sand holidays for families with young kids.

The All-Inclusive Style

Attitudes to all-inclusives often vary depending on whether you're staying in them or not. If not, you find them infuriating, as they go all out to close off some of the most beautiful places on the coast to everyone else. Many resorts are also among the region's worst perpetrators of environmental damage. But, if you do stay (especially with kids), you might find the all-round convenience and the invitation to just lie back and forget everything simply irresistible.

Some points on all-inclusives. Resorts sell themselves on convenience, especially that of paying for everything in one go. But this doesn't necessarily come cheap, if you break down prices and compare with the cost of tours or eating locally. The enclosed feel of resorts also appeals to a notion of safety, of being insulated from an everyday Yucatán that by implication is full of dangers and diseases. Some resorts state this semi-openly, to dissuade guests from spending money anywhere else. Two things on this:

Basic resort prices include rooms, meals, drinks, and use of most facilities; however, some things – diving, tours, sometimes fancier cocktails – are usually extra. Resorts are designed to be booked as part of a package with flights and other essentials, and so (in contrast to most independent hotels nowadays) you will nearly always get better prices booking through travel agents or online travel services rather than with the resort direct. Travel websites and agents also often have handy special-offer deals for many resorts.

a) the Yucatán is not remotely threatening, and b) major cases of food poisoning and infections can occur in the big kitchens and water systems of resorts, more frequently than they do in local restaurants.

Some people stay at all-inclusives, then find them claustrophobic. But, despite first impressions, staff cannot stop you wandering out of the movie-set gateways, and combining a resort stay with a look around outside.

A Short Selection

The Riviera now has so many resorts it's only possible to list a few here, but here are some, contrasting, options.

Akumal Beach Resort
South of Akumal village, at Highway 307 km 255; tel: (984) 875 7500; www.ventaclub resorts.com; $$$; Map p.135 D2
A long-running, popular family resort with rooms in modest-sized villas, all with balconies, on one of Akumal's loveliest beaches (some rooms face a garden). It's excellent for kids, with plenty to do and great, easy snorkeling. Relaxation is the keynote, but there's an entertainment program when you need it. Accessible rates make it very good value.

Price ranges are based on prices per night in US dollars for a double room, meals, drinks, and use of most facilities, in the winter-spring (but not Christmas peak) season. Note that prices at all-inclusives vary a lot by how you book them *(see above)*:
$$$$	over $300
$$$	$200–$300
$$	under $200

Left: the discreet architecture of the Riu Cancún.

luxury **Grand Hotel Paraíso** for couples to low-priced, family-oriented **Paraíso del Mar**. The whole place is vast, so this is no intimate hide-away, but it offers loads of options, with almost theme-park style facilities for kids.

Maya Koba Resorts
Highway 307 km 298, 9km north of Playa del Carmen; central tel: 1-800 828 0639; http://rivieramayakoba.com; $$$$; Map p.135 D3
The Riviera's most ambitious, most sophisticated develop-ment, with five varying resorts in villas, and a Greg Norman golf course; it has even won some praise from ecologists for the way the layout has fol-lowed the flow of mangrove channels. This refinement comes at high prices.

The Reef Playacar
Avenida Xaman-Ha, Playacar, Playa del Carmen; tel: (984) 873 4120; www.thereefplayacar.com; $$$$; Map p.135 D2
Nothing fancy, but this 210-room resort in Playacar, on the south side of Playa del Carmen, is a family favorite, and very competitively priced, especially in low seasons. Friendly staff and a relaxed, kid-friendly atmosphere have won it many return customers.

Azul Hotel & Beach Resort
Highway 307 km 324, 4km north of Puerto Morelos; tel: (998) 872 8080; www.karismahotels.com/azul; $$$$; Map p.135 E3
A 'boutique resort,' this stylish, smaller all-inclusive has three pools and 96 rooms under palapa-style roofs. Some are plainish, and the hotel is often taken over by weddings, but its fans love the friendly feel, and chic lounging-cabañas on the white powder beach.

Excellence Riviera Cancún
Highway 307 km 323, 3km north of Puerto Morelos; tel: (998) 872 8555; www.excellence-resorts.com; $$$$; Map p.135 E3

A romantic, adults-only luxury resort, where arriving guests are greeted with a glass of champagne, and which prides itself on exceptional service. Six beautiful pools wind through the resort, and there's a superior choice of restaur-ants, and a sumptuous spa.

Iberostar Playa Paraíso
Off Highway 307, 17km north of Playa del Carmen; tel: (984) 877 2800; www.iberostar.com; $$$$; Map p.135 D3
Iberostar, one of the Spanish hotel conglomerates that are now the Riviera's biggest builders, has all of five resorts at this huge property, from the

Below: three views of Puerto Aventuras.

Bars and Nightlife

Night-owls on the Riviera Maya have two big options to pick from: Cancún and its party bars and spectacular megaclubs, and the far more cool-and-chic style of Playa del Carmen, with venues around the walkway of Quinta Avenida. Besides these main dishes there are other appetizers on the menu, like salsa bars in Mérida, or beach parties in Tulum. For more traditional Mexican drinking-places like bar-restaurants and cantinas, mainly open during the day, *see Restaurants, Cafés, and Cantinas, p.104–13.*

Cancún

Cancún's Hotel Zone geography encourages a certain scale (big: some of the biggest multi-space clubs on the planet are here) and style, with taxis often needed to get around. Handily, though, the most popular venues are clustered together near **Forum by the Sea** (more a fun-center than a shopping mall), around Boulevard Kukulcán km 9.5.

Azúcar

Dreams Cancún, Punta Cancún, off Boulevard Kukulcán at km 9; tel: (998) 848 7000; www.cancun-dreaming.com; Thur–Sat restaurant 6–9.30pm, music 10pm–4am; entrance charge; Map IBC

Below: your caipirinha awaits.

This elegant club beside the Dreams Cancún resort (with its own entrance) is the city's best live Latin dance venue, and the biggest names in Latin music play here. It's much loved by well-heeled locals of all ages (don't be intimidated by the fantastic footwork). One place in Cancún to dress sharp and show off your jewelry.

The City

Boulevard Kukulcán km 9; tel: (998) 848 8380; www.thecity cancun.com; daily 10pm–4am; entrance charge; Map IBC
Less well known than the Coco Bongo, this is actually bigger, with four dance floors and nine bars, and has a more adventurous music policy. A beach club hosts pool parties on Tuesdays, and there are different theme nights through the week.

Coco Bongo

Boulevard Kukulcán km 9.5; tel: (998) 883 5061; www.coco bongo.com.mx; daily 10pm–4am; entrance charge; Map IBC
The Cancún strip's most famous venue is a show as well as a club, with eye-and-ear-boggling presentations nightly at 10.30pm that feature

Left: awesome: part of the show at the Coco Bongo.

Anyone who feels like a break from the Hotel Zone's international club-odromes and something more Mexican should head for **Avenida Yaxchilán** in Ciudad Cancún. It has ever lively restaurants, salsa clubs, discos like the wonderfully named Bum-Bum, sports bars where you can catch up with Mexican games, and even the local musicians' union, where you can hire a guitar trio or a mariachi for the night. Nearby, the newly refurbished **Parque de las Palapas** has more bargain restaurants, and a few relaxed bars.

acrobats, dancers, and very convincing lookalikes of Beyoncé, Madonna, Elvis, Ricky Martin, and other superstars (you couldn't tell the difference if the real ones *were* here, given the fantastic lighting effects). After this sensory bombardment, without letting the energy fade, you can dance on to salsa, rock, hip hop, 80s retro and more in the club's several spaces.

Congo Bar
Boulevard Kukulcán km 9.5; tel: (998) 883 0563; www.congo bar.com.mx; daily 9pm–4am; free entrance; Map IBC
A relative newcomer, but this high-energy bar has become a very buzzing, popular alternative to the big clubs nearby, especially for young locals. There's no cover, three dance floors (including an outdoor terrace under the stars), and an inventive music mix.

Dady'O
Boulevard Kukulcán km 9.5; tel: (998) 883 3333; www.dadyo. com.mx; daily 10pm–5am; entrance charge; Map IBC
The biggest rival to the Coco Bongo (*see p.30*), with a more classic big-club style, and

long lines outside every Spring Break. It offers a choice of spaces: the main **Dady'O** is a giant disco; **Dady Rock** is a smaller, still louder downhome party club (Wet Body night, Thursday). Lately, perhaps stung by the idea its approach was no longer cool, Dady'O has added the more stylish **O Ultra Lounge**, with House and Trance sounds, and **Terrasta**, with R&B, reggaeton and similar.

Fat Tuesday
Embarcadero, Boulevard Kukulcán km 4; tel: (998) 883 2676; daily 10am–3am; entrance charge some nights; Map IBC

The all-time favorite Spring Break party bar, which hosted MTV's Spring Break shows several times. Money problems led to a move to this new location, but it's still a prime home to the giant daiquiri and the beach bikini party.

Pat O'Brien's
Plaza Flamingo, Boulevard Kukulcán km 11.5; tel: (998) 883 0832; www.patobriens.com.mx; Sun–Thur 10am–4am, Fri–Sat 10am–5am; free entrance; Map IBC
XXL-size all-American sports bar and restaurant – a good place to keep up with scores, including English soccer.

Below: out for the night on the Cancún strip.

Above: dance on tables, wave your arms in the air… another night at Señor Frog's.

Señor Frog's

Boulevard Kukulcán km 9.7; tel: (998) 883 1092; www.senor frogs.com; daily noon–3/4am; free entrance; Map IBC

Flagship venue of Grupo Anderson, which hit the jackpot with its bar-restaurants, all with jokey names like Señor Frog's, Carlos'n'Charlie's or El Shrimp Bucket and Mexican-themed décor, mostly Mex food and all-out party atmosphere (music can be shamelessly cheesy, you have been warned). There are branches in Cozumel and Playa del Carmen. Spring Break is (of course) a main event.

Terraza Chacmool

Hostal Chacmool, Calle Gladiolas 18, by Parque de las Palapas, Ciudad Cancún; tel: (998) 892 1462; daily 9am–2am; free entrance; Map IBC

Mellow little bar and terrace attached to one of Ciudad Cancún's more enterprizing budget hostels. Open for breakfast, lunch and until late, with ambient music and sofas for lounging.
SEE ALSO HOTELS, P.76

The Islands

ISLA MUJERES

Like the island, the scene is far smaller than Cancún, with a laid-back, off-the-beach style.

Buho's

Playa Norte, by Cabañas María del Mar; no phone; daily 9am–9pm; free entrance; Map p.8

The archetypal beach-hut bar, with rope seats to swing on under the droopy palapa roof. After beach erosion there is now little space between bar and water, but hopefully this will not be permanent.

Nitrox Club VIP

Avenida Guerrero 11, off Avenida Matamoros; tel: (998) 887 0568; Wed–Sun 9pm–3am; entrance charge; Map p.8

Isla's biggest, most energetic club venue: Friday is salsa-Latin night, other days there's lots of dance and techno.

Om Bar and Chill Lounge

Avenida Matamoros, between Avenidas Juárez and Hidalgo; tel: (998) 820 4876; daily 8pm–3am; free entrance; Map p.8

A more mellow alternative, with kind-of Moroccan décor and herbal teas as alternatives to cocktails and beers (which you serve yourself, from taps at each table). The music range includes acid jazz and Brazilian.

COZUMEL

In line with its family-resort style, nightlife on Cozumel is more conventional, more restrained, than in Cancún or Playa, and even in the party bars the dancing on tables is less energetic.

Hard Rock Café

Avenida Melgar, corner of Calle 1 Sur; tel: (987) 872 5271; www. hardrock.com; daily 10am–1am; free entrance; Map p.9

Below: one of cozy Cozumel's social hubs, the Hard Rock.

Unmissable for new arrivals on the island, as it's right at the end of the ferry dock. Chain bar-restaurants play a big part in Cozumel's unfussy nightlife, and the Hard Rock is regularly packed to the walls. No departures from the estalished Hard Rock style, except for a ceiling mural of coral reefs.

1.5 Tequila
Avenida Melgar, corner of Calle 11 Sur; tel: (987) 872 4421; www.1punto5.com; daily noon–3am; entrance charge on some nights; Map p.9

A stylish venture for Cozumel, a chic upstairs lounge bar with soft seating, sushi, great cocktails and a fabulous view (especially at sunset). Ambient and lounge music feature, with guest DJs sometimes raising the energy level.

Viva Mexico
Avenida Melgar, by Avenida A. Rosado Salas; tel: (987) 872 0799; daily 10am–3am; entrance charge on some nights; Map p.9

A big, rumbustious Malecón restaurant-dance club, popular with locals and tourists, who come to eat, drink, and dance to an irresistible mix of Mexican-Latin pop, salsa, merengue, and the like.

HOLBOX
Disco Carioca's
Calle Damero, by the beach, on the east side of the village; tel: (984) 875 2210; no fixed schedule; free entrance; Map p.9

'Nightlife' on Holbox usually means sitting over a beer, but it also has this loveable venue, more a bar-restaurant on the beach, which unpredictably (but often on Sundays) hosts live salsa bands and DJs.

Riviera Maya: Playa del Carmen

The headliners in Playa are stylish venues that (unlike many Cancún bars) follow global clubbing trends and

Above: chilling out at the Blue Parrot.

import leading DJs, from Mexico City, the US or Europe. Another part of Playa style is that most venues are along Quinta Avenida, so you walk between them. The most happening are even closer together in the same spot, at the crossing of Avenidas 1 and 5 with Calle 12.

There are also unfussy leftovers from Playa's hippy past with their unpretentious rock and reggae cover bands, and regular beach parties at **Mamitas** and **Kool** on Mamitas beach.
SEE ALSO BEACHES, P.38

Alux
Avenida Juárez, between Avenidas 65 and 70; tel: (984) 803 0713; daily 6pm–2am; free entrance; Map p.10

Playa's unique cave bar, a labyrinth of wonderfully intimate spaces deep down in a real cave. It's a spectacular spot for a romantic encounter, but inland of the Highway, far from the main Playa scene, so to get there you need a taxi.

Bali Club
Calle 12 Norte, between Avenidas 5 and 10; tel: (984) 803 2864; www.baliclub.com.mx; daily 10.30pm–6am; entrance charge; Map p.10

Big, high-tech club with live acts, water sprays, and so on to go with non-stop dancing. Playa's nearest thing to a Cancún megaclub.

Blue Parrot
Avenida 1 bis, corner of Calle 12 Norte; tel: (984) 206 3350; www. blueparrot.com; daily 8am–4am; free entrance; Map p.10

It's probably a bad idea for cool bars to tell you how old they are. The Blue Parrot, founded 1984 and once voted 'one of the 10 best beach bars in the world' in a magazine

SEE ALSO HOTELS, P.79

Left: dress suitably to match the *feng shui* at Om.

divans to lounge on, and a style-conscious crowd. Not a place to be too lively, though.

Fah Bar at Siesta Fiesta
Avenida 5, between Calle 8 and 10 Norte; tel: (984) 803 1166; daily 8am–midnight, music from 7pm; free entrance; Map p.10
Not everything is cool in Playa. On many nights when the trendier bars are quiet, this big terrace on the Quinta, part of a budget hotel, will be packed with drinkers boogieing along to live bands playing covers of Bob Marley or Steve Miller.

Kartabar
Avenida 1, corner of Calle 12 Norte; tel: (984) 873 2228; www.kartabar.com; daily restaurant 6pm–1am, bar 6pm–3.30am; free entrance; Map p.10
An especially mellow chill-out bar by 'Blue Parrot corner', with a Middle Eastern theme that includes hookahs to suck on while you sit back on big, comfortable divans and sample the Mediterranean menu. Sometimes belly dancers, too.

Mambo Café
Calle 6 Norte, between Avenidas 5 and 10; tel: (984) 803 2656; www.mambocafe.com.mx; Tue–Sun 10pm–4am; entrance charge; Map p.10
A must for salsa and Latin fans, one of a chain of clubs across Mexico, with great live bands from Mexico, Cuba, Colombia, and further afield. There are also salsa classes.

poll, was long the beginning and end of Playa nightlife. Nowadays, it's more like one of the crowd. It's still a good call, though, with one of the best beach dance floors, mostly with pop and hip hop. Landwards, there's a rooftop bar and a lounge-style (but sand-floored) space under a big palapa, with progressive dance and ambient sounds.

La Bodeguita del Medio
Plaza Paseo del Carmen, near Cozumel ferry terminal; tel: (984) 803 3950; daily 11am–2am; free entrance; Map p.10
Unnoticed, maybe, by global politics, the famous Havana bar has become a franchise, with branches in several Mexican cities. There's Cuban rum, snacks and mojitos, and superb live bands for sinuous dancing in the intimate space.

Coco Maya
Avenida 1 bis, corner of Calle 12 Norte; tel: (984) 111 9361; daily 9pm–4am; entrance charge some nights; Map p.10
Muscling in on the Blue Parrot next door, this big beach club brings in a more adventurous slate of US, Mexican and European DJs for parties that often go on until sunrise. A raised chill-out deck with a great view is another asset.

Deseo Lounge
Avenida 5, corner of Calle 12 Norte; tel: (984) 879 3620; www.hoteldeseo.com; daily 9am–midnight/1am; free entrance; Map p.10
The pool-deck bar in Playa's sleekest designer hotel is the town's pinnacle of cool, with ambient music, old movies flickering on a wall, giant

Below: not every Playa bar has designer décor.

Above: La Zebra's beach bar.

Om
Avenida 1 bis, corner of Calle 12 Norte; tel: (984) 879 4784; www.omplaya.com; daily 5pm–4am; free entrance; Map p.10
Another chilled out bar like near-neighbor Kartabar *(see left)*, with a design (supposedly with good *feng shui)* that mixes oriental, Mexican and Middle Eastern. Fine cocktails are the drinks to go for.

La Santanera
Calle 12 Norte, between Avenidas 5 and 10; tel: (984) 803 2856; daily 8pm–4/6am; entrance charge; Map p.10
The wildest, most cutting-edge club in Playa, with a very original Mexican take on club culture (like DJs dressed as masked Mexican wrestlers). Dynamic and full of surprises.

Riviera Maya: Tulum
Lack of electricity limited life after dark in Tulum, but lately it has developed a beach-party scene. There are also DJ sessions on some Saturdays at **Ah'Kiin** (km 9.5).

Mezzanine
Beach road, km 1.5; tel: (998) 112 2845; www.mezzanine.com.mx; daily 8am–11pm, DJs Fri 9pm–2am; entrance charge Fri; Map p.12
This very chic little design

hotel hosts Ibiza-style house-and-ambient beach parties every Friday. Big-name international DJs show up, and it has a growing reputation among Riviera party animals.
SEE ALSO HOTELS, P.81

La Zebra
Beach road, km 8.5; tel: (998) 112 3260; www.lazebra.com.mx; Mon–Sat 8am–10pm, Sun 8am–11pm; salsa nights Sun 7–11pm; free entrance; Map p.12
This more-stylish-than-most cabaña hotel and bar goes for a more Latin approach, with salsa parties every Sunday on its mid-beach dance floor. Free salsa classes Thur–Sat.
SEE ALSO HOTELS, P.81; RESTAUR-ANTS, CAFÉS, AND CANTINAS, P.109

Mérida
Mérida provides so much free entertainment *(see Festivals, p.62)*, that nightlife venues attract less interest. The main clubs are in the wealthy part of town, on or near Prolongación de Montejo (a continuation of Paseo de Montejo). Hotel bars, like the one in **Piedra de Agua**, are upscale meeting-points. For clarification of local addresses, *see box, p.19.*
SEE ALSO HOTELS, P.84

The block on Calle 60 between Calles 55 and 57 has a special place in Mérida nightlife. One building houses **El Nuevo Tucho**, a cantina-style dance hall that fills up with locals to see live acts from salsa bands to Yucatecan comedians; **¡Ay Caray!**, a popular upstairs bar; **Azul Picante** salsa bar; and **KY60**, a dive-like disco.

El Cielo
Prolongación de Montejo 83, x 15 & 17; tel: (999) 944 5127; www.elcielobar.com; daily 7pm–3am; entrance charge some nights; Map p.18
The favored haunt of well-heeled local youth, an all-white minimalist bar-club with a stunning outside terrace. Also has a branch in Playa.

Pancho's
Calle 59 no. 509, x 60 & 62; tel: (999) 923 0942; daily 6pm–2am; free entrance; Map p.18
Its Mexican Revolution-themed décor may be kitschy, but Pancho's is a likeable city-center institution. Staff are friendly, the food tasty, and the dance floor is open to the stars. Music is eclectic/Latin pop, always lively, and fun.

Below: one way to learn about Mexican history, at Pancho's.

35

Beaches

White, softer than fine carpet, deliciously cool as the sand wraps around your feet: the beaches of Yucatán's Caribbean coast are something special. They're made up of ultra-fine silicate sand, which always stays cool, even when the thermometer tops 40°C. Beyond the sand is a perfect-temperature sea that shades from deep blue to brilliant turquoise, calm enough for easy swimming and clear enough for great snorkeling and diving. Some beaches have to be shared with the crowds, but elsewhere you can still find that longed-for stretch of beach with not much for company except palm trees and the birds.

Cancún

Beaches facing north, along the top of the '7' of Cancún Island, are compact but have calm waters; east-facing beaches are more beautiful and more spacious, but also have more surf and sometimes undertow (look out for red-flag safety warnings).

The post-Wilma restoration of Cancún beach *(see box, right)* has been so complete it's hard to see the difference. However, erosion is still a problem, especially round Punta Cancún, where the beach is very thin in parts.

Resort hotels may seem to close the way to the beach, but the whole length of it is public *(see box, p.38)*, and there are public-access points all along the island. **Playa Langosta** (km 5) and **Playa Tortugas** (km 6) have the most rides and fun things of the north beaches. The finest ocean beach, **Playa Delfines** (km 17–18), is a superb white bank with a spectacular view.

The Islands

ISLA MUJERES
Map p.8

The island's jewel is **Playa Norte**, across the top of Isla town, with the oval inlet of **Playa Secreto** – ideal for kids – at its east end. Snug and shallow for lazy swimming and lounging, Playa Norte has the added attraction of **Buho's** and other bars.

Lately the shifting of sand between Playa Norte and the less attractive **Playa Caribe**, facing Cancún, has become more extreme, and Playa Norte has shrunk severely at times. The charge is made that this is due to the dredg-

Below: Holbox's shell-covered beach.

Left: the Tulum idyll.

east side. Rough seas make swimming dangerous in places, but every so often (such as by **Chen Río** restaurant) there are lovely sheltered bays, with just a few people.
SEE ALSO CHILDREN, P.45; RESTAURANTS, CAFÉS, AND CANTINAS, P.106

HOLBOX
Map p.9
Holbox faces the Gulf, not the Caribbean, so the sea is very shallow, and opal rather than turquoise: there are miles of tranquil, palm-lined sands to pick from.

Riviera Maya: Cancún to Playa del Carmen
From north to south.
PUERTO MORELOS
Map p.10
A fine long beach, broad to the north, with unfussy bars and other facilities – so that it never gets crowded. A rich reef only just offshore makes for excellent snorkeling.

PUNTA BETE
Off Highway 307 at km 295, 7km north of Playa del Carmen, signposted to Tides Riviera Maya; Map p.10
Building has moved fast on these curving beaches since the dirt road was paved, with the **Tides Riviera Maya** and

---

Shifting Sands
Because the sand here is so soft it is also relatively unstable. Beaches change shape a little year by year, and can be altered drastically by hurricanes. Hurricane Wilma, especially, in 2005 stripped away part of Cancún beach, which was 'rebuilt' by dredging sand from the sea bed. This was amazingly effective, but may also have had unexpected consequences (*see left, Isla Mujeres*). Shortcuts are used in places to stabilize beaches: as well as being ugly, this can cause long-term damage.
See also Environment, p.56.

COZUMEL
Map p.9
Cozumel's favorite beaches, long, white and very safe, face the mainland north and south of San Miguel. Those north are mostly taken by hotels; the most popular are to the south, like **Playa Paraíso** (by **Chankanaab** snorkel park) and **Playa Palancar**. Access is often through beach clubs, with restaurants, kayaks, snorkels, and other facilities. Noisy in peak seasons, they're low-key at other times.

A different experience can be found just over on Cozumel's wind-blown, empty

---

ing done to remake Cancún beach, which (it is said) has destabilized the ocean floor. Hopefully a solution will be found, but for now the beach has lost some of its charm.

The main beaches along Isla's west side are **Playa Lancheros** and **Playa Indios**, near Hacienda Mundaca. Often visited by day-trips from Cancún, they're much less crowded at other times.
SEE ALSO BARS AND NIGHTLIFE, P.32

Below: Holbox at sunset.

Norte; tel: (984) 803 2867; www.mamitasbeachclub.com; daily 9am–6pm, later for club nights; Map p.10
Playa institution tha has gone upscale, with decadent loungers, global food, and Ibiza-style beach raves.

Riviera Maya: South of Playa to Tulum

From north to south.
PAAMUL
Off Highway 307 at km 273; Map p.135 D2
Not the trendiest beach, with an RV park, but a fine arc of sand, with a turtle beach.

PUERTO AVENTURAS
Off Highway 307 at km 270; Map p.135 D2
This purpose-built holiday village has a long, calm main beach (open to non-residents), and sheltered coves, mostly tied to condos or resorts.

XPU-HA
Off Highway 307, between km 260 and 265; Map p.135 D2
Much of this 7km row of exquisite, curving beaches is now dominated by all-inclusives. Three of the seven access roads (signed X-4, X-6 and X-7) are still open to everyone, and lead to small restaurants and basic hotels.

AKUMAL
Off Highway 307, between km 253 and 255; Map p.135 D2

Topless bathing is tolerated in Playa, Tulum, and many other places on the Riviera: take your cue from people around you. There are also remote beaches where nude bathing is possible, and clothing-optional resorts. Elsewhere, attitudes are more conservative.

---

other resorts, but there are also still cabañas and basic palapa restaurants.
SEE ALSO PAMPERING, P.103

PLAYA DEL CARMEN
Map p.10
Playa has also been affected by shrinking beaches. Its best and softest beaches are to the north. South of the town, the resorts of Playacar have a narrow beach, which is narrower still after recent hurricanes.

With its zooming growth, Playa is not a place to get away from it all. It has much less beach frontage than Cancún, and the first hotels here grabbed the best spots. The main access point for anyone from hotels not on the beach is **Mamita's Beach** and **Playa Tukan** (really one beach) at the end of Calle 28. Consequently, the beach from there to the town plaza is the Riviera spot where sun-worshippers most often line up elbow to elbow.

All-inclusive resorts often give the impression they have exclusive rights to the beaches in front of them, and try to restrict access for non-guests. However, all beaches in Mexico are public property, open to all. No one can stop you walking over to a beach from an open-access beach alongside.

Undaunted, Playa makes a virtue of this agglomeration with beach clubs that encourage a cool, sexy party buzz, and offer (expensive) loungers.

Kool by Playa Tukan
Playa Tukan, end of Calle 28 Norte; tel: (984) 803 1961; daily, beach club 9am–7pm, restaurant 9am–midnight; bar 9am–3am; Map p.10
A designer variation on the Playa beach club, with divans as well as loungers, and a sleek, international restaurant.

Mamita's Beach Club
Playa Mamita's, end of Calle 28

All the essentials: dazzling sea, graceful curves of sand, plenty of palms for shade, untarnished tranquility. While mainly a vacation community, Akumal's layout leaves you far more space to move than the newer resort complexes. This is also a turtle-breeding beach. SEE ALSO DIVING, SNORKELING, AND WATERSPORTS, P.54; WILDLIFE AND NATURE, P.127

PUNTA SOLIMÁN AND TANKAH

Off Highway 307 by km 237, 8km north of Tulum; Map p.135 D2
An easily missed track runs to the jungle beach at Punta Solimán, identified with **Oscar y Lalo's** restaurant. Just south, another track (signed Tankah Tres) leads to a coastal cenote and hotels. Head right to walk to a little-used forest beach. SEE ALSO RESTAURANTS, CAFÉS, CANTINAS, P.108

TULUM
Map p.12
Tulum beach is one of the glories of the world. It has plenty of competition, but this has to be the Riviera's finest beach. Closer to Tulum ruins, the beach is relatively narrow; it widens further down, towards Sian Ka'an, so for space and seclusion, head south. Plus no other beach offers the same range of cabañas to stay in, from mellow retreats to chic beach-party venues, with diving and (now) kiteboarding too.

For really empty beaches, cross over into Sian Ka'an, or carry on down to Punta Allen. SEE ALSO BARS AND NIGHTLIFE, P.35; DIVING, SNORKELING, AND WATER-SPORTS, P.55

Yucatán State
Map p.16–17
Beaches line the northwest coast, facing the opal Gulf, shallow and often amazingly

One special beach is on the uninhabited barrier island across the lagoon from **San Felipe**, west of **Río Lagartos**. The local boatmen who give flamingo tours will take you there. Often, you can have the island to yourselves. Take everything you need with you, and arrange with the *lanchero* when to be brought back. You can also camp there overnight – but take plenty of bug repellent. *See also Wildlife and Nature, p.129.*

still when not whipped up by a *norte* wind. **Progreso** and its smaller neighbors are Mérida's favorite beach towns. Go on a Sunday for a different style of beach, a slice of Yucatecan life, as the seafood restaurants fill up with noisy family groups.

All along this coast there are beach houses, often available at low rents. To the west, laidback **Celestún**, known for flamingos, has a fine, white, utterly relaxing beach, and a few simple restaurants. SEE ALSO WILDLIFE AND NATURE, P.129

Costa Maya
Map p.22
Beaches here don't quite have the Riviera's magnificence, and have a bit more seaweed, but they give you a greater feel of escape from the everyday world, and are great for easy swimming. In **Mahahual** the best spots are south of the village, with sandy bays for miles. The vegetation, usually lush, is recuperating rapidly after Hurricane Dean.

Xcalak is a fair model for an ideal beachcomber village – with superb diving at Banco Chinchorro, and snorkeling in the lagoons around Xcalak – and on the beaches north of town you can easily feel you have a world to yourself. SEE ALSO HOTELS, P.84

Below: a color range that repays contemplation.

Caves and Cenotes

The Yucatán is a unique landscape. It is one vast slab of limestone, which does not retain surface water, so there is not a single river north of Champotón on the west coast and Chetumal on the east. From the surface it can seem to be just a great flat expanse of forest, with no natural landmarks. These are below ground, in vast networks of caves and underground rivers, reached through holes in the rock called *cenotes* (a Spanish version of Mayan *dzonot*). They can be huge pools open to the sky, or narrow tunnels that lead down into underground cathedrals. Spellbinding to explore, they are magical places to swim and snorkel.

Riviera Maya: Cancún to Playa del Carmen

PUERTO MORELOS
Cenotes inland from Puerto Morelos, such as **Siete Bocas** or Deep Blue, have been opened up by a newly-paved road to Central Vallarta (signed off Highway 307). The closest cenotes to Cancún, they get a growing number of tours.
Boca del Puma Eco Park
Central Vallarta road, 16km from Puerto Morelos; tel: (998) 886 9869; www.bocadelpuma.com; daily 9am–5pm; entrance charge; Map p.135 D3
An adventure park around a cenote: cycle jungle trails and wall-climb as well as snorkel.

Most cenotes are on private or village community *(ejido)* land, so you normally pay a small fee to use them, often 30–50 pesos per person. Some now have 'eco-parks' around them, with jungle trails, snack stands, and other things as well as the cenote; others are still very simple, with just someone to take the money, steps to the water and (maybe) toilets. Take your own snorkel to basic cenotes.

Riviera Maya: South of Playa to Tulum

These are some of the Yucatán's best-known cenotes Areas listed from north to south.

AROUND XPU-HA

A popular clutch of cenotes is by Highway 307 from Puerto Aventuras down to Xpu-Ha. Most have broad entry pools, and so are lovely for casual swimming and snorkeling. From the north, the most enticing are: **Chac Mool**, two

well-developed rock pools; **Ponderosa**, one of the best for snorkeling, with an island in the middle; **Cristalino**, little-visited, placid, but near the road; and **Taj Mahal**, where you swim underwater to emerge into a cavern.

Eco Park Kantun-Chi
Highway 307 km 266.5; tel: (984) 873 0021; www.kantunchi.com; daily Nov–Mar 9am–5pm, Apr–Oct 9am–6pm; entrance charge; Map p.135 D2
Four cenotes and a cavern, bike or horse rides, and a local

Below: exploring Dos Ojos Cenote from Hidden Worlds.

Left: Cenote Samula.

THE TULUM–COBÁ ROAD

Some famous cenotes are along the road to Cobá, but several are best for divers and adventurous swimmers. The best open pools are the **Gran Cenote** (5km from Tulum) and **Aktun-Ha** (also known as Carwash). There are two off Highway 307 4km south of Tulum, **Cristal** and **Escondido**, but they can be hard to find.

Chichén Itzá

Chichén Itzá's **Sacred Cenote** is the most famous of all, but you can only look at it.
SEE ALSO CHICHÉN ITZÁ, P.15

Balankché
Highway 180, 5km east of Chichén Itzá; no phone; museum daily 9am–5pm; guided tours daily in English at 11am, 1pm, 3pm, in Spanish at 9am, noon, 2pm, 4pm, in French at 10am; entrance charge; Map p.134 B3
Most famous of the dry caves, this maze of dramatic cham-

The longest underwater cave systems in the world have been discovered in the eastern Yucatán, around Tulum. They are intricately linked. In 2007 **Sac Actun** cave was found to join the **Nohoch Nah Chich** cavern, forming one system 154km (95 miles) long. Nearby **Ox Bel Ha** cave – previously held to be the longest – is not much shorter at 145km (90 miles). As a result, this is the most exciting area in the world for cave-diving. *See also Diving, Snorkeling, and Watersports, p.52–5.*

zoo. Popular, so the water can get murky for swimming.

AKUMAL TO TULUM

Tulum is surrounded by the most awe-inspiring cave systems of all, extending north towards Akumal. Entrances to some caverns are small and hard to find, so they are better for divers and experienced snorkelers. **Hidden Worlds** center is an easy access point to some spectacular caverns, and local dive shops offer good-value snorkel tours as well as diving. There is also a

big, easily swimmable cenote behind the beach at **Tankah**, with fresh and salt water.
SEE ALSO DIVING, SNORKELING, AND WATERSPORTS, P.54

Aktun-Chen

Highway 307 km 250; tel: (984) 884 0444; www.aktunchen.com; daily Sept–May 9am–4.30pm, June–Aug 9am–6pm; entrance charge; Map p.135 D2
Not a cenote but a giant cave (unsuitable for swimming) with a forest park, a zoo of local animals, and lively tours.

Dos Ojos/Hidden Worlds

Dos Ojos Cenote, Highway 307 km 242, 11km north of Tulum; tel: (984) 877 8535; www.hiddenworlds.com.mx; daily 9am–3pm; entrance charge; Map p.135 D2
Dos Ojos, best-explored of the giant cenote systems, has fabulous big, snorkel-friendly caverns as well as tunnels down below. You can visit by yourself for a small fee, but Hidden Worlds provides a fine taster of cenote snorkeling (and diving), with cenote and jungle tours through stunning caverns, in other systems as well as Dos Ojos. Other adventures to try include 'sky-cycling' in the forest at treetop height.

Below: Mayan incense burners at Balankché.

Cenotes have always played a central part in the life of the Maya. In typical Mayan style, they are ambiguous: essential sources of water – and so life – but also gateways to *Xibalba*, the sinister underworld. Since ancient times they were places of refuge, and of special rituals to make contact with the gods.

Above: one of the great natural swimming pools, Cenote Samula.

bers, stalagmites and stalactites has served the Maya since long before the building of nearby Chichén Itzá, while in the chamber known as 'The Sanctuary' there are incense burners from the time of the Spanish Conquest. Humidity in the cave is often fierce.

SEE ALSO MAYAN RUINS AND RELICS, P.90

Cenote Ikkil

Highway 180 km 122, 4km east of Chichén Itzá; daily 8am–6pm; entrance charge; Map p.134 B3

Remarkably round, ringed by creepers, this is a huge well cenote as at Chichén, but here a stairway allows you to swim. At the top there's a restaurant.

Cenote Yokdzonot

Highway 180 km 100, 18km west of Chichén Itzá; daily 9am–5pm; entrance charge; Map p.134 B3

In 2005 a group of Mayan women decided Yokdzonot's village cenote was underused, and began to clear it up for opening. They care for it very well, so it's beautifully clean to swim in. They also offer local snacks, and snorkels and even bikes to rent. Local men also act as forest guides.

Yucatán State

Yucatán actually has many more cenotes than Quintana Roo – nearly every village has one – including some of the most spectacular, and huge, mysterious dry caverns. Villages have lately been keener to open their cenotes to visitors, as at Yokdzonot *(see left)*, and signs to them are often seen along roads.

AROUND VALLADOLID
Cenote Dzitnup and Cenote Samula

Dzitnup, off Highway 180 7km west of Valladolid; daily 8am–5pm; entrance charge; Map p.134 B2

Natural masterpieces, these subterranean basilicas are next to each other in little Dzitnup, west of Valladolid. The passageway into the main cenote gives no sign of what's ahead, as you emerge into a vast, arching cavern above perfectly clear, cool turquoise water. A shaft of light from a hole in the roof falls straight into the pool. Chichén Itzá tours often visit around 11am, but rarely give time to swim; at other times it's far quieter. Neighboring **Samula** is an equally dramatic vision of the underworld, with the roots of a giant *ceiba* – tree of life for the Maya – reaching far down to the water's surface.

Right: an easy way in to Yokdzonot cenote.

Above: the mysterious depths of Loltún.

Cenote Zací
Calle 37, between Calles 36 and 38, Valladolid; daily 8am–6pm; entrance charge; Map p.134 B3

Two blocks from Valladolid's main square is the town's chasm-like original cenote, earlier that of Mayan *Zací*. No longer good for drinking or swimming, but fascinating.

CENTRAL YUCATÁN
Cenote Xlacah, Dzibilchaltún
Off Mérida–Progreso road at km 12; daily 8am–5pm; entrance charge; Map p.133 D3

Dzibilchaltún is unique among Mayan ruins in still having its cenote fully open. A bottomless pit, explored so far down to 44m, Xlacah is a popular swimming hole (especially on Sundays, as locals get in free) but still very clean, and with shallow areas for swimming.
SEE ALSO MAYAN RUINS AND RELICS, P.90

Finding village cenotes can be an adventure, and can drive you crazy – as you try to pick out unmarked forest trails on empty roads. A guide can make things a lot easier. For cenote tours from Mérida, *see Tours and Guides, p.121.*

Cuzamá
45km southeast of Mérida on road via Acanceh; daily 9am–5pm; entrance charge; Map p.133 E3

The area south and east of Mérida is riddled with cenotes, and Cuzamá's three forest pools have rapidly become the best-known. The village is well organized: signs direct you to local guides, who take you by horse-drawn cart on an old light rail line about 12km to each cenote in turn. Access is steep, down metal ladders. The pools are exquisite, but can get crowded.

Uxmal and the Puuc Cities
No swimmable cenotes, but vast cave systems.

Grutas de Calcehtok
Off Highway 180 Mérida–Campeche road: turn east north of Maxcanú to Calcehtok village, then follow signs for 'Grutas de Calcehtok-Oxkintok'; Map p.133 D2

One of the most extraordinary Yucatán caves, a giant pit big enough to house trees, as well as weird cave plants, birds, bats, and strange air currents to add to the unearthly feel. It's unsafe to go beyond the main cave without a guide.

Loltún
Junction of Puuc Route and Xul–Oxcutzcab road, 12km east of Labná; tours daily in English at 9.30am, 11am, 1pm, 3pm, in Spanish at 9am, 12.30pm, 2pm, 3pm, 4pm; Map p.133 D2

The most jaw-dropping of all the Yucatán's giant caves, used by the Maya from earliest prehistory to the 1840s Caste War. Loltún is a vast labyrinth, where tiny passages lead into soaring caverns with columns of frail light to reveal strange cave ferns. Also bizarre are the shifts in temperature. Guides are only paid if they take a tour, so a good tip is in order.
SEE ALSO MAYAN RUINS AND RELICS, P.91

Campeche
Grutas de Xtacumbilxunaan
3km south of Bolonchén de Rejón on Highway 261; Tue–Sun 9am–5pm; Map p.133 D1

Stephens and Catherwood visited this deep cave in 1842, and saw, amazed, that it was Bolonchén's only source of water, with relays of men carrying it up a huge stairway. This is no longer intact, so visitors can usually only enter the upper chambers.

Below: Catherwood's famous engraving of Xtacumbilxunaan.

43

Children

A s major resort areas Cancún, Cozumel, and the Riviera Maya naturally have plenty of places to entertain kids – fun parks, water slides, zoos, dolphin pools – if they ever run out of things to do on those beaches. Local specialities are snorkel parks and 'eco-parks' like Xcaret, which provide a fascinating first look at tropical nature – forest walks, turtles, toucans, and other birds and animals, coral lagoons – in a safe, family-oriented setting. Away from the coast, keeping children enthralled is less a matter of finding specific attractions than of hooking up to the very child-friendly nature of Yucatecan life.

Cancún

Aquaworld

Boulevard Kukulcán km 15.2; tel: (998) 848 8327; www. aquaworld.com.mx; daily 8am–9pm; charges vary for different activities; Map IBC
Cancún's biggest water-based fun center faces placid Nichupté lagoon: for smaller children there are easy, stable kayaks and underwater rides in the 'Subsee' glass-sided boat; older kids are drawn to snorkeling, sailing, the 'sky rider' ride and a jungle tour by wave-runner.

Wet'n'Wild

Boulevard Kukulcán km 25; tel: (998) 881 3000; www.wetnwild cancun.com; daily 10am–5pm; entrance charge; Map IBC
This giant family water park at the bottom end of Cancún island has all the classic rides required for maximum fun-while-wet: interlinked wave pools, whirlpools, and four multilevel slides for real dare-devils. For a more gentle time there's a 'lazy river' for swimming, and a fun area for younger children. On-site restaurants are routine, but handy. There's also a Delphinaris dolphin pool, *see p.46.*

The Islands

ISLA MUJERES
El Garrafón Reef Park

Carretera de Garrafón; tel: (998) 877 1100; www.garrafon.com; daily 10am–5pm; entrance charge; Map p.8
One of the first Riviera 'snorkel parks,' created round Garrafón lagoon, a once-beautiful rock pool that's very placid and safe for children. However, due to hurricane damage and excessive visitor numbers it now has far less coral or fish, so snorkelers are often disappointed. Kayaks, banana boats and so on can be rented on the beach, at high rates.

Below: getting to grips with a few of the options at Aquaworld.

Left: enjoying the
Carnaval spirit in Mérida.

Discover Mexico
Carretera Costera Sur km 5.5; tel:
(987) 857 2820; www.discover
mexico.org; Mon–Sat 8am–6pm;
entrance charge; Map p.9
This curious, recently opened
park brings together monu-
ments from all over Mexico –
Mayan and Aztec pyramids,
Mexico City's Palace of Fine
Arts – in miniature. There's
also a handicrafts museum, a
very large souvenir store, and
a restaurant with food specialties from around the country.

Parque Chankanaab
Carretera Costera Sur, 9km south
of San Miguel; tel: (987) 872
0914; www.cozumelparks.com;
daily 7am–5pm; entrance charge;
Map p.9
One of Cozumel's most popular attractions, centered on
Laguna Chankanaab, a lovely
rock-and-coral bowl. There's
also a dolphin pool, a botanical garden, a playground, and
a fine, calm beach, with children's area. Hurricanes have
damaged the coral at nearby
Paraíso reef, but you can still
see all kinds of colorful fish a
few feet from the beach – if
this is a first try at snorkeling,
then the sights seen here just
by poking a mask below water
have guaranteed wow-factor.

Parque Punta Sur
Carretera Costera Sur km 27; tel:
(987) 872 0914; www.cozumel
parks.com; admissions daily
9am–3pm; entrance charge,
children under 8 free; Map p.9
A much larger park covering
the island's southern tip:
there's a (climbable) lighthouse
and a tiny Mayan ruin, and
well-marked nature trails that
lead to a crocodile lagoon,
bird-filled woods and fabulous
snorkeling beaches, where
you can also rent kayaks.
SEE ALSO WILDLIFE AND NATURE,
P.126

Above: choices, choices…

Tortugranja Turtle Farm
Carretera de Sac Bajo; tel: (998)
877 0595; daily 9am–5pm;
entrance charge; Map p.8
This official centre breeds and
raises sea turtles until they are
ready to be released into the
wild, in an effort to repopulate
the region's seas with these
endangered animals. Visitors
can usually see turtles at many
stages of development, from
eggs in incubators to newly
hatched babies to near-full-
grown leatherback and
hawksbill turtles, and there's
an informative exhibition.

The Yucatán's thousands of
snack stands provide plenty of
treats for kids. *Churros*, which
came directly from Spain, are
sticks of soft, sweet batter,
served dusted in sugar; more
local are *marquesitas*, sweet
waffle-like wafers rolled into a
cone and usually filled with
cheese or *cajeta* (sweet, milky
toffee). *Garapinados*, sugar-
roasted peanuts, are another
option. Of course, all this sugar
and frying doesn't exactly make
for health food (but they're
prepared fresh, and generally
additive-free). For more balance, find a *Paletería-Nevería*
or ice-cream stand, which will
have great fresh fruit juices,
nieves (water ices) and *paletas*
(popsicles or lollipops). *See
also Food and Drink, p.66.*

COZUMEL
Cozumel has the region's
most family-oriented beaches
on its sheltered southwest
coast, with beach clubs that
offer facilities for different ages
such as snorkeling, kayaks,
banana boats, and so on. The
further south you go, the less
likely they are to be crowded.

45

Riviera Maya: Cancún to Playa del Carmen

Crococún

Highway 307 km 323, 3km north of Puerto Morelos; tel: (998) 850 3719; www.crococunzoo.com; daily 8.30am–5.30pm; entrance charge, children under 6 free; Map p.135 E3

One of the Riviera's older attractions, but this crocodile farm is always among its most popular, and very well-kept. As well as crocodiles of various ages – from little ones to old monsters – there are local animals such as snakes, deer, and monkeys. Kids love it as there's plenty of opportunity to get close to small crocs and harmless animals like coatis.

Rancho Loma Bonita

Highway 307 km 315, 5km south of Puerto Morelos; tel: (998) 887 5465; www.rancholoma bonita.com; daily 10am–7pm; entrance charge; Map p.135 D3

Horseback rides through the jungle, along the beach and through the water. The Rancho now also has noisier ATV jungle tours, and wave-runners.
SEE ALSO SPORTS, P.119

Riviera Maya: From Playa del Carmen to Tulum

Laguna Yal-Ku

At north end of Media Luna Bay road, Akumal; no phone; daily 8am–5.30pm; entrance charge; Map p.135 D2

Below: Yal-Ku lagoon.

Above: kids love colors.

Akumal's lovely Media Luna bay is closed off to the north by this huge, shallow, very calm turquoise lagoon. It's a wonderful place to swim and snorkel with young children, as it's very safe, yet the lagoon is still full of fish and marine life. Tour groups sometimes come here around midday, but it's rarely crowded at other times. Admission is charged, but facilities are simple: take snorkel gear with you.

Punta Laguna Spider Monkey Reserve

On road between Cobá and Nuevo Xcan, 17km north of Cobá; no phone; charge for guides and canoe hire; Map p.135 C3

The forest northeast of Cobá is among the best places in

The Dolphin Downside

Swim-with-dolphin operations are heavily criticized for disregarding the animals' health. Wild dolphins swim huge distances, and when confined to small, shallow pools they are prone to a range of diseases. Most of these cute critters live shortened lives. For a summary of the argument, see *Dolphins are Dying to Amuse You*, issued by the US Animal Welfare Institute, www.awionline.org.

Dolphins

Dolphin pools are some of the Riviera's most prominent – but most expensive – family attractions. Most offer a show, when the animals do tricks with their trainers, and the opportunity to swim with dolphins and (for a higher charge) do some tricks yourself such as riding on their backs. They are run by three companies, **Dolphin Discovery** (www.dolphindiscovery.com), at Isla Mujeres, Cozumel, and Puerto Aventuras; **Delphinaris** (www.delphinaris.com) at Wet'n'Wild in Cancún and Cozumel; and **Delphinus** (www.delphinusworld.com) at Dreams Cancún Resort, Xcaret, Xel-Ha, and near Mahahual on the Costa Maya. There's also a cramped dolphinarium in La Isla mall in Cancún. Dolphin Discovery is a bit cheaper, beginning at $69 for a basic 45min swim ($59, under-12s); Delphinus has a higher reputation. At all sites, more advanced programs are around $130–160 an hour. *See also box, below, and for places to see wild dolphins, see Wildlife and Nature, p.127.*

the Yucatán to see spider monkeys. Tours are run by the Mayan village of Punta Laguna, which provides guides. Canoes can be rented on a cenote-style lagoon.
SEE ALSO WILDLIFE AND NATURE, P.128

Xcaret

Highway 307, 6km south of Playa del Carmen; tel: freephone 1-800 292 2738; www.xcaret.com; daily Nov–Mar 8.30am–9pm, Apr–Oct 8.30am–10pm; entrance charge; Map p.135 D2

The Riviera Maya's biggest family attraction, the original 'eco-park' offers lots of different things to to do in a complete day out, to match the high prices. One of the most popular is the 'snorkeling

Right: some of the options in a day at Xcaret.

river', which winds through the park to the beach; there's also a large dolphinarium. Centered on a natural lagoon, the park also contains the remains of the Mayan city of **Polé**, a big stretch of forest, and a botanical garden. It's one of the easiest places for most visitors to catch sight of the Yucatán's more exotic (so more elusive) wildlife such as pumas, rare parrots, and jaguars, with a fine zoo, aviary, and aquarium. Rarer attractions include the astonishing *mariposario* or butterfly garden. Restaurants are high-standard, and the day ends with a spectacular live show. Transport is provided to Xcaret from Cancún and various points on the Riviera.
SEE ALSO MAYAN RUINS AND RELICS, P.89

Xel-Ha

Highway 307 km 245, 15km north of Tulum; tel: freefone 1-800 009 3542; www.xel-ha. com.mx; daily 9am–6pm; entrance charge; Map p.135 D2
Part of the same organization as Xcaret, this park focusses more on snorkeling, kayaking, 'sea trek' undersea walks and many other activities in an exquisite natural lagoon. There's an excellent separate pool for young kids.

Mérida

Parque del Centenario
Calle 59, at Avenida Itzaes; tel (zoo): (999) 928 5815; www. merida.gob.mx/centenario; park daily dawn–dusk, zoo Tue–Sun 6am–6pm; free; Map p.18
Loved by local kids, Mérida's biggest park has a zoo, boating lake, a miniature train, and ample space to run around in.

SEE ALSO MAYAN RUINS AND RELICS, P.89

Street Rides and Fiestas
Kids' entertainments– bouncy castles, carrousels – appear in the squares and paseos of many Mexican towns every weekend. There are naturally more things to see and do in the bigger regular events, such as the **Mérida en Domingo** fiesta every Sunday. As well as towers of bright balloons for sale, snack stands, music, and captivating street life, there are dances, shows, and other events for kids, and – old favorites – rides in horse-drawn carriages or rented cycle-carts along traffic-free streets. There are hundreds more rides during each town's annual fiesta, when traveling funfairs take over whole squares.
In Mérida, the second day of **Carnaval** is 'Children's Day,' with a special kids' parade, and there are other attractions all week. *See also Festivals, p.62.*

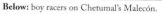

Below: boy racers on Chetumal's Malecón.

Churches

The Spanish missionary friars sent to establish Christianity in the Yucatán left a legacy in stone every bit as solid as that of their Mayan predecessors – and often far more visible, since colonial churches anchor the squares of most towns and villages. The Spanish crown allotted each of its new American lands to different missionary orders. The whole of the Yucatán was entrusted to the Franciscans, and its first churches reflected the austere traditions of the order: plain, massive, and with little decoration. These giant, solid temples have become an inseparable part of the Yucatecan scenery.

Yucatán State

IZAMAL
Convento de San Antonio de Padua
Plaza Mayor, Calle 31, corner of Calle 30; daily 6am–8pm; Map p133 E3

The greatest creation of the Franciscan builders was founded by Father Landa *(see p.51)* in 1549 and begun by Friar Juan de Mérida. The first thing to notice is its huge size: painted yellow and white like the rest of Izamal, it dominates the town, with its *atrio* court-yard entirely covering a former Mayan pyramid-platform. The

Above: San Bernardino Sisal.

Below: in San Servacio.

church and cloister are solid and simple in Franciscan style, but this adds to its grandeur, and scattered around there are fascinating pieces of fresco. It contains the Yucatán's official patroness, Our Lady of Izamal, and Pope John Paul II visited here in 1993.

VALLADOLID
Catedral de San Servacio
Parque Principal, corner of Calle 42; Map p.134 B3

Valladolid's lofty white cathedral was built during the second wave of Yucatán church building in the mid-17th century and not finished until the 18th, and so has a

much lighter, more elegant style than the early churches.
San Bernardino Sisal
Calle 41A (Calzada de los Frailes), corner of Calle 49; Map p.134 B3

In contrast, the town's oldest church was begun as part of a monastery by Friar Juan de Mérida in 1552. Its fortress-like appearance was no accident: it was built on the edge of newly founded Valladolid, then a Spanish reserve closed to the untrustworthy Maya, so that it could both serve local Spaniards and act as a mission to the Maya. It has an ornate baroque altarpiece, and a massive cloister and well, built in 1613 over a cenote.

Left: leaving the great atrium of Izamal after a dance display.

Churches are usually open daily from around 7am–1pm, and again around 4–9pm (so there is no point in trying to visit at lunchtime). Some city churches may be open all day, and keep more precise hours. In country churches, hours depend on the local *sacristán*, and so often vary. Entrance is always free.

Friar Juan's Designs

The Spanish friars brought their resources with them – including architects. For the Franciscans in Yucatán, their principal early architect was Friar Juan de Mérida, believed to have been an architect and soldier before he joined the order. He was chief builder of the monasteries of Maní, Sisal, and Izamal. The actual work was carried out by the Maya, as forced labour.

In style, Friar Juan and other Franciscans had little interest in current fashions, and their plain churches are far more 'medieval'-looking than others built at the same time back in Spain. An innovation of their own, unknown in Spain, was the huge *atrio* or courtyard in front of many churches, as seen at Maní and, above all, Izamal. These were built to enclose vast Masses for thousands of newly converted Maya, too many to fit in the church. Many early churches have an altar built into their outside walls. Called a *capilla de indios* or 'Indian chapel' and once protected by a palm roof, this was used for these open-air services.

Mérida

Catedral de San Ildefonso

Plaza Mayor, corner of Calles 60 and 61; daily usually 6am–1pm, 2–8pm; Map p.18

The oldest cathedral on the American mainland – its only predecessor in the continent is in Santo Domingo – was begun in 1562 and finished in 1598. The bishop at the time complained to his superiors at the extravagance of building such a thing in one of Spain's poorer colonies, but Yucatán's *conquistadores* were determined to have it. The usual severity of Franciscan building was lightened by Renaissance touches and Plateresque carving, but it doesn't conform to any one style (and the two main towers are not identical). The interior is plain and white, having lost most of its images during the Mexican Revolution, except for the shrine of the *Cristo de las Ampollas* (Christ of the Blisters).

Ermita de Santa Isabel

Calle 66, corner of Calle 77; Map p.18

This charming little chapel and cloister were built in 1748 at the (then) starting point of the Camino Real to Campeche, for travelers to pray for a safe journey or give thanks for their arrival. It feels very secluded.

Iglesia de Jesús (Tercer Orden)

Parque de la Madre, Calle 60, corner of Calle 59; Map p.18

The Franciscans were followed into the Yucatán by other Catholic orders such as the Jesuits, who inaugurated this church in 1618. Characteristically it is in a far more ornate style than the early churches, and is a favorite for weddings. Its other name comes from the 'Third Order' (Tercer Orden) of Franciscans, to whom it passed after the Jesuits were expelled from the Spanish Empire in 1767. In the wall facing Parque Hidalgo

Below: the Iglesia de Jesús.

49

Above: the massive, but not symmetrical, facade of Mérida cathedral. *See p.49.*

there are easily visible stones with Mayan inscriptions, since like many colonial buildings the Jesús was built with stones from Mayan temples.

La Mejorada
Parque de la Mejorada, Calle 50, corner of Calle 59; Map p.18
Church building never ceased in colonial Mérida, and this suitably massive, plain church, consecrated in 1640, is the biggest surviving part of one of the two huge Franciscan monasteries that existed in the city. Most of the monastery behind it is now a college.

Las Monjas
Calle 63, corner of Calle 64; Map p.18
'The Nuns' church was built in the 1590s as part of one of the first closed convents of Nuns in the Americas. Imposing metal grills created a separate area so nuns could take part in services without mixing with other worshippers, while above the church is a pillared *mirador* watchtower where they could get some air without leaving the convent.

Santa Lucía
Calle 60, corner of Calle 55; Map p.18
In colonial times the Barrio de Santa Lucía was home to Mérida's black population, and this simple church was built to serve them. Today –

inexplicably painted pink – it's very popular for weddings.

Uxmal and the Puuc Cities
Maní
Off Highway 18, 14km east of Ticul; Map p.133 D2
Few buildings evoke the history of the Conquest as much as Maní, oldest of the big missionary monasteries, founded in 1547. The Franciscans came here invited by Tutul Xiu, lord of Maní and first of the Mayan lords to accept Spanish rule and Christianity. It was built remarkably quickly by Friar de Mérida, and its style is particularly plain and massive

Below: an 18th-century portable altar from Santa Elena.

– the cloister almost feels like a giant cave. The unenclosed *atrio* in front, once the plaza of Mayan Maní, was the site of Father Landa's great bonfire of Mayan artifacts in 1562 *(see box, right)*. Maní does not get many visitors, which only heightens the atmosphere.

Santa Elena
Highway 261, 16km southeast of Uxmal; Map p.133 D2
A fine example of a village church: like many villages, Santa Elena, near Uxmal, did not acquire a permanent stone church until late – the 1750s – having earlier made do with wooden huts. It has scarcely changed since, with a venerable sacristy and altars, and a museum with grisly remains from burials in colonial times.

Teabo
Off Highway 18, 12km east of Maní; Map p.133 E2
Many southern Yucatán towns built grand new churches in the 17th century, in a more baroque style than that of the post-Conquest era. Built from 1650–95, Teabo is one of the largest, and has remarkable murals in the sacristy.

Tekax
Highway 184, 18km east of Oxcutxcab; Map p.133 E2
Another very refined, basilica-like small-town church, completed in 1692.

The Many-Sided Father Landa

Father Diego de Landa (1524–79), first head of the Franciscans in Yucatán, is an inescapable, ever-controversial figure in the region's history. He is inseparable from the great monastery in Izamal, which he founded in 1549. Without Landa we would know far less about the Maya, for in 1566 he wrote a painstaking report, the 'Relation of the Affairs of Yucatán.'

Full of all kinds of details of Mayan life at the time of the Conquest, it has also provided the essential basis for all later understanding of Mayan writing and inscriptions. But it was also Landa who was responsible for the single greatest act of destruction of Mayan culture. In 1562 he discovered that many supposedly Christianized Maya were still performing their old rituals in secret. Enraged, he organized a mass *auto da fé* in front of the monastery at Maní, where Mayan backsliders were tortured into repentance. He also had his men search out every Mayan idol and ceramic pot they could find, and hundreds of manuscripts, and burned them, which had 'an extraordinary effect' on the watching Maya, causing them 'great sorrow.' Today, there are only four known Mayan manuscripts left.

Costa Maya and Río Bec

FELIPE CARRILLO PUERTO
Balam-Na (Santa Cruz)
Plaza Principal, Calle 67, corner of Calle 68; Map p.139 D4

This is, in legend, the only church in the Yucatán built by white slaves (Yucatán army prisoners) under Mayan command, rather than vice versa. When the rebel Maya established their 'capital' here in 1851 they built a central temple-church, the Balam-Na or 'jaguar house.' They did not, though, build anything recognizably Mayan, but a version of the most simple of Franciscan chapels. Since the 1940s, it has been a Catholic church.

Santuario de la Cruz Parlante
Calle 69, corner of Calle 58; Map Map p.139 D4

The actual 'Sanctuary of the Talking Cross' is on one side of Carrillo Puerto, in a small park. A chapel was built around it in 2004, and people still often leave offerings and observe *cruzob* ceremonies.

Campeche

Catedral de La Inmaculada
Parque Principal, Calle 55; daily usually 6am–1pm, 2–8pm; Map p.24

Campeche's cathedral had a very different history to that of Mérida: it was begun in the 1630s, but work was often

Above: Campeche cathedral.

interrupted, and it was not finished until the 1850s. The central facade is one of the oldest parts, from the 1650s, while the north tower dates from the 1760s, and the south tower from the 1840s.

San Francisco
Avenida Miguel Alemán, corner of Calle Mariano Escobedo; Map p.24

The first of all the Franciscan buildings in the Yucatán was begun just north of recently conquered Campeche in 1546. Its massive, plain walls long served the people of the city as a refuge against pirate attacks. Part of the original cloister survives, and there's also the font where a grandson of Cortés was baptized.

San Francisquito
Calle 59, corner of Calle 12; Map p.24

A dazzling little showpiece of full-on, 18th-century Mexican baroque, with altarpieces and chapels in red, white and gold that have recently been beautifully restored.

San José
Calle 63, corner of Calle 10; Map p.24

This huge 18th-century church is now used for art exhibitions, but its great attraction is its unusual façade, decorated with blue and white tiles.

Below: the *Cruz Parlante* (Talking Cross) itself.

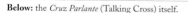

51

Diving, Snorkeling, and Watersports

One of the richest underwater environments in the world flanks the Yucatán's east coast, an extraordinary diversity of coral reefs and chasms full of life. It has just as much to offer complete beginners and experienced divers – who can also try out the world's best cave-diving. You can even see plenty in these waters with just a snorkel, and the fishing – both fly and deep-sea – is superb.

Diving and Snorkeling

Most dive centers offer plenty of options, starting with one-day 'Discover Scuba' or 'Resort' sampler courses for complete beginners (usually around $60–$80). Open-water certification courses cost from about $350, two-tank dives for certified divers around $60. Night and wreck dives, advanced courses, and more are also available. The best-prepared dive centers tend to cost a bit more; this is generally a price worth paying.

Virtually all dive masters will have an international NAUI or PADI certificate, and you should only ever dive with one who does. Another thing to look for is the number of students to each instructor: four is the maximum acceptable for beginners. Most diving here is drift diving (the current carries you, without needing to swim, so it is important to follow the lead of a dive master.

Dive shops also offer **snorkel** trips, from around $25. This is by no means second best, as you can see an abundance of marine life with no need for heavy equipment.

CANCÚN

Not favored by serious divers: dive trips from here often go to Isla or Cozumel in any case.

Aquaworld
Boulevard Kukulcán km 15.2; tel: (998) 848 8327; www.aquaworld.com.mx; daily 8am–9pm; Map IBC
This big family fun center has a large, rather impersonal scuba facility. Snorkel trips can be a better bet here.
SEE ALSO CHILDREN, P.44

THE ISLANDS
ISLA MUJERES

The best diving center near Cancún, with sites for every level of expertise, and small operators with personal service at decent rates. The shallow **Manchones** reef is great for snorkelers and scuba novices, and further out there are more testing sites such as **Sleeping Sharks** cave, where (harmless) reef sharks bask in the current. Most dive shops also offer fishing trips.

Coral Dive Center
Avenida Matamoros, off Avenida Rueda Medina; tel: (998) 877 0763; www.coralscubadive center.com; office daily 8am–10pm; Map p.8
One of Isla's longest-running dive operators, but still with

Below: a typical dive shop, Cozumel's Studio Blue.

Above: one of Cozumel's many low-cost snorkel tours.

Left: cavern-diving in the Dos Ojos Cenote near Tulum.

Dive schools can normally arrange accommodations packages with local hotels for customers taking 4–5-day certification or longer courses, and some have their own hotels. Check the possibilities when booking.

and you can see a lot from **Chankanaab** snorkel park or on one of the cheap snorkel tours run from San Miguel. More advanced reefs further south such as **Palancar** and **Punta Sur** are in a far better state, and are a divers' must. Some can be visited with (pricier) snorkel tours.

Cozumel has the region's most comprehensive diving infrastructure, with several specialist dive hotels. Many other hotels also offer good-value diving packages.

SEE ALSO CHILDREN, P.45

Aqua Safari
Avenida Melgar 429, between Calles 5 and 7 Sur; tel: (987) 872 0101; www.aquasafari.com; office daily 8am–8pm; Map p.9
The longest-running dive shop on Cozumel: individual service, with accommodation.

Deep Blue
Calle Adolfo Rosado Salas 200, corner of Avenida 10; tel: (987) 872 5653; www.deepblue cozumel.com; office daily 9am–8pm; Map p.9
Top of the line in dive shops: first-rate staff and equipment, and every option right up to advanced specialist courses.

Studio Blue
Calle Adolfo Rosado Salas, between Avenidas 5 and 10; tel: (987) 872 4414; http://cozumel-diving.net/studio-blue; office daily 8am–8pm; Map p.9
Straightforward, good-value operator offering basic dives and low-cost instruction.

very accessible rates. 'Adventure dives' to the many wrecks and wall dives around Isla are a specialty.

Diving Safety
Special measures should be observed to avoid accidents between divers and small boats. Areas used for diver training should be closed to other boats, dive masters should instruct students to look around when surfacing, and the dive center's boat should stay close to warn off other craft. In case of pressure accidents there are high-standard facilities in Cancún, Cozumel and Playa del Carmen.

Mundaca Divers
Avenida Madero 10, off Avenida Guerrero; tel: (998) 877 0607; www.mundacadivers.com; office daily 8am–5.30pm; Map p.8
A wide range of diving, snorkel and fishing options.

COZUMEL
The most famous dive area of all, with reefs of every degree of difficulty. Some are astonishingly close inshore, and are superb for snorkeling as well as diving. Well-known inshore reefs such as **Paraíso** just south of San Miguel have lost much of their coral thanks to recent Hurricanes, but the sea around them is still full of fish,

53

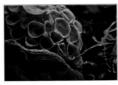

Above: some facets of the underwater kaleidoscope.

HOLBOX

There is no air compressor on Holbox, so diving is only possible with operators – often from Playa del Carmen – that bring equipment with them. But it's superb for snorkeling – in the June–September whale shark season, and year-round at **Isla de Pájaros** and places around Laguna Yalahao. The **Faro Viejo** and **Posada Mawimbi** offer excellent trips.

SEE ALSO HOTELS, P.78; TOURS AND GUIDES, P.120

RIVIERA MAYA: CANCÚN TO PLAYA DEL CARMEN

Listed from north to south.
PUERTO MORELOS
One of the most vibrant inshore reefs – now a specially protected area – on the main-

land side of the Cozumel channel makes this a wonderful spot for easy snorkeling as well as all levels of diving, in a much more laid-back setting than the bigger diving centers.
Almost Heaven Adventures
Avenida Rojo Gómez, off plaza; tel: (998) 871 0230; www.almost heavenadventures.com; office daily 9am–6pm; Map p.10
Dive master Enrique Juárez and his staff offer individual attention and abundant local knowledge, at good prices.
Dive Puerto Morelos
Avenida Rojo Gómez, north of plaza; tel: (998) 206 9084; www.divepuertomorelos.com; office daily 9am–6pm; Map p.10
Friendly, and with a full mix of diving, snorkeling, and fishing.

PLAYA DEL CARMEN

The base for some of the most experienced dive operators, who run trips to many parts of the coast. Costs can be higher than elsewhere.
Phocea Riviera Maya
Avenida 1 bis, between Calles 10 and 12 Norte (entrance to Hotel Colibrí); tel: (984) 873 1210; www.phoceariveramaya.com; office daily 9am–7pm; Map p.10
High-quality French-run company with an exciting range of dive packages, including cenote and reef dives.
Yucatek Divers
Avenida 15, between Calles 2 and 4 Norte; tel: (984) 803 2836; www.yucatek-divers.com; office daily 9am–5pm; Map p.10
Expert international divers who share space with **Casa Tucan** hotel, and offer great room-and-dive packages.
SEE ALSO HOTELS, P.78

RIVIERA MAYA: FROM PLAYA DEL CARMEN TO TULUM

Listed from north to south.
AROUND AKUMAL
There are dive shops on most beaches in the southern

Riviera, and exquisite reefs – despite the loss of coral caused by excessive hotel building onshore. This area also has some of the best cave-diving operators.
Akumal Dive Shop
Akumal village; tel: (984) 875 9032; www.akumal.com; office daily 8am–5pm; Map p.12
Well-equipped, long-running local operator.
Aquatech-Villas De Rosa
Aventuras Akumal; tel: (984) 875 9020; www.cenotes.com; office daily 9am–5pm; Map p.12
Owner Nancy De Rosa is a cave-diving expert, and has the Villas de Rosa hotel, so a comprehensive service is available, with every level of snorkeling, open-water and cave-diving, and a big range of packages.
SEE ALSO HOTELS, P.80
Pro Dive Mexico
Puerto Aventuras; tel: (984) 873 5491; www.prodivemex.com; office daily 9am–5pm; Map p.12
A very high-tech operator

> **Cavern- and Cave-Diving**
> The Yucatán's underground labyrinth of cenotes and water-filled caves makes this the most important area in the world for cavern- (in chambers still open to natural sunlight) and cave- (beyond the reach of natural light) diving. To try either, one must have completed at least an open-water certification course. Many dive operators now offer cavern dives, but it's best to go with one of the area's skilled cave and cavern specialists, such as **Aquatech** or **Cenote Dive Center** in Tulum. Prices begin at around $60 for an introductory cavern dive; cave-diving courses cost from around $650, with discounts for groups.
> **Hidden Worlds** (*see p.41*) also offers a taste of cavern-diving at lower prices. *See also Caves and Cenotes, p.40.*

Above: cave-diving with Aquatech from Akumal.

based at Puerto Aventuras, with an enterprising range of snorkel trips as well as dives.

TULUM
Divers are most drawn by the cenotes and caves, but there's good offshore diving as well.
Cenote Dive Center
Avenida Tulum, corner of Calle Osiris; tel: (984) 871 2232; www.cenotedive.com; office daily 9am–5pm; Map p.12
Cavern and cave specialists, who also provide excellent cenote snorkeling trips.
Maya Diving
Avenida Tulum, between Calles Orion and Centauro Sur; tel: (984) 871 3333; www.mayadiving.com; office daily 9am–5pm; Map p.12
Good-value operator with a full range of services.

COSTA MAYA
Far from crowds, so wonderfully mellow, and with a special draw in **Banco Chinchorro** – one of the Yucatán's unknown jewels, a huge ring of islands and pristine coral 20km offshore, with shallow reefs, wall dives, and wrecks from pirate ships to World War II relics.
Casa Carolina
Beach road, 4km north of Xcalak; tel in US: (610) 616 3862; www.casacarolina.net; Map p.22
Owner Bob Villier is a highly

trained dive master, so this ultra-tranquil hotel is an ideal spot to learn or try new dives.
SEE ALSO HOTELS, P.84
XTC Dive Center
Xcalak village; tel: (983) 831 0461; www.xtcdivecenter.com; office daily 9am–6pm; Map p.22
Xcalak's friendly, low-key dive shop has the best boat for visiting Chinchorro, and excellent snorkel tours, too.

Fishing
Fishermen discovered these coasts even before divers did. Offshore, there is fine **deep-sea fishing** for barracuda, snapper, sierra and (from April to June) marlin, sailfish, and dorado. Onshore, the flats around **Ascension Bay** south of Tulum, and further south behind **Xcalak**, contain some of the world's best **fly-fishing** grounds, above all for permit, tarpon and bonefish. Also excellent for fly-fishing is the lagoon around **Holbox**, especially for tarpon and snook.
Most dive shops will also arrange fishing trips with expert local boat captains.
Cuzan Guest House
Punta Allen; tel: (983) 834 0358; www.flyfishmx.com; Map p.12
A magnet for fly fishermen in the coast's most remote village, with pretty rooms, too.

Holbox Tarpon Club
Holbox; tel: (984) 875 2144; www.holboxtarponclub.com; Map p.9
Alejandro 'Mr Sandflea' Vega is a superb fishing guide, with many return customers.
3 Hermanos
Cozumel; tel: (987) 872 6417; www.cozumelfishing.com; Map p.9
Well-equipped deep-sea and fly-fishing trips from Cozumel.

Sailing and Kayaks
The best place to rent sailboats is **Puerto Aventuras**. **Windsurf** boards are available on Isla Mujeres, Holbox, and in Playa del Carmen.
Kayaks can be rented on many beaches, but some of the most enjoyable places to explore this way are the lake at **Bacalar**, **Xcalak**, and **Sian Ka'an**, where **CESiak** offers unforgettable kayak tours.
SEE ALSO TOURS AND GUIDES, P.120

Kiteboarding
Extreme Control
El Paraíso, Beach road km 2, Tulum; tel: (984) 745 4555; www.extremecontrol.net; Map p.12
Learn how to fly up out of the waves and never look back: they also operate from chic La Zebra hotel, down the beach.

Below: waiting for the wind on Holbox.

Environment

Very few people who see the Yucatán and its coast fail to recognize its exquisite beauty – a blend of explosive green plantlife, soft white sand, and a gem-like sea, with still more color in the coral and marine life just below the water's surface. This beauty is the result of a unique, complex balance, between thin, dry limestone rock, the fresh water in the maze of caves just a few feet beneath it, the mangrove fringes and lagoons around the coast, and the life of the reefs offshore. This makes it an especially delicate environment, and yet in the last 30 years it has been subjected to unprecedented pressures.

The Riviera Maya: Booming until it Busts?

The scale and pace of development between Cancún and Tulum since the mid-1990s have been mind-boggling. The mushrooming of towns such as Playa del Carmen has been matched by the march of the giant all-inclusive resorts, which are now spreading inland with rows of condos. Over and beyond the abuses alleged against specific resorts, there is a more general question as to just how long this kind of no-holds-barred development can be kept up. Concern centers particularly on four main areas.

SHEER SCALE: LAND USE

One is simply the extent and manner of resort building. The Riviera Maya is a long strip of beach backed by mangrove on one side, and the reef on the other. The vibrancy of the reef is due to the supply of nutrients from the rocky land mass, as filtered through coastal mangroves. Resorts, though, crave beach frontage, and many build right next to the shore, draining or obliterat-

ing mangroves, and so cutting the region's natural flow. This has been a major cause of reef loss all along the Riviera.

The growth in cruise traffic also contributes to reef loss, especially round Cozumel.

HURRICANES AND BEACH MANIPULATION

Argument goes on over whether the greater frequency of Caribbean hurricanes in the last few years is due to global warming, but it is undeniable that hurricanes have had a severe effect on the Riviera, especially Wilma in 2005.

Because the sand here is so soft, it shifts easily in storms, and Wilma stripped away large parts of Cancún beach. Beaches also become less stable when they are separated from mangroves by hotel building. Hotel and resort owners, however, don't like to accept this unpredictability – or the long-term planning that might ensure beaches revive naturally – and many use a range of shortcuts to try to fix the shape of 'their' beaches.

One is the deposit of 'sac-sab,' cheap powdered stone,

Above: drainage comes in many forms.

in place of lost sand, and to 'mold' open beaches into enclosed bays. At first this seems only like coarse sand, but after it has got wet a few times it's as hard as cement. Still more drastic is the use of geotubes, plastic sacks filled with cement, to create beach barriers. Apart from being miserable to walk on – and so destructive of the charm of the very beaches they're supposed to protect – both methods are harmful to reef life and breeding turtles.
SEE ALSO BEACHES, P.37

Left: building never stops.

GARBAGE

The Riviera's residents and tourists produce mountains of trash, and it has run out of landfill sites to put it in. This is a crisis local authorities cannot ignore: new waste-handling and recycling programs have begun, but this is an uphill struggle, and a permanent solution is still to be found.

Positive Steps

Such is the role played by heavy-duty tourist development in the local economy that those who question how it's done often get short shrift, and the obvious argument that an ecologically harmed Riviera will no longer be an attraction long-term is usually ignored. Local groups focus on tightening of Mexican law and enforcement of ecological standards, and certification schemes for eco-acceptable resorts, but a lot more needs to be done.

Thankfully, there are still huge areas that haven't been built on, as well as examples of 'better practice' – a way to find them is to check Google Earth, and just see which resorts are built back from the beach. For more information see the Centro Ecológico Akumal site, www.ceakumal.org, or www.saverivieramaya.org.

The Golf Issue

There's only one way to say it: no one who cares one whit about the environment expects to come to the Yucatán and play golf. Golf courses are alien growths here: most of the Riviera Maya is made up of mangrove or *selva baja*, low jungle. This is naturally invasive, as you can see on the sides of any road after rain. In order to keep it back and create the clear, neat fairways and greens demanded by golfers, a common practice is to drain mangrove and import unnaturally solid soil, then ring the course with a ferocious barrier of chemicals and pesticides, which is regularly renewed.

Some courses are built over cenote systems, blocking the natural flow of rainwater, while allowing a drip-drip of pesticides into the underground water system and on to nearby reefs. Despite publicity claims, only one Riviera course, at Maya Koba, has been built with significant awareness of local ecology. And yet, golf-course building has exploded on the Riviera since 2000. Only a drop in demand will counteract the process.

DRAINAGE

Because the Yucatán is so fragile, a crust of rock above an underground water network flowing out to coral reefs, drainage systems here should be especially secure. Mexican law, however, has not kept up with the pace of building, and many towns and resorts do as little as possible even within current law. Many complaints are heard of resorts that have only semi-enclosed drainage systems, and allow semi- (or un-) filtered waste to flow into cenotes and out to sea. This is a major cause of reef loss and damage to sea life.

Below: solid sacsab on the beach at Cancún.

57

Essentials

The Yucatán is an easy-to-handle destination: small towns and villages may sometimes look as if they're sunk in a sleepy past, but alongside the palm trees and wooden Mayan houses there is a full set of modern communications, and should you ever be unable to find any service locals will point the way with habitual courtesy. This section gives you the basic orientation you need to get money, check your email or deal with medical and other emergencies. For information on getting around the region, *see also Transportation, p.122;* for useful phrases for travelers, *see Food and Drink, p.71, and Language, p.86.*

Climate and Clothing

As a tropical region the Yucatán has two main seasons: a dry season that gets hotter roughly from November to late June, then a hot, wet season from June to October. Things are not as predictable as the names suggest, though, and you can get bone-dry hot days in September and brief downpours in March. The weather is usually ideal in December–February, with daytime temperatures of mid-20s °C (75°–85° F). This is also the peak tourist season.

Casual clothing is generally all you need, with maybe something 'smart-casual' for some nightspots or restaurants, and a light sweater for the occasional cool evening. It is good to have at least one long-sleeved shirt, to protect against the sun and scratches while exploring Mayan ruins. Don't bother to pack a sunhat: you can buy better ones here.

HURRICANES

The official Atlantic hurricane season runs from June to November, but whether there will be a major storm in that time is unpredictable beyond a few days. If there is one, Mexico now has some of the best hurricane precautions and safety procedures anywhere in the Caribbean, and visitors are warned well in advance of any dangers.

Consulates

Canada
Honorary Consul, Plaza Caracol II, 3rd floor, no. 330, Boulevard Kukulcán km 8.5, Cancún; tel: (998) 883 3360; www.dfait-maeci.gc.ca; Map IBC

Below: hurricane warnings are very thorough.

UK
Honorary Consul, Royal Caribbean, Boulevard Kukulcán km 17, Cancún; tel: (998) 881 0100; email: ion@british consulate.cancun.com; Map IBC

US
Cancún: Honorary Consul, Plaza Caracol II, 3rd floor, no. 323, Boulevard Kukulcán km 8.5; tel: (998) 883 0272; Map IBC
Cozumel: Honorary Consul, office 8-9, Villa Mar mall, main plaza; tel: (987) 872 4574; Map p.9
Mérida: US Consulate-General, Paseo de Montejo 453; tel: (999) 925 5011; http://merida.us consulate.gov; Map p.18
Playa del Carmen: Honorary Consul, The Palapa, Calle 1 Sur, between Avenidas 15 and 20; tel: (984) 873 0303; Map p.10

Left: services to meet all needs in Tulum.

for travel to the Yucatán, but it is a good idea to be immunized against tetanus, typhoid, and hepatitis A. The risk of stomach complaints here is generally wildly exaggerated. The main health precaution to observe while here is to drink only purified water (*agua purificada*), which is provided automatically in most hotels.

It is important to have a fully comprehensive travel insurance policy, which will cover you for theft, lost baggage, and all medical eventualities. For scuba diving you may need extra cover.

Emergencies

A common number (**066**) is now in use in most parts of Mexico for calling emergency services, but it's often more effective, if possible, to call the nearest local service direct.

Cancún, Mérida, and some other towns have English-speaking 'tourist police,' who are generally the best to turn to if you are a victim of any kind of crime. You must also report any theft to the local prosecutor's office (Ministerio Público) to get the statement required for insurance claims. If you lose a passport, inform your consulate immediately.

EMERGENCY NUMBERS
General emergencies: 066
Tourist Police: Cancún 066; Playa del Carmen (984) 873 4000; Mérida (999) 930 3200
Ambulance (Red Cross): Cancún (998) 884 1616 Mérida (999) 924 9813

Gay and Lesbian Travelers

The Riviera gay scene is small, with a few, long-running venues in Cancún and Playa del Carmen, but has been get-

Metric to Imperial Conversions
1 meter = 3.28 feet
1 kilometer = 0.62 mile
1 hectare = 2.47 acres
1 kilogram = 2.2 pounds

ting more upfront, and Cancún hosts a gay festival each May that involves non-strictly gay venues as well as the known gay clubs. Elsewhere, gay life is less overtly visible, but there are quite a number of venues that are relatively gay-friendly.
SEE ALSO BARS AND NIGHTLIFE, P.33

Health and Insurance

There are no inoculations or special precautions required

THINGS TO PACK

A small **first-aid kit** is very useful, above all if you expect to spend time in forests and at more remote Mayan ruins. It should include bite lotion, antiseptic wipes and band-aids for minor cuts and scratches, and **bug repellent**. The strongest types all contain the chemical ingredient DEET. There are natural alternatives to DEET, but unfortunately they're often less effective.

HEALTH FACILITIES

If you have a medical problem, and have the required travel insurance, the best places to turn will be the high-quality

Below: Mérida's police are now bike-friendly.

private clinics found in main cities, such as those listed here. If you cannot get to one, local public health centers (*centros de salud*) provide an adequate emergency service, or call the nearest Red Cross clinic (*see Emergencies, p.59*).

Cancún:
American Hospital
Calle Viento 15, off Avenida Tulum; tel: (998) 884 6133; Map IBC
Mérida: Centro Médico de las Américas
Calle 54 no. 365, between Avenida Pérez Ponce and Calle 33A; tel for emergencies (24hrs): (999) 927 3199; Map p.18

PHARMACIES

Pharmacies, many open 24 hours daily, are easy to find in cities and even small towns. As well as a huge range of drugs and medicines, they always stock purified water.

Internet

Internet cafés are still not quite as abundant as pharmacies in Mexico, but even the smallest town seems to have at least one, so checking your email is not a problem.

For those who travel with laptops, a remarkable number of even cheap hotels now offer wireless (WiFi) connections, often for no extra charge.

Money

The Mexican currency is the **peso**, which usually stands at around 11 to the US dollar. It 'tracks' the dollar, so Canadians and Europeans have lately found the value of their money

Below: a Mérida ATM.

increasing in Mexico. There are coins for 1–20 pesos, and notes for 20 to 1,000 pesos.

US dollars are accepted in many shops in Cancún, Cozumel and the Riviera, but note that if you use dollars you end up paying slightly more. **Credit cards** are widely accepted across the region.

BANKS AND ATMS

Banks traditionally open Monday to Friday 8.30am–1pm and Saturday 9am–1pm, but many now stay open much later. However, many do not change cash or travelers' cheques through their opening times, so check before joining the line, and try only to use larger branches. If traveling from Europe, take travelers' cheques in US dollars, as Mexican banks give poor rates against other currencies. Outside bank hours, there are many small exchange offices open in tourist areas.

ATMs (cash machines) are plentiful in cities, and there are even one or two in many small towns, so, given the inconveniences of using banks, this is often the best way to get cash. Note that due to security concerns you may need to

Above: the local Internet shop has become a Mexican institution.

notify the card company that you are traveling to Mexico, or your card can be cut off. Also, there are still areas where ATMs are hard to find, *see below*.

Post

Email has ended any incentive to improve the erratic Mexican postal service. Try to use only main post offices; most open Monday to Friday 8am–6pm, Saturday 9am–1pm.

Main Post Offices
Cancún: Avenida Sunyaxchén, corner Avenida Xel-Ha; Map IBC
Mérida: Calle 53; Map p.18
Campeche: Avenida 16 de Septiembre, by Calle 53; Map p.24

ATM-free zones

Cards and ATMs may usually be a handy way to get money, but it's a good idea to have extra cash or travelers' cheques too, as it can happen that the town ATM breaks down or runs out of cash. Also, ATMs are still scarce in some areas, notably southern Quintana Roo and rural Campeche. There are no banks or ATMs on the Costa Maya or the Río Bec, so when traveling there you need to take adequate cash (in pesos) and check with hotels what to do if you go short.

Time

Yucatán and most of Mexico are usually in the same band as US Central time (so 6hrs behind GMT). However, Mexico goes to daylight-saving time a few weeks later than the US and Canada in April, and comes off it a little earlier in October.

Telephones

White *Lada* public phones are plentiful in cities and towns. They work with phone cards *(tarjetas lada)*, available for 30, 50 or 100 pesos (most pharmacies sell them). There are also phone offices *(casetas telefónicas)*, where you call from a booth and pay when you have finished. These are cheaper for international calls.

To make a call within Mexico but outside the immediate area, you must first dial an access code (**01**), followed by a 3-figure area *(lada)* code, as given with all numbers listed in this guide (998 Cancún, 999 Mérida, and so on). Cell (mobile) numbers have the same area codes, but to call them you may need another access code, **044** or **045**. **0800** numbers are toll-free.

Cellphone coverage is now pretty good in most of the Yucatán. However, charges are high for foreign users.

Tipping

Many Mexicans rely on tips to make up for low wages, so a good principle to follow is to tip generously, and keep a stock of loose change. One group doesn't usually expect extra tips: taxi drivers.

Tourist Information

Local tourist offices here are not well informed, especially on the Riviera. Those in Mérida and Campeche are a bit better. Much more useful are the local English-language free magazines, such as *Cancún Tips* (handed to all new arrivals at Cancún airport) and in Mérida *Yucatán Today* and *Explore Yucatán*, especially for upcoming events and maps. Local tour agencies are also far better information sources than official tourist offices. SEE ALSO TOURS AND GUIDES, P.120.

Main Tourist Offices

Cancún: Convention Center, Boulevard Kukulcán km 9.5; Mon–Fri 9am–5pm, Sat 9am–1pm; Map IBC

Mérida: Palacio Municipal, Plaza Mayor; Teatro Peón Contreras, Calle 60, x 57; both daily 8am–8pm; Map p.18

Campeche: Casa Seis, Parque Principal; Kiosk, Parque Principal, both daily 9am–9pm; Plaza Moch-Cuouh (state tourist office), daily 8am–8pm; Map p.24

Useful Websites

www.visitmexico.com official Mexico Tourism site
www.mexicotravel.co.uk for Mexico Tourism in Europe
www.cancun.net information on Cancún and the Riviera
www.mayayucatan.com.mx Yucatán State Tourism site
www.campechetravel.com Campeche State tourism
www.yucatantoday.com the site of the best local free magazine
www.yucatanliving.com excellent site by Mérida-based expats

Visas and Customs

US, Canadian, British, and other EU citizens do not need a visa to enter Mexico, but all must now have full passports. On the incoming flight you will be given a **Mexican Tourist Card** to fill in, which the immigration officer will stamp with your permitted stay (usually 90 or 180 days). Keep this with your passport and give it up when you leave the country.

You must also fill in a **customs form**. As you hand it in, after clearing immigration, you will be asked to press a button by a kind of traffic light. If it comes up green, you go straight through; if red, your bag will be searched. The theory is that this makes searches completely random.

Below: free magazines like *Yucatán Today* are a traveler's standby.

61

Festivals

Celebration is an essential part of Mexican life, as essential as family and tortillas. Every village, every trade, has its special fiesta to mark out the year, usually around the day of its patron saint, an occasion to step out of the everyday and spend time decorating the streets, mingling with neighbors, and enjoying music, food, and fireworks. An intricate blend of Hispanic and Mayan traditions, fiestas are vibrantly colorful. And, not content to wait for these main events, cities such as Mérida and many towns put on smaller celebrations every week. For the outsider, they are a warm, bright welcome mat to the Yucatecan way of life.

Weekly Fixtures

Some of the most charming events are not quite festivals but permanent dates in the weekly calendar. Nor are they just shows for tourists – rather, they are a demonstration of how much Yucatecans enjoy their own culture. Mérida and Campeche host most events, but many towns put on something, such as band concerts on Sundays. And all are free.

MÉRIDA
Map p.18
As the Yucatán's cultural capital, Mérida hosts the most extensive program, every week, all year round. For the first-time visitor, this creates a very full schedule.

Monday:
Vaquería Regional
Plaza Mayor, in front of the Palacio Municipal; 9pm
Performances of *jarana* folk dances, with a live band, in front of the town hall.

Tuesday: Remembranzas Musicales
Parque de Santiago, Calle 59, x 70 & 72; 8.30pm
Nostalgic music from local boleros and trios to Artie Shaw, in a charming square.

Wednesday: Concerts and Exhibitions
Centro Cultural Olimpo, Plaza Mayor; from 9pm
A quieter night, with a varied mix of events and temporary art exhibits in the Olimpo center on Plaza Mayor.

Thursday:
Serenatas Yucatecas
Parque de Santa Lucía, Calle 60, x 55; 9pm
One of the great must-sees of Mérida, held every Thursday for over 40 years and a wonderful showcase for the whole world of Yucatecan music and dance. Musicians,

Below: *jaranas* and poetry at Thursday's Serenatas Yucatecas in Santa Lucía.

Left: enjoying the heart of Mérida on a Saturday night.

The best sources of information in English on upcoming events in and around Mérida are the free magazines *Yucatán Today* and *Explore Yucatán*. If you can read any Spanish, the *Diario de Yucatán* has announcements of fiestas all around Yucatán state.

Friday:
Viernes Folclóricos
Casa 6, Parque Principal, Calle 57, between Calles 8 and 10; 8pm; Map p.24
Also in Casa 6, but this time focussing on folk dances.
Saturday–Sunday:
Fiestas en el Centro Histórico
Parque Principal, between Calles 8 and 10; Sat 6–11pm, Sun 9am–11am; Map p.24
At weekends Campeche's main plaza hosts concerts, kids' shows, exhibitions, and dance bands in the evenings.

Local Fiestas

Town and village fiestas go on year-round, somewhere in the Yucatán. Some are very local, others are shared by several places. Some are rooted in Mayan folklore, others at least seem more conventionally

Below: plenty to keep the kids happy on a Mérida Sunday.

For more on the *jarana* and the other dances seen and heard at Yucatecan fiestas, *see Music and Dance, p.100.*

dancers, and poets all perform with great sincerity, to a mainly local audience. An enormously charming event, and, again, completely free.
Friday:
Serenata Universitaria
Patio of the Universidad Autónoma de Yucatán, Calle 60, x 57; 9pm
For once, not Yucatecan music but traditional dances and music from all over Mexico, performed by very high-standard student groups.
Saturday:
Corazón de Mérida
Calles 60 and 62 between Calles 63 and 53; 8.30pm–1am; Map ??
Noche Mexicana
Paseo de Montejo, by Calle 47; from 7pm
Saturdays see two events. For the **Corazón** (heart) the city centre is closed to traffic (except horse buggies and *tricitaxis*) and taken over by dance bands, mariachis, cafés, and wandering crowds.

The **Noche Mexicana** is a celebration of everything Mexican – especially mariachis and marimbas – with yet more food, held at the bottom of Paseo de Montejo.
Sunday:
Mérida en Domingo
Plaza Mayor and up Calle 60 to Calle 53; all day
Mérida's all-day Sunday fiesta, again with the center closed to traffic, is a great fixture of local life, another real must-see. Events include *jarana* dances in the Plaza Mayor (around noon), and mariachis and dance bands in Parque Hidalgo and Santa Lucía. There are also clowns and other shows for children, and an array of street stalls.
SEE ALSO CHILDREN, P.47

CAMPECHE
A more limited calendar, but still an engaging program.
Thursday:
Jueves Culturales
Casa 6, Parque Principal, Calle 57, between Calles 8 and 10; 8pm; Map p.24
Traditional music, boleros, and tríos in the charming setting of the patios of Casa 6.

Left: the crazy excitement of a village corrida in Cuzamá.

National Holidays
On official holidays all banks and public offices are closed, but they get less attention than local holidays. Jan 1 **Año Nuevo**; Feb 5 **Día de la Constitución**; Mar 21 **Nacimiento de Juárez**; **Semana Santa** (Easter Thursday, Good Friday, Easter Saturday); May 1 **Día del Trabajo**; May 5 **Batalla de Puebla**; Sept 16 **Día de la Independencia**; Oct 12 **Día de la Raza**; Nov 20 **Día de la Revolución**; Dec 12 **Nuestra Señora de Guadalupe**; Dec 25 **Navidad**.

La Candelaria
Valladolid, Temax, Kanasín; around Feb 2; Map p.134 B3
The main fiesta of Valladolid and several other towns.

Carnaval
Mérida, Campeche, and other towns; late Jan–Mar
The biggest event of the year – Mérida's Carnaval is one of the biggest in Latin America, but with a friendly style that one can't imagine is quite the same in Río. Everyone gets dressed up, there are parades daily for a week, and even when there isn't one there are dance bands on street corners. Highlights include the 'burning of bad moods' on the first night, the delightful children's parade the next day, and the 'Regional Parade' the night before Mardi Gras, when Mayan spirits get out to play.

Campeche and **Cozumel** are also big Carnaval cities, and even **Cancún** now hosts a growing event.

The Equinox at Chichén Itzá and Dzibilchaltún
Chichén Itzá and Dzibilchaltún; Mar 21; Map p.14, p.16
Thousands flock to Chichén Itzá on the spring equinox to see the 'Descent of Kukulcán'

Catholic. Most go on for several days around the day of the local patron virgin or saint. In towns, trades *(gremios)* like bakers or taxi drivers often have a special fiesta as well.

Everything stops for a fiesta, as the village square is decked out in bright colors. On the main day there's a religious procession, while for the whole of fiesta week there are fairground rides, folk dances, food, dancing to salsa bands until early morning, and (among men) stiff drinking.

A central part of Yucatán village fiestas is a corrida, a **bullfight**, but this is a wilder, more raucous affair than its remote Spanish parent. The ring, built on the first day, is a precarious structure of poles and sticks. The bull often isn't killed (it may be too valuable), and the bullfighters are often amateurs, spurred on by a barrage of catcalls from their neighbors in the stands.

If you hear of a nearby fiesta, do what you can to get to it. Foreigners will be met (like bullfighters) with a bit of giggles and banter, but this needn't be taken as unwelcoming. Many are announced in the *Diario de Yucatán*.

The Annual Calendar
This can only include a few of the events through the year.
JANUARY–MARCH
Año Nuevo and Día de Reyes
All over the Yucatán; Jan 1, Jan 6
The old year is seen out at parties and burned at midnight, then on January 6 the Three Kings bring children presents. It's an especially big, 10-day fiesta in **Tizimín**.
Festival Internacional de las Artes
Various venues, Mérida; two weeks early Jan; Map p.18
Mérida hosts a varied, international program of art, film, music, and dance.

Above: after the equinox.

as the sun picks out the great serpent on the Castillo. Get there early, and be ready for crowds. Another phenomenon occurs at Dzibilchaltún, where the dawn sun strikes directly through the Temple of the Seven Dolls. Both effects can also be seen (but less clearly) on surrounding days, and again, but also less clearly, on and around September 21.
SEE ALSO CHICHÉN ITZÁ, P.15; MAYAN RUINS AND RELICS, P.90

Semana Santa (Easter)
All over the Yucatán; Mar–Apr
A less intense religious festival than in many parts of México – many people just head for the beach – but there are passion plays in **Acanceh** and **Mani**.

APRIL–JUNE
Santa Cruz
Celestún, Chumayel, and other towns; around May 3; Map p.16

The main patron-fiesta for many towns and villages.

JULY–SEPTEMBER
San Román
Campeche; Sept 14–30; Map p.24
Campeche's biggest religious fiesta is also the occasion for a big *feria*, with processions and all the usual entertainment.
Cristo de las Ampollas
Mérida; Sept 27–Oct 13; Map p.18
Mérida's chief religious fiesta is a special occasion for the city's *gremios* (trades), who all put on colorful displays.

OCTOBER–DECEMBER
Otoño Cultural
Yucatán State; Oct–Nov
A lively arts program, with events all around the state.
Day of the Dead
All over the Yucatán; Oct 31–Nov 2 and surrounding days
The most famous of Mexican festivals comes in the special Yucatecan form of the *Hanal Pixán*, little altars to commemorate and evoke the dead and so welcome back their spirits, around which families gather with special foods for their dead children (on the night of Oct 31) and adults (on Nov 1). This is an intimate family occasion, but visitors are welcome to see the beautifully dressed graves in cemeteries, and there is a display of *Hanal Pixán* in Mérida's Plaza Mayor.

Feria Yucatán X'matkuil
Xmatkuil, 9km south of Mérida; Nov–Dec; Map p.133 D3
The village of Xmatkuil just about lives for the Yucatán state fair, and it's huge: four weeks of concerts, displays, discos, cattle shows, and the state's largest fairground.
Festival de Aves Toh
Mérida and Izamal; end Nov–early Dec; www.yucatan birds.org.mx
The arrival of migrant birds from North America is marked with a range of events.
Riviera Maya Jazz Festival
Mamita's Beach, Playa del Carmen; end Nov–Dec; www.riviera mayajazzfestival.com; Map p.10
Three days of free concerts on the beach in Playa.
Vírgen de Izamal (Immaculate Conception)
Izamal; around Dec 8; Map p.16
A huge fiesta in Izamal, with general parades and still more presented by local *gremios*.
Vírgen de Guadalupe
All over Mexico; Dec 12
On the roads in the preceding weeks you can see *Guadalupanos*, running long distances as pilgrimages to the Virgin.
Navidad (Christmas)
All over Mexico; Dec 25
Nacimientos (Nativity scenes) appear, and groups called *posadas* go from door to door singing carols, before ending with a dinner and the breaking open of a goodie-filled *piñata*.

Below: putting on a show for Carnaval in Mérida.

Food and Drink

People often think they know their way around Mexican food – the familiar *tacos*, *burritos*, *fajitas*, and the rest. Mexico, though, is big enough to contain several different cuisines, and the food of the Yucatán, *la cocina yucateca*, has long been regarded as one of its most distinctive, most varied, and most sophisticated. It blends together indigenous Mayan, Spanish, Caribbean, and even Lebanese influences. Like any great cuisine, it makes fine use of the local ingredients it has at hand – Gulf seafood, subtle herbs and chilis, fabulous fresh fruit, lime, and cilantro. Exploring local food is one of the Yucatán's great pleasures.

Dining out in the Yucatán

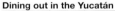

Eating in Mexico is a very social activity, to be treasured and enjoyed. There is an amazing variety of places to eat – charming traditional restaurants in bougainvillea-lined gardens, shiny tourist restaurants, beachside tables with fine fresh seafood, basic cheap cafés with plastic chairs with beer logos, taco stands, and more. Even the smallest village will have at least one simple *lonchería*.

Places called *restaurantes* generally serve alcohol, and many have bars attached. Cheap *loncherías* (so-named because they serve *lonch*) and *cocinas económicas* ('cheap kitchens') normally have only sodas and juices. There's always a cluster of *cocinas económicas* in and around markets, which are among the cheapest places to eat well.

One oddity of eating in the Yucatán is that price, quality, and status are more than usually disconnected. In an upscale restaurant, the service might be all over you, but the food may be mediocre; while some of the best local dishes

– especially seafood – are to be found in basic street-corner bars. It's just one of the local idiosyncrasies.

THE EATING SCHEDULE

The traditional Yucatecan meal schedule is distinctive, born of tropical tradition. People here get up early, and breakfast *(desayuno)* is a major meal. Restaurants accordingly open early, around 7am. The main traditional meal, though, is the *comida fuerte*, starting around 2pm. Whenever there's time, as on Sundays, it lasts long into the afternoon, and may be followed by a siesta. After that, dinner *(la cena)* is a far lighter meal, after 9pm. The most traditional (and commonly the best) Yucatecan restaurants open only for breakfast and the *comida fuerte*, and close around 6–7pm. This is why it's hard to find a good, genuine Yucatecan meal for dinner.

Foreigners, though, find this incomprehensible, so on the Riviera virtually all restaurants follow more international timings for dinner, and many stay open late. In any case, strict timings are not part of

Above: you're never far from a *taco* stand.

the culture, and throughout the region most mid- to cheaper-range restaurants are simply open all day, every day – though *loncherías* in smaller places still tend to close early, around 7pm. At midday many cheaper restaurants offer bargain set menus, called a *menú del día* or *comida corrida*.

SNACKING

Places where you sit down to eat make up only some of the options, for Mexicans are among the world's most devoted snackers. Every town,

Left: essentials: fresh pepper, onion, cilantro, and lime.

But the old cantina-model has softened at the edges, and there are also comfortable versions that have plenty of women customers, and 'family days' at weekends. Cantinas serve special foods, *botanas*, small dishes a bit like Spanish tapas. They are enormously varied – marinated cucumbers, grilled fish, savory pancakes – and among the most intriguing Yucatecan dishes. As tradition dictates, you get a few with your first drink, bigger ones with your second, and so on; it's also traditional you pay only for the drink, not the *botana*, so this is an amazingly cheap, enjoyable way to eat.

Another cantina tradition is live music, from trios to dance bands in big, family-sized venues like Mérida's wonderful **Eladio's**. There are upscale cantinas (Mérida's **Lucero del Alba**) and historic survivors like the **Rincón Colonial** in Campeche. Whichever, they are some of the most atmospheric places to eat in the Yucatán. One more cantina feature is that, like traditional restaurants, they mainly open during the day, and tend to close up around 7–8pm.
SEE ALSO RESTAURANTS, CAFÉS, CANTINAS, P.104–113

The Food of the Yucatán

Yucatecan cooking is a rare historical mix. Mayan tradition is the basis for many dishes – in basic ingredients like corn, beans and chillis, in complex marinades and spices – combined with contributions from the Spaniards. For years Yucatán had little contact with the rest of Mexico, but instead received many influences from Cuba, and from new migrants like the highly influential Lebanese community.

Hot, or Not

People often assume that all Mexican food is going to be seriously spicy, but this is not so. Many Yucatecan dishes, especially, are essentially more fragrant than fierce. Hot spice is an optional extra: in traditional restaurants, there will usually be two little bowls of sauce in the middle of the table *(see below)*. The red one is a medium-strength chili sauce; the green one is made with the Yucatán's specialty *habanero* chilis, and if you're not a chili fan is liable to blow your head off. Locals often spoon out lashings of the stuff, but there's no pressure to join in.

every village, has a few stands and tiny shops selling *tacos*, *tortas* (filled bread rolls), local specialties like *panuchos*, and *salbutes* or treats for kids like sweet *marquesitas*. At weekends and during fiestas there are even more, as well as old women selling peeled fruit or potato chips. The overall word for snacks is *antojitos*, 'something on a whim,' which sums up their role in local eating.

Some visitors are suspicious of all these snacks on health grounds, but they can be nutritious fillers when a full local meal is too much (as well as very cheap). And some are unquestionably healthy, such as those sold by the juice and ice-cream stands, *see p.70*.
SEE ALSO CHILDREN, P.45

CANTINAS AND BOTANAS

The cantina, the traditional Mexican bar, stands out from other places to eat and drink. Most traditionally, cantinas were places where men (and only men) went to drink and sing away their sorrows, and there are still many of this rough-and-ready type around (they're easily recognizable).

F

Above, from top: *panuchos,*
salbutes, and *ceviche.*

Learning More
Anyone interested in finding out
more about the intricacies of
Yucatecan cooking should seek
out the courses at **Los Dos**, a
cookery school in an exquisite
old Mérida patio house run by
American chef David Sterling.
There are one- and half-day
'taster' courses, and longer
workshops, packages, and seasonal courses. All courses begin
with a market tour, and end with
a fine meal. *Los Dos, Calle 68
no. 517, x 65 & 67, tel: (999)
928 1116, www.los-dos.com.*

While there are local specialties, similar dishes tend to
appear on menus across the
Yucatán. One variation is the
food of Campeche, *cocina
campechana*, which has many
distinctive dishes, especially
using fish and seafood.

STAPLES
The same trinity that forms
the historic basis of cooking
across Mexico – corn (maize),
beans, and chilis – is found in
the Yucatán. Corn tortillas
have traditionally been part of
every meal, but with the
recent rise in corn prices they
have – unprecedentedly –
become something of a
luxury, so you may often be
served bread, and have to ask
if you want real tortillas.

A huge range of chili
peppers is used in Yucatecan
cooking, including mild *chile
x'katik* ('pale chili') and hotter
serrano. Most characteristic is
the tiny, supercharged green
habanero chili, as used in the
ferocious green sauce that

adds explosive power to
otherwise mild dishes *(see
box, p.67)*. *Chipotle*, used as a
seasoning, is made of ground,
smoked *jalapeño* peppers.

The signature Yucatecan
seasoning, though, is *achiote*,
ground seeds of the annatto
tree mixed in a paste with
cumin, garlic, onion, and pepper. It is used in many marinades, and it is this, together
with the juice of the local bitter
oranges *(naranjiles)* and limes,
that gives so many Yucatecan
dishes a distinctive fragrance.
Another specialty is *chaya*, a
vegetable rather like spinach.
It is very high in nutrients, and
has been important in the
Mayan diet for centuries.

SOUPS AND MEATS
Strangely, maybe, for a hot
country, Yucatecans often
start a meal with soup *(sopa)*,
especially one of their great
culinary creations, *sopa de
lima* – actually a chicken soup,
with strips of crisp tortilla, and
subtly flavored with lime.

Staple meats here are pork,
chicken, and turkey, though
beef is becoming more common. The classic way to pre-
pare meat is as *cochinita* (if
with pork) or *pollo* (chicken)
pibil, marinated in *achiote* and
bitter orange juice, then baked
wrapped in banana leaves.
Pibil comes from the Mayan
for an earth oven made in the
ground, so this is a cooking
style that's centuries-old, even
though today it's more often
done with a conventional
oven. *Cochinita* and *pollo pibil*
can be served as a main dish
(with the usual accompani-
ments, like refried beans), or
as a *taco* ingredient.

Another common favorite
is *poc chuc*, thin-sliced pork
marinated in bitter oranges
and cooked with onions,
garlic, and herbs. Some of the
most intricate dishes, which

Below: *queso relleno*, one of the Yucatán's subtle surprises.

often require a blend of 10 or more different chilis, spices, and juices, are only done well in the best traditional restaurants, such as chicken or turkey *en relleno negro*, in a thick black sauce of minced pork, chilis, mixed herbs and spices, grated egg, and more, or *queso relleno*, ground pork and a whole range of other ingredients in melted cheese – which, when done well, is far more delicate than it sounds.

FISH AND SEAFOOD

Excellent fish and seafood are almost the basis of the diet all around the Yucatán coast. Grouper *(mero)*, gray mullet *(mojarra)*, and red snapper *(huachinango)* are some of the most common fish; shrimp *(camarones)*, conch *(caracol)*, octopus *(pulpo)*, and lobster *(langosta)* the most-seen shellfish.

Fish is most often served simply, either plain-grilled, *empanizado* (breaded), or *al mojo de ajo* (pan-fried in oil and garlic), but it can also be

Above: tequila comes under many labels.

marinated in *achiote*. For more variety head for Campeche, which has attractive fish dishes such as *pan de cazón* (young shark in tomato sauce, cooked between tortillas).

The most popular way to eat local seafood is also very simple, in a *ceviche* – marinated in lime juice (which partially cooks the seafood) and served with tomato, onion, and cilantro (coriander). With good *camarón* or *caracol*, lashings of fresh cilantro, nachos, and a cold beer, a *ceviche* makes an irresistible lunch by the beach.

YUCATECAN ANTOJITOS

The Yucatán also has its own snacks to go alongside pan-Mexican *tacos*: the double act of *panuchos* and *salbutes*. The former are small, crisp tortillas, topped with refried beans and such things as shredded chicken or pork, red onion, chili, and avocado; *salbutes* are very similar but with a softer, uncooked tortilla base. Other (very filling) 'snacks' of Mayan origin are *papadzules*, large tortillas stuffed with a sweet pumpkin-seed sauce with mild chili, onions, and tomatoes.

DESSERTS

In general, the best thing to go for is some of the superb local fruit – often, the only alternative will be the universal His-

panic *flan* (crème caramel). More refined spots may have a refreshing *manjar blanco*, of rice, cinnamon, and coconut.

Mexican Dishes

For all the self-contained tradition of Yucatecan cooking, all sorts of dishes from the rest of Mexico are of course available here. Beyond the inescapable *taco* – any kind of ingredient, served in a rolled tortilla – Mexican favorites are essential for breakfast: *huevos rancheros*, *huevos revueltos* (scrambled, with various other things mixed in), or *huevos a la mexicana* (scrambled with hot chili and chorizo sausage). *Chilaquiles* are a hefty breakfast dish of slivers of tortilla baked with meat and cheese.

Below: one of Mexico's many classic beers.

Vegetarian Options

There are few truly vegetarian-friendly (let along vegan) traditional dishes in Mexican or Yucatecan cooking, as many vegetable or fruit-based dishes have a little meat and/or fish in them to add flavor. The best bet is usually to find restaurants that have vegetarian specialties – sometimes based on traditional dishes – like the **100% Natural** chain in Cancún or Playa del Carmen, or **Amaro's** in Mérida. Look out for dishes made with the great local vegetable, *chaya*. If you eat cheese and/or eggs, other dishes become possibilities, such as *quesadillas* (but check they don't also contain ham) or Yucatecan *papadzules* (*see right*). See also *Restaurants, Cafés, Cantinas, p.104.*

Above: when the heat is up, find the nearest juice-and-ice stand.

Beef is more common in central Mexico than in the Yucatán, so popular 'Mexican' dishes include *arracheras*, thin-cut steaks, or *puntas de res*, chargrilled strips of beef with tomatoes and onions. Always worth trying are *pollo con mole*, fried chicken with the classic savory chocolate sauce of Oaxaca, and *pescado a la veracruzana*, fish in a tomato, caper, olive, and cinnamon sauce. Plus, of course, there are all the familiar *fajitas* and *enchiladas*, especially on the Riviera Maya.

Drinks

BEER

Mexico's most popular drink, and its number-one export. Light *(clara)* beers like Corona or the more substantial Superior may be the best-known brands, but there are satisfying Mexican dark *(negra)* beers such as Negra Modelo or León Negra. In tourist bars you are normally served beer in just the bottle, with a slice of lime in it. You'll know if you're in a mainly Mexican venue, because you'll probably be offered a glass, and no fruit.

If you want fruit in your beer, the popular way to do it is to ask for a *michelada* (or a *chela*), beer with lime, salt and often a dash or worcestershire or similar spicy sauce.

TEQUILA AND SPIRITS

There are hundreds of labels of Mexico's most famous drink, and many Riviera barmen will be happy to take you through a tasting. Tequila comes in three basic grades: clear, unaged *blanco*; *reposado*, aged for 2–11 months in oak casks; and *añejo*, aged for 1–5 years. A ritual has arisen around tequila-drinking – in a *caballito* shot glass, preceded by a pinch of salt and followed by sucking a slice of lemon or lime – but it's just as popular in cocktails, such as a margarita.

Tequila comes from Jalisco in central Mexico, and a more traditional drink in Yucatán is actually local rum. Cuban rum is also popular, in mojito cocktails. Another native drink

is sweet, honey-based *Xtabentún*, a refined version of the historic mead of the Maya.

Juices, *Aguas*, and Ice Cream

Mention apart must go to one of the Yucatán's greatest glories – its fabulous fruit, whether familiar melons or pineapples or more exotic papaya, *mamey* or *guanábana*.

Fruit can be eaten, or tried in different ways at neighborhood *juguerías*, juice shops, or *paletería-neverías*, ice-cream stands (which often sell juices too). Many tropical fruits are more enjoyable juiced than to eat. You can have them as straight juices, as *licuados* (put through a blender and mixed with a little water, or sometimes milk) or as an *agua*, diluted with water and ice. Some of the most interesting can only be had as *aguas*, such as the wonderfully refreshing *agua de jamaica*, made with hibiscus flowers, tamarind water, or *agua de chaya*. Other variations are *raspados*, mixtures of fruit juice and crushed ice.

Ice-cream stands, meanwhile, offer a big choice of *paletas* (popsicles or lollipops) and *nieves* (tubs of water ices), again made with fresh fruit. Have a few *aguas* every day,

Below: *agua de jamaica.*

> **Wine** does not go particularly well with Mexican or Yucatecan food. This is all to the good, as good wine is either hard to find here, or expensive. Upscale restaurants with international cuisine should have a decent range of mainly US, Chilean, or Argentinian wines, but mid- to lower-range restaurants will scarcely have any. When eating local, it's best to stick to beer, cocktails, or juices.

Above: chillis come in many different kinds.

and you need never be short of vitamins ever again. And while the local juice stand is the easiest place to find them, refined *aguas* such as *jamaica* are also specialties at the Yucatán's luxury haciendas.

Food Vocabulary

BASIC TERMS/PHRASES
desayuno **breakfast**
almuerzo, comida fuerte **lunch**
cena **dinner**
postres, dulces **desserts**
plato **plate**; *vaso* **glass**
taza **cup**; *copa* **wine glass**
tenedor **fork**
cuchillo **knife**; *cuchara* **spoon**
pan **bread**; *miel* **honey**
sal **salt**; *pimienta* **pepper**
azúcar **sugar**; *hielo* **ice**
mantequilla **butter**
queso **cheese**
huevos **eggs**; *ensalada* **salad**
mesero/a **waiter, waitress**
¿tiene una mesa para dos (cuatro)? **do you have a table for two (four)?**
carta, menú **menu**
menú del día, comida corrida **set meal**
¿qué hay de bueno hoy? **what's good today?**
la cuenta/la nota, por favor **the check (bill) please**
¿puedo pagar con tarjeta de crédito? **can I pay by credit card?**
cambio **change**
propina **tip**

MEATS *(CARNES)*
arracheras **thin steak**
asado/a **roast**
chorizo **spiced red sausage**
chuleta **chop**; *jamón* **ham**
lomo, lomitos **pork loin**
longaniza **mildly spiced pork sausage**
pavo, guajolote **turkey**
pollo, gallina **chicken**
puerco, cerdo, cochino, cochinita **pork**
res, carne de res **beef**
tocino **bacon**

FISH AND SEAFOOD
(PESCADO Y MARISCOS)
atún, bonito **tuna**
calamares **squid**
camarones **shrimps, prawns**
cangrejo **large crab**
caracol **conch**
cazón **hammerhead shark, dogfish**
corvina, corbina **sea bass**
esmedregal **black snapper**
huachinango, pargo **red snapper**
jaiba **small crab**
langosta **lobster**
lisa, mojarra **gray mullet**
mero **grouper**
ostiones **oysters**
pámpano **pompano**
pez espada **swordfish**
pulpo **octopus**; *tiburón* **shark**

VEGETABLES *(VERDURAS)*
aceite (de maíz) **(corn) oil**
aguacate **avocado**
ajo **garlic**
alcaparras **capers**
arroz **rice**
calabaza **pumpkin/zucchini**
canela **cinnamon**
cebolla **onion**
chaya **spinach-like vegetable**
chícharos **peas**
cilantro **cilantro, coriander**
clavos **cloves**; *comino* **cumin**
elote **corn cob**
frijoles (refritos) **(refried) red beans**
jitomate **tomato**
lechuga **lettuce**
nopalitos **nopal cactus (similar to palm hearts)**

papas (fritas) **(fried) potatoes**
pepino **cucumber**
pimientos (morrones, verdes) **(red, green) peppers**
totopos **nachos, tortilla chips**

FRUIT *(FRUTA)*
chicozapote, zapote **fruit of the sapodilla tree**
coco **coconut**
durazno **peach**
fresas **strawberries**
guanábana **soursop, a type of Caribbean custard apple**
guayaba **guava**
jamaica **a type of hibiscus; its dried flowers are used to make *agua de jamaica***
lima **lime**; *limón* **lemon**
mamey **similar to a mango, but smaller**
mango **mango**
manzana **apple**
melón **melon**
naranja **orange**
naranjil, naranja agria **small, bitter orange**
papaya **papaya, paw paw**
plátano **banana**
piña **pineapple**
sandía **watermelon**
tamarindo **tamarind**
toronja **grapefruit**
uvas **grapes**

DRINKS *(BEBIDAS)*
agua **water**; *café* **coffee**
cerveza **beer**; *coca* **any cola**
jugo **juice**; *leche* **milk**
refresco **soft drink, soda**
vino (tinto, blanco) **(red, white) wine**

Below: *papadzules.*

Haciendas

Relics of colonial Yucatán, the aristocratic haciendas built amid huge estates from the 16th to the 19th centuries have some of Mexico's most gracious architecture, with lofty ceilings and broad, shaded terraces, ringed by exuberant tropical gardens. For years they sank into atmospheric decline, until it was realized that, carefully restored and re-landscaped, they would make exceptional hotels. You can now choose between luxury hacienda-hotels with fine restaurants and spectacular pools, and more modest country retreats; whichever you go for, a stay in a hacienda is one of the Yucatán's most seductive experiences.

Hacienda Hotels

Several luxury haciendas were all restored by the Plan group, and are also marketed as part of Starwood Hotels' 'Luxury Collection' (www. starwoodhotels.com/luxury).

YUCATÁN STATE
Hacienda Chichén at Chichén Itzá also now offers hacienda-style luxury after recent renovation.
SEE ALSO HOTELS, P.82

Hacienda San Antonio Chalanté
2.7km east of Sudzal village, 8km south of Izamal; tel via Mérida: (999) 132 7411; www.hacienda chalante.com; $$; Map p.133 E3
A very charming estate that gives a real taste of rural Yucatán at amazingly low prices. There are 10 comfortable rooms and a pool; birdwatching, nature trails and horse-riding are specialties.
SEE ALSO SPORTS, P.119

Hacienda San José Cholul
Off road to Izamal via Tixkokob, 38km east of Mérida; tel: (999) 910 4617; www.thehaciendas. com; $$$$; Map p.133 E3
A very tranquil Plan group hacienda, in deep country-

Above: San Antonio Chalanté.

side between Mérida and Izamal. The 17th-century main house has been beautifully restored, and the master suite has a pool to itself.

Hacienda San Pedro Nohpat
Off Highway 180, 3km east of Mérida; tel: (999) 988 0542; www.haciendaholidays.com; $$–$$$; Map p.133 D3

Price bands based on rates per night in US dollars for a standard double room, without breakfast unless stated:
$$$$ over $200
$$$ $100–$200
$$ $50–$100
$ under $50

This Canadian-owned hacienda is cozy rather than chic: rooms come in several sizes and colors, and there are good rates for longer stays. It's right on the edge of Mérida, but inside the garden it's tranquility itself.

Hacienda Santa Cruz Palomeque
14km south of Mérida; tel: (999) 910 4549; www.haciendasanta cruz.com; $$$; Map p.133 D3
An attractive smaller hacienda that has just reopened under new owners, with a fine restaurant promised. There are just five rooms and one large *casita*, in a magnificent garden.

Hacienda Santa Rosa
10km west of Highway 180 (Campeche road) near Maxcanú, 65km south of Mérida; tel: (999) 910 4875; www.thehaciendas. com; $$$$; Map p.133 C2
The smallest Plan group hacienda – with just 11 ample rooms and suites – sits in deep seclusion just west of the Puuc hills. The pool and the bar, in a former chapel, are especially striking, and the light in the garden at sunset is exquisite.

Left: Temozón's fabulous pool.

Hacienda Museums

Some haciendas are now fascinating rural museums.

Hacienda Ochil
Highway 261 km 176 (32km north of Uxmal); tel: (999) 910 6035; www.haciendaochil.com; entrance charge unless dining; daily 11am–7pm; Map p.133 D3

Also run by the Plan group, Ochil has been restored only as a fine restaurant, and a museum with a beautiful display of Mexican handicrafts.
SEE ALSO RESTAURANTS, CAFÉS, AND CANTINAS, P.112

Hacienda Sotuta de Peón
29km south of Mérida; tel: (999) 941 8639; www.haciendatour.com; entrance charge; tours Tue–Sat 10am, noon; Map p.133 D3

One of very few haciendas that still work henequen cactus. The lively tours include a meal and a swim in a cenote.

Hacienda Yaxcopoil
Highway 261, 33km south of Mérida; tel: (999) 900 1193; www.yaxcopoil.com; entrance charge; Mon–Sat 8am–6pm, Sun 9am–1pm; Map p.133 D3

A great stop-off on the way to Uxmal, Yaxcopoil gives a wonderful insight into hacienda life. It also has a guest house available, at very good prices.

For truly exclusive luxury, you can have a whole hacienda to yourself, at **Petac**, 20km south of Mérida, with full service for $8,400 a week. *Hacienda Petac, tel: (999) 911 2601, www.haciendapetac.com.*

Hacienda Temozón Sur
8km east of Highway 261 (Uxmal road), 43km south of Mérida; tel: (999) 923 8089; www.thehaciendas.com; $$$$; Map p.133 D3

The first Plan group hacienda set the style, especially in its sumptuous bathrooms. The main house is magnificent, and delicious food is served on a terrace above a stunning pool. There's a luxury spa, and lots of tours and activities, but many find, once here, that they don't want to move.

Hacienda Xcanatún
Carretera Mérida–Progreso km 12; tel: (999) 941 0273; www.xcanatun.com; $$$$; Map p.133 D3

An independent hacienda in a village north of Mérida. The grounds are not as broad as at more remote haciendas, but the spa is superb, and it has one of Mérida's best restaurants, the **Casa de Piedra**.
SEE ALSO PAMPERING, P.102; RESTAURANTS, CAFÉS, AND CANTINAS, P.111

CAMPECHE
See also Hacienda Puerta Campeche, Hotels, p.85.

Hacienda Uayamón
28km south of Campeche; tel: (981) 829 7526; www.thehaciendas.com; $$$$; Map p.132 C1

The most remote Plan hacienda is the most stylish: some buildings have been left as ruins, to add to the atmosphere. A very chic rural retreat.

Below: the atmospheric terraces of Hacienda Uayamón.

History

c.20000–10000 BC
Tribes of hunter-gatherers move across the Bering Strait from Asia to North America, and then spread south to occupy the whole continent.

c.4000 BC
The Nomadic tribes in Mesoamerica (modern Mexico and Central America) first begin to settle, grow crops, and make ceramics.

c.2000 BC
Nixtamal flour is invented, a mix of maize flour and powdered lime. Much more nutritious than maize alone, it is used to make corn tortillas, the basic food of Mesoamerica for the next 4,000 years.

c.1800–300 BC
The Preclassic Era of Mesoamerica: the Olmecs form the region's first city-based civilization, at San Lorenzo (Veracruz) and La Venta (Tabasco), with many features inherited by later civilizations: the basics of mythology and the calendar, cities centered on symbolic pyramids, and the ball game.

c.300 BC–AD 250
The Late Preclassic: a distinctive Mayan civilization takes shape in communities from Guatemala, Chiapas, and Belize into Yucatán. The Mayan Long Count calendar and Mayan writing system develop.

250–800

The Classic Era of Mayan civilization, which flourishes in over 60 independent city states, each under a sacred ruler, above all in the Guatemalan Petén, the Usumacinta valley (Chiapas) and the Río Bec region. The largest Mayan cities are Calakmul, Tikal (Guatemala), and Palenque (Chiapas).

592–695
Calakmul is the most powerful city in the Petén. From 650–800, warfare intensifies between Calakmul and Tikal and their various different allies for dominance in the region.

700–950

In the Terminal Classic Era, Mayan cities grow rapidly in the previously less populated northern Yucatán, especially Uxmal and the Puuc cities and Chichén Itzá, which from 850–950, after defeating Cobá in war, is the dominant city in the north.

780–1000
The Mayan Collapse: Mayan civilization disintegrates, for reasons still open to argument – the most likely causes were a complex mix of inter-city warfare, overpopulation, soil exhaustion, and drought. Most of the great southern cities like Calakmul fall apart by 850 or earlier, and never revive; in northern Yucatán, the Collapse arrives 50–100 years later, and is never as complete. However, the Long Count calendar and much else of Classic Mayan culture are abandoned.

c.1150–1520
The Postclassic Era: Mayan culture revives in northern Yucatán, though towns are never as big as the Classic cities. From around 1200–1441 Mayapán functions as a 'capital' of the Yucatán. From 1400 trading cities such as Tulum and El Rey (Cancún) develop steadily on the Yucatán coast, as important links on a trade route between South America and the Aztec Empire in central Mexico.

1517
Francisco Hernández de Córdoba makes first Spanish landing in Mexico, on Isla Mujeres.

1519
Hernán Cortés and his men land briefly on Cozumel before going on to conquer central Mexico.

1526–42
Spanish Conquest of the Yucatán, led by three men all called Francisco de Montejo (father, son, and nephew). The Maya resist longer than any other Pre-Columbian American culture, and it is only at the third attempt that the Montejos are victorious and found their capital, Mérida, in 1542.

1562
Father Diego de Landa, head of the Franciscan order in Yucatán, discovers that many apparently Christian Maya are still holding traditional rituals in secret, and orders a mass *auto da fé*, burning hundreds of Mayan manuscripts and other relics.

1821

Mexico becomes independent. Yucatán, which had had its own administration within the Spanish Empire, grudgingly accepts to join the new state.

1838–42

Yucatán declares its independence from Mexico, and beats off an army sent to restore central control at Campeche in 1842.

1839–42

John Lloyd Stephens and Frederick Catherwood travel throughout the Yucatán, searching for ruins. Stephens's subsequent books with Catherwood's remarkable drawings first make the existence of Mayan ruins widely known in the outside world.

1847–50

Yucatán's 'Caste War': the Maya revolt across the peninsula in the largest – and most nearly successful – indigenous rebellion anywhere in the Americas since the 1540s. White Yucatecans flee in panic, and sovereignty over the Yucatán is offered to Spain, Britain, and the US, whichever would 'save the civilized population from their fate.' But in May 1848, when the Maya are about to take Mérida, the planting season comes early, and the rebel army dissolves as men return to their villages to sow corn. Yucatán accepts reintegration into Mexico in return for aid against the Mayan rebellion.

1850–1901

Rebel Maya retreat into the southeast of the Yucatán peninsula and create their own state around the cult of the 'Talking Cross', with a capital in Chan Santa Cruz (now Felipe Carrillo Puerto) and known as the *Cruzob* (people of the Cross).

1863

Campeche becomes a separate Mexican state.

1860–1910

World demand rockets for sisal rope made from the henequen cactus, the 'green gold' that revolutionizes the Yucatán economy. Henequen hacienda-owners become immensely rich, which is

reflected in the palatial mansions, theatres, and other new buildings that spring up in Mérida.

1901

Mexican army re-establishes control over Chan Santa Cruz, but most of the *Cruzob* Maya retreat into the forest and still reject the Mexican state. Quintana Roo is separated off from Yucatán State as a federal territory controlled from Mexico City.

1910–20

Mexican Revolution ends the 34-year dictatorship of Porfirio Díaz. Fighting goes on between different factions for 10 years, as the country collapses into chaos. In Yucatán, the wealthy henequen elite manage largely to retain power until 1915, when a revolutionary army arrives to take control.

1921–4

Yucatán state has a socialist government, led by Felipe Carrillo Puerto. He is murdered during a failed military revolt in January 1924.

1929

Partido Nacional Revolucionario (PNR), later to become the *Partido Revolucionario Institucional* (PRI), takes power as the 'official party' of the Mexican Revolution, ending the period of revolutionary disorder. In the 1930s, large areas of land are redistributed to village communities in Yucatán.

1971

First hotel opens in Cancún, beginning the era of tourism in the Yucatán.

1974

Quintana Roo finally becomes a Mexican state.

2000

Vicente Fox is elected President of Mexico for the PAN *(Partido de Acción Nacional)*, ending 71 years of PRI rule.

2005

Hurricane Wilma rages over the Riviera Maya and eastern Yucatán for 65 hours, causing severe damage to buildings, forests, and reefs, but remarkably few casualties. Reconstruction begins immediately.

Hotels

The Yucatán can cater for pretty much all tastes: in rooms, options run from glittering beach palaces to quirky small-town hotels with whirring roof-fans. For extra graciousness, there are elegant hotels in restored colonial haciendas (*see p.72*), and there's a growing number of charming, individually run small hotels and B&Bs, especially in Mérida. As alternatives to the big resorts, the coasts and islands offer a seductive variety of romantic palm-roofed cabins by the beach – from basic to luxury-standard – and some of the most enjoyable places to stay are in the most apparently remote locations.

Cancún

HOTEL ZONE

Hotels listed all take non-all-inclusive bookings.

Ambiance Villas at Kin-Ha
Boulevard Kukulcán km 8.5;
tel: (998) 891 5400;
www.ambiancevillas.com;
$$$–$$$$; Map IBC
An attractive complex with rooms and suites in three-story villas, and moderate rates. They're spread around a garden on a good beach on the north side of Cancún island, so you have tranquility and all the Hotel Zone buzz within walking distance.

Avalon Baccara
Boulevard Kukulcán km 11; tel: (998) 881 7180; www.avalon vacations.com; $$$; Map IBC
Easy to miss beside the Avalon Grand all-inclusive, the Baccara has the essentials of the Hotel Zone experience – the beach below, great views,

Most of the big hotels and resort complexes in Cancún and the Riviera Maya are available only on an all-inclusive basis. *See also All-Inclusives, p.28.*

a pool with swim-up bar – at a smaller scale. It's near the nightlife hub around the Coco Bongo, but within its walls you can even feel secluded.

Fiesta Americana Grand Coral Beach
Boulevard Kukulcán km 9.5;
tel: (998) 881 3200; www.fiesta americana.com; $$$$; Map IBC
A candidate for the grandest of Cancún's top-line hotels, with an unrivaled location at Punta Cancún and plenty for those after a real splurge: fine restaurants, a superb **spa**, a pool winding through a garden, and an air of class not found in all of its neighbors.
SEE ALSO PAMPERING, P.102

CIUDAD CANCÚN

Hostel Chacmool
Calle Gladiolas 18, by Parque de las Palapas; tel: (998) 887 5873; www.chacmool.com.mx; $; Map IBC
One of the brightest budget hostels, with dorm beds ($10 a night) and rooms with or without bathrooms (from $29). All have air-con, breakfasts are included, it's in the middle of town, and also has the Terraza Chacmool bar.
SEE ALSO BARS AND NIGHTLIFE, P.31

Hotel Alux
Avenida Uxmal 21, near corner of Avenida Tulum; tel: (998) 884 0556; www.hotelalux.com; $; Map IBC

Below: Cancún's Hotel Zone is a land of giants.

Left: the patio at Mérida's Hotel Marionetas, *see p.83.*

Prices, Regions, and Seasons
Hotel prices are higher overall – often a lot higher – in Cancún, Isla Mujeres, Cozumel, and the Riviera Maya than in the rest of the Yucatán, and have soared recently in Tulum. However, there are welcome exceptions. Seasons vary for each hotel, but generally high season prices apply from mid-December to March or April, and in some hotels during August, with additional peak hikes for Christmas-New Year and Easter, which periods need to be booked well ahead. Low-season rates (usually May–July, Sept–early Dec) are a good deal lower. Again, seasonal increases are more marked on the Riviera than in other areas, where some hotels keep the same rates all year. Extra discounts may be on offer in deep low season (June, October), and many hotels now give discounts for booking online.

The Alux has two great things going for it: a location right next to the bus station, and great-value prices. Rooms are simple but quite bright and well kept, with decent bathrooms, TV, and air-con. In great demand, so book early.

Hotel El Rey del Caribe
Avenida Uxmal 24, corner of Avenida Nader; tel: (998) 884 2028; www.reycaribe.com; $$; Map IBC
A charming little hotel with spacious rooms around a garden (with pool) that feels like a peaceful haven in central Cancún, still not far from the bus station. The owners try hard to keep to high ecological standards, breakfast is included, and other extras include free WiFi.

Price ranges, given as a guide only, are based on prices per night in US dollars for a standard double room, without breakfast unless stated, in the main winter-spring (but not the Christmas peak) season:

$$$$	over $200
$$$	$100–$200
$$	$50–$100
$	under $50

The Islands
ISLA MUJERES
Casa de los Sueños
Carretera a Garrafón; tel: (998) 877 0651; www.casadelos suenosresort.com; $$$$; Map p.8
Dazzling boutique retreat on a bluff south of Isla town, with eight rooms and one suite, each a showcase of Mexican style. There's also a very sexy pool, and the '**Spa Zenter**' for total indulgence.
SEE ALSO PAMPERING, P.103

Hotel Secreto
Playa Secreto; tel: (998) 877 0139; www.hotelsecreto.com; $$$$; Map p.8
Showered with awards by travel and design magazines, the Secreto features ultra-chic design and state-of-the-art facilities. With just nine minimalist rooms, it's intimate in scale (some find the rooms small). A fabulous pool makes up for the now sad state of Playa Secreto below.

Hotel Villa Kiin
Calle Zazil-Ha 129; tel: (998) 877 1024; www.villakiin.com; $$–$$$; Map p.8
Colorful rooms in a main building and more spacious bungalow-style cabañas, all

different sizes, next to Secreto beach. There's a lounge and open kitchen, and breakfast is included.

COZUMEL
Amigo's B&B
Calle 7 Sur no. 571A, between Avenidas 25 and 30; tel: (987) 872 3868; www.bacalar.net; $–$$; Map p.9
A great pool is one plus of this lovely guest house. There are just three rooms around a garden, all with kitchenettes, and breakfast (included) is served under a big palapa. Dive packages are available. The owners also have B&Bs in Bacalar and Holbox; details are on the website.

Hotel Flamingo
Calle 6 Norte, off Avenida Melgar; tel: (987) 872 1264; www.hotel flamingo.com; $$; Map p.9

77

Above: Holbox style.

A long-running divers' hotel that has been renovated in 'boutique hotel' style, but still with a laid-back feel and very decent rates. Rooms are bright, stylish, and decorated with original art. High-standard diving and fishing packages are still offered, but there's also the Aroma day spa and Aqua Cuban restaurant.

Tamarindo Bed and Breakfast

Calle 4 Norte no. 421, between Avenidas 20 and 25; tel: (987) 872 6190; www.tamarindo cozumel.com; $–$$; Map p.9

French owner Eliane Gode-ment serves great breakfasts at her welcoming, tranquil guest house. She has four rooms and a suite that share an open kitchen, and two larger rooms with kitchen-ettes. A fine bargain.

Ventanas al Mar

Carretera Costera Oriente km 43.4; tel: (044 987) 105 2684; www.ventanasalmar.com.mx; $$–$$$; Map p.9

The only hotel on Cozumel's east coast offers romantic isolation, with just a couple of restaurants for company, and a swimmable little beach. It's a bit eccentric: rooms are large and wind-battered, with balconies to take in the view, one for lovers of infinite sea and sky. List rates seem high, but discounts may be had.

HOLBOX

CasaSandra

Calle Igualdad, at the beach; tel: (984) 875 2171; www.casa sandra.com; $$$–$$$$; Map p.9

Holbox's most opulent hideout occupies a palapa-roofed beach mansion, with lounges that summon up almost a country-house feel. Suites are utterly stunning: rooms are more conventional but still beautiful. Also a spa, a full range of tours, and a fine restaurant with a Cuban chef.

Hotel Faro Viejo

Avenida Tiburón Ballena; tel: (984) 875 2217; www.faroviejo holbox.com.mx; $$; Map p.9

The oldest hotel on Holbox has a prime beach location, a beach bar and restaurant, and pretty rooms with balconies or large suites with beachside terraces. Also snorkel and whale-shark tours.

Posada Mawimbi

Calle Damero, by the beach; tel: (984) 875 2003; www.mawimbi.net; $$; Map p.9

One of the most enjoyable of Holbox's cabaña-style hotels: owners Ornella and Carmelo have seven relaxing rooms in beachcomber style and two cabañas, and a beach garden for watching the day slide by. They also offer some of Hol-box's best whale-shark watch-ing, snorkel, and other trips.

SEE ALSO TOURS AND GUIDES, P.120.

Rentals and Condos

With the boom in condo and holiday-home building since the 1990s – especially around Playa del Carmen and Akumal – there is a huge choice of fully equipped properties for rent, from very short to longer term. Many rentals can also be found in Yucatán coast towns such as Progreso and Telchac, where winter rents are a specialty, and in Mérida. They cover a full range of sizes and prices, and can be far more economical than hotels. Many websites offer Yucatán rentals, but check out www.vacationrentals.com, www.perfectplaces.com, and www.akumal-rentals.com. For Yucatán state, look at www.yucatanliving.com.

Riviera Maya: Cancún to Playa del Carmen

Listed from north to south.

PUERTO MORELOS

Hotel Ojo de Agua

Avenida Rojo Gómez, north of the plaza; tel: (998) 871 0027; www. ojo-de-agua.com; $$; Map p.10

Popular beach hotel with big rooms with air-con and sea views, a funky bar-restaurant, and low-cost diving, snorkel-ing and fishing. A good call for no-frills beach relaxation.

Rancho Sak-Ol

Beach road, south of the port; tel: (998) 871 0181; www.rancho sakol.com; $$; Map p.10

Below: at Rancho Sak-Ol.

Left: the stunning pool deck at Deseo.

4448; www.hotelbasico.com), deals in post-industrial cool ('distressed' exposed pipes, gas-tank-tubs as a rooftop pool). In both, giant windows in many rooms face right onto bar-restaurants (Básico's seafood bar, the very hip **Deseo Lounge**), but then, these are not hotels where you sit in your room with a book.
SEE ALSO BARS AND NIGHTLIFE, P.34

Las Palapas
Calle 34 Norte, off Avenida 5; tel: (984) 873 4260; www.laspalapas. com; $$$–$$$$; Map p.10
Once outside Playa to the north, Las Palapas has been surrounded by the town's growth, but inside the fabulous tropical garden it remains a wonderfully tranquil reserve. The 70 rooms are in luxurious cabañas or palm-roofed villas. The restaurants, pools, and beach bar are also lovely, and, having got here first, it has one of the best stretches of beach.

Playa Palms
Avenida 1 bis, between Calles 12 and 14 Norte; tel: (984) 803 3966; www.playapalms.com; $$$; Map p.10
This suite-hotel is just up the street from the hub of Playa nightlife on Calle 12, and yet inside it's remarkably quiet. The studios and suites all have kitchenettes and balconies for taking in the sea view, and down below is a tiny pool, and steps down to the beach.

A likeable cabaña-style hotel that invites you to settle in on the beach south of the town, with simple rooms around a big, palapa-roofed building, some with great views. Breakfast is included, and there's an open kitchen and free use of snorkels, bikes and WiFi. The owners are quietly charming, the atmosphere enormously relaxing.

PLAYA DEL CARMEN
Cabañas La Ruina
Calle 2 Norte, below Avenida 5; tel: (984) 873 0405; email: laruina @prodigy.net.mx; $; Map p.10
Playa's growth has been so fast it has passed some places by, like La Ruina (so called as there's a tiny Mayan ruin in the garden). Here since the 1980s, it still offers beachside or garden cabins (with or without air-con and showers) at low prices, and even still has space to camp or sling a hammock. There's also a fun beach bar-restaurant.

Casa Tucán
Calle 4 Norte, between Avenidas 10 and 15; tel: (984) 873 0283; www.casatucan.de; $; Map p.10
One of Playa's best-value options. Rooms are colourful and comfortable, and there's a lush garden with a much better pool than you find in many newer hotels. Alongside is one of the best local dive operators, **Yucatek Divers**, and packages are available.
SEE ALSO DIVING, SNORKELING, AND WATERSPORTS, P.54

Deseo
Avenida 5, corner Calle 12 Norte; tel: (984) 879 3620; www.hotel deseo.com; $$$–$$$$; Map p.10
Playa's status as the Riviera's hippest spot was confirmed by the style hotels opened by Mexico City design gurus the Habita group. Deseo is all brilliant-white minimalism, with rooms round an ultra-sleek pool ringed by divans for decadent lounging. Habita's other hotel, **Básico**, a block along at Calle 10 (tel: 984-879

Price ranges, given as a guide only, are based on prices per night in US dollars for a standard double room, without breakfast unless stated, in the main winter-spring (but not the Christmas peak) season:

$$$$	over $200
$$$	$100–$200
$$	$50–$100
$	under $50

Shangri-La Caribe

Calle 38 Norte; tel: (984) 873
0611; www.shangrilacaribe.net;
$$$–$$$$; Map p.10

Like its neighbor Las Palapas,
the Shangri-La staked a claim
on the beach when Playa del
Carmen was still a kilometre
away, and has charms newer
hotels can't match. Around a
garden are some of the Rivi-
era's most upscale cabañas.
All are pretty, but they vary in
size and view, and therefore
price. Fine restaurants and
pools complete the picture.

Above: cabañas with a view at Shangri-La Caribe.

Riviera Maya: South of Playa to Tulum

From north to south.
AKUMAL
Villas De Rosa
Aventuras Akumal; tel: (984)
875 9020; www.cenotes.com;
$$–$$$; Map p.12

Distinctive hotel on one of the
best Akumal beaches, with
spacious condos with dazzling
sea views, a pool and a
rooftop bar for catching sun-
sets. Owner Nancy De Rosa is
a cave diver, and the hotel is
also base for her **Aquatech**
dive center, so dive packages
are a specialty, but it also wel-
comes non-divers and fami-
lies, with a babysitting service.
SEE ALSO DIVING, SNORKELING, AND
WATERSPORTS, P.54

TULUM

Most places on Tulum beach
do not have mains electricity,
but most have their own sup-
plies – from generators or

solar – for some hours each
day. Air-conditioning is rarely
necessary, if a cabaña is
properly ventilated. For
Tulum's geography, *see p.13*.
Azulik/Ecotulum
Beach road, km 3.3; for phone
lines, see website: www.eco
tulum.com; $$$$; Map p.12
Romantic beach cabañas
square-set at couples and
honeymooners: 15 tropical-
fantasy all-wood villas on a
rocky crag. The Ecotulum
group also caters to other wal-
lets with **Cabañas Copal**
(simpler cabins with or without
showers, $–$$) and **Zahra**
(more family-oriented cabins,
$–$$$). Cabañas at Copal and
Zahra vary a lot in size and
attractiveness, so make sure
you know what you're getting.
Casa Magna
Beach road, km 9.5; tel: (998)
185 7430; www.casamagna
tulum.com; $$$–$$$$; Map p.12
Tulum's most spectacular
option has to be the former
beach hideaway of late
Colombian drug kingpin
Pablo Escobar. Seized by the
Mexican government on his
death in 1993, it was derelict
for years, but the American
owner of **Amansala** has now
beautifully renovated it, play-
ing up to the casa's history
with rooms like the 'king pin
suite.' The megalomaniac
architecture is astonishing,

Palapas and Cabañas

A *palapa* is the tightly bound
palm roof typical of the
Yucatán. When it's on a hut
placed next to a beach, this is a
cabaña. The first beach
cabañas were just simple
stick-and-palm huts, with just
candlelight, a mattress, or
hammock hooks. From these
rough beginnings, though,
cabañas have sprouted walls,
bathrooms, porches, bright
Mexican-themed décor, solar
power and even (horrors) air-
con. Some are truly luxury-
standard. Prices have risen
accordingly, especially in the
cabañas' original home, Tulum.
Anyone after a more basic style
can still find it – at least for the
moment – at the north end of
Tulum beach, at **Cabañas Zazil-
Kin** (www.zazilkintulum.com) at
km 0.5, which has both rooms
and cabins with or without
showers, and the simpler still
Mar Caribe, which still has no
electricity. Even here, cabañas
are around $50 in peak season.
Another growing cabaña clus-
ter, at Mahahual, was badly hit
by Hurricane Dean, but may
revive. Cabañas can also be
found dotted around the less
developed parts of the coast,
such as Holbox. And staying in
a cabaña – with whatever
degree of added comforts – is
always a delicious experience.

Price ranges, given as a guide
only, are based on prices per
night in US dollars for a stan-
dard double room, without
breakfast unless stated, in the
main winter-spring (but not
the Christmas peak) season:
$$$$ over $200
$$$ $100–$200
$$ $50–$100
$ under $50

the rooms stunning, and it faces a fabulous stretch of open beach. There's also a striking restaurant, open to non-guests.

SEE ALSO PAMPERING, P.103

Hemingway
Beach road, km 6; tel: (984) 114 2321; www.mexonline.com/hemingway; $$$; Map p.12

Ten exceptionally pretty, large cabaña-style villas – each has two bedrooms, a living area, and terraces with the essential hammocks – facing a beautiful, quiet stretch of the beach. Fruit-filled breakfasts are included.

Mezzanine
Beach road, km 1.5; tel: (998) 112 2845; www.mezzanine.com.mx; $$$$; Map p.12

No cabañas, but Tulum's first modern design hotel, with just four rooms combining beach chic and minimalist luxury. As well as admiring the styling, guests can enjoy a sleek pool deck, and the beach. It also has Tulum's most stylish (Thai) restaurant and bar, **Ph**, with weekend DJ nights on the beach popular with party animals.

SEE ALSO BARS AND NIGHTLIFE, P.35; RESTAURANTS, CAFÉS, CANTINAS, P.108

Piedra Escondida
Beach road, km 3.5; tel: (984) 100 3826; www.piedra escondida.com; $$$; Map p.12

A very enjoyable beach hotel at Punta Piedra, with eight rooms in two-story palapa-roofed villas. All have terraces or balconies, looking onto a lovely white-sand cove. Italian-owned, it has a pleasant Italian-Mexican restaurant.

Villa Matisse
Avenida Satélite 19, Tulum Pueblo; tel: (984) 871 2636; email: shuvinito@yahoo.com; $; Map p.12

A star among the low-cost options in Tulum village. Hostess Lourdes runs her place

Above: Cabañas Copal.

with flair: the six rooms are bright and fresh, and there's an open kitchen, and free bikes for getting to the beach.

La Zebra
Beach road, km 8.5; tel: (998) 112 3260; www.lazebra.com.mx; $$$–$$$$; Map p.12

La Zebra seeks to combine the cabaña format and hip modernity in a more Latin fashion than Mezzanine *(see left)*. The cabañas, stretching back from a superb beach, are lovely, with 24-hr power. Next to the cantina-restaurant and tequila bar there's a super-cool lounging deck, and on the beach there's even a dance floor, for salsa nights.

SEE ALSO BARS AND NIGHTLIFE, P.35; RESTAURANTS, CAFÉS, CANTINAS, P.109

Below: beachfront luxury at La Zebra.

BOCA PAILA
Boca Paila Camp
Beach road, 15km south of Tulum; tel: (984) 104 0522; www.cesiak.org; $$–$$$; Map p.12

CESiak, which runs tours into Sian Ka'an reserve, also has rooms at its study center, built within the reserve to low-impact standards: they are 'tent-cabins,' but beneath permanent palapa roofs, and have bathrooms, balconies, and other facilities. There's an almost bizarrely refined restaurant, and the location, above a majestic empty beach, is another world.

SEE ALSO TOURS AND GUIDES, P.120

COBÁ
Club Med-
Villas Arqueológicas
Cobá village; tel: (984) 206 700; www.clubmedvillas.com; $$; Map p.135 C2

With only a slight connection to Club Med, the Villas Arqueológicas are three near identical hotels beside major Mayan sites at Cobá, **Chichén Itzá** (tel: 985-856 6000) and **Uxmal** (tel: 997-974 6020). Run with an old-fashioned charm, and exceptional value, they're especially pretty, with charming rooms and pools and garden restaurants that are perfect for cooling brain and body after pyramid-climbing.

Right: Izamal's Macan Ché.

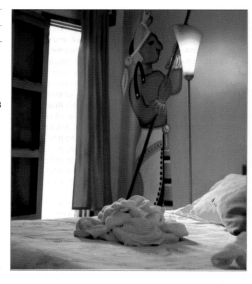

Around Chichén Itzá

SEE ALSO COBÁ, P.81

Hacienda Chichén
Off Highway 180, by the east ruins entrance; tel in Mérida: (999) 920 8407; www.hacienda chichen.com; $$$; Map p.134 B3
The most characterful hotel next to Chichén has been imaginatively renovated. Its core is the original Chichén Hacienda, used by the first archaeologists excavating the site in the 1920s. Its use as a hotel long predates recent hacienda-makeovers *(see p.72)*, but its cottage-style rooms have been beautifully redecorated in similar fashion. The many activities include birding and cultural tours; or, you can just enjoy the luscious gardens and terraces, and the very gorgeous pool and spa.

Hotel Dolores Alba
Highway 180 km 122, near Balankanché; tel: (985) 858 1555; www.doloresalba.com; $; Map p.134 B3
On its own about 4km east of Chichén Itzá, this is far the best of the area's lower-cost options. Rooms are pretty, and there are all of two garden pools, and an enjoyable restaurant. A free bus runs to the ruins each morning. The same owners have a hotel in Mérida *(see opposite)*.

Yucatán State

SEE ALSO HACIENDAS, P.72

CELESTÚN
Eco Paraíso Xixim
Carretera Antigua de Sisal, 9km north of Celestún; tel: (988) 916 2100; www.ecoparaiso.com; $$$; Map p.132 C3

> Some of the most memorable rooms in Yucatán state and Campeche are in beautifully restored colonial haciendas. For these, *see p.72.*

In a wonderfully remote spot 9km up a bumpy sand track from Celestún is this seductive 'eco-resort.' Though built to low-impact standards, the 15 cabañas are very comfortable, all with terraces from which to enjoy the vast beach and absolute peace. An exciting range of tours is available, including visits to parts of the Celestún dunes and lagoons ignored by standard boat trips.

IZAMAL
Macan Ché
Calle 22 no. 305, x 33 & 35; tel: (988) 954 0287; www.macan che.com; $; Map p.133 E3
A lovely B&B-hotel with a fine sense of Yucatecan tranquility. Rooms and suites, all distinctively decorated, are in little bungalows around an exquisite garden, a few blocks from the town centre. There's a rock swimming pool, and breakfast is served in a palm-shaded space, where evening meals can also be ordered. Owners Emily and Alfred and their staff are extra-welcoming.

RÍO LAGARTOS
Hotel Punta Pontó
Calle 7 Diagonal no. 140, corner of Calle 19, Río Lagartos; tel: (986) 862 0509; www.rio lagartos.com; $; Map p.134 B4
Simple but bright little hotel in Río Lagartos village. Nothing fancy, but a handy base for taking a full lagoon tour.

VALLADOLID – EK-BALAM
Casa Quetzal
Calle 51 no. 218, x 50 & 52, Valladolid; tel: (985) 856 4796; www.casa-quetzal.com; $$; Map p.134 B3
In a tranquil old house by San Bernardino Sisal, with a colonnaded garden around a pool, this little hotel is ideally pretty, with six bedrooms decorated with traditional textiles.

Genesis Retreat
Ek-Balam Pueblo; tel: (985) 852 7980; www.genesisretreat.com; $; Map p.134 C3
An 'eco-cultural' venture in the Mayan village of Ek-Balam (a walk from the ruins), with cabañas around a garden, with solar-powered showers

and chemical-free pool. Activities include birdwatching and cenote trips, cycling (with free bikes), and a distinctive choice of tours. The restaurant has Mayan and vegetarian food.

Mérida

SEE ALSO HACIENDAS, P.73

Casa Ana

Calle 52 no. 469, x 53 & 51; tel: (999) 924 0005; www.casaana.com; $; Map p.18
A star budget choice, four blocks from Calle 60. Hidden behind a traditional Mérida façade is a lush garden-patio, where breakfast is served. There's even a pretty pool, and around the garden are five bright, well-equipped rooms.

Casa Esperanza

Calle 54 no. 476, x 55 & 57; tel: (999) 923 4711; www.casa esperanza.com; $$; Map p.18
A giant old house that Mexican-Canadian owners Sergio and Claudette Terrazas have turned into an individual B&B. Beyond the grand entrance patio are just three rooms, beautifully decorated with Mexican antiques and craftwork. There's a pool in one of several patios, the Terrazas couldn't be more welcoming, and breakfasts are fabulous.

Cascadas de Mérida

Calle 57 no. 593C, x 74A & 76; tel: (999) 923 8484; www.cascadas demerida.com; $$; Map p.18
Not an old mansion, but an all-new house built by long-time New Yorker Chucho Basto and his wife Ellyne a few years

Price ranges, given as a guide only, are based on prices per night in US dollars for a standard double room, without breakfast unless stated, in the main winter-spring (but not the Christmas peak) season:

$$$$	over $200
$$$	$100–$200
$$	$50–$100
$	under $50

ago. It's an original: the four guest rooms are each at a corner of the pool, and have great showers surrounded by little waterfalls (the 'cascadas'). Abundant breakfasts, served at one convivial table, sum up the generosity of the operation.

Hotel Dolores Alba

Calle 63 no. 464, x 52 & 54; tel: (999) 928 5650; www.dolores alba.com; $; Map p.18
One of the most popular of Mérida's traditional hotels, despite being four blocks from the Plaza Mayor. Newer rooms around the pool are a bargain; rooms in the older building are well used and a bit cheaper, but also have more character. The owners also have a hotel at Chichén Itzá (see opposite).

Hotel Marionetas

Calle 49 no. 516, x 62 & 64; tel: (999) 928 3377; www.hotel marionetas.com; $$; Map p.18
One of the most charming of the small hotels that make the most of Mérida's architecture.

Below: Casa Esperanza.

In the eight rooms subtle colors and floor tiles are set off against lofty wood-beamed ceilings. In mid-patio is the pool, beside which is a pretty terrace where refreshing breakfasts (included) are served. Owners Sofi (from Macedonia) and Daniel (from Argentina) Bosco run their hotel with individual verve.

Hotel MedioMundo

Calle 55 no. 533, x 64 & 66; tel: (999) 924 5472; www.hotel mediomundo.com; $$; Map p.18
The place that perhaps set the mold for Mérida's small hotels, with 12 rooms in sumptuous colors around tropical-blue patios that catch the light wonderfully. At the back is the pool, and a café and breakfast bar. Owners Nelson and Nicole are especially helpful.

Luz en Yucatán

Calle 55 no. 499, x 58 & 60; tel: (999) 924 0035; www.luzen yucatan.com; $–$$; Map p.18
Mérida is a city of urban oases, and Luz is one of its finest. Founder Madeline Parmet took off in 2006, but new owners Tom and Donard have pledged to keep up its easygoing feel, while adding new rooms and renovating. The rambling old house, incorporating part of the convent of Santa Lucía, is huge. At the back there's a pool, and guests have the run of a huge kitchen, as well as free beers in the fridge on arrival.

Piedra de Agua

Calle 60 no. 498, x 59 & 61; tel: (999) 924 2300; www.piedra deagua.com; $$$; Map p.18
A novelty in Mérida, a 'boutique hotel' in a lofty building on the Plaza Mayor. Rooms

83

are understated-chic and have state-of-the-art features, but can be cramped. Its best feature is the cocktail bar at the back, by a pocket-size pool.

Uxmal and the Puuc Cities

SEE ALSO COBÁ, P.81

Flycatcher Inn B&B
Calle 20 no. 223, Santa Elena; tel: (997) 102 0865; www.flycatcher inn.com; $–$$; Map p.133 D2

Below: at Sacbé Bungalows.

The creation of American Kristine Ellingson and husband Santiago Domínguez, the Flycatcher – signposted on the Uxmal road through Santa Elena – has spacious rooms, a suite and a cottage. Great breakfasts are included, they have their own nature trail from the garden, and guests benefit from the owners' vast local knowledge of wildlife, fiestas, and more.

Sacbé Bungalows
Highway 261 just south of Santa Elena, 16km from Uxmal; tel: (997) 978 5158; www.sacbebun galows.com.mx; $; Map p.133 D2
The best budget choice in the Puuc region. Annette and Edgar Portillo have seven rooms in cabins in a garden. All have good showers and fans, and power is provided 24 hours by solar panels. A larger house is also available with kitchen, but bargain breakfasts are also provided. It's on the west side of Highway 261 south of Santa Elena: look for the 'Hotel Sacbé' sign.

Left: Hotel Marionetas. *see p.83*

Costa Maya and Río Bec

CHETUMAL AND BACALAR
Casita Carolina
Costera Bacalar, Bacalar; tel: (983) 834 2334; www.casita carolina.com; $; Map p.139 C2
A bright, friendly guest house on Bacalar lake, with five cosy rooms facing a garden leading down to the water. Kayaks are available for guests' use.
Hotel Los Cocos
Avenida Héroes 134, Chetumal; tel: (983) 832 0544; www.hotellos cocos.com.mx; $$; Map p.139 D2
Chetumal's most prominent hotel has been unattractively renovated, but it's still a handy base for visiting the area.

COSTA MAYA
Casa Carolina
Beach road, 4km north of Xcalak; tel in US: (610) 616 3862; www.casacarolina.net; $$; Map p.139 D2
Four airy rooms, with kitchens, 24-hr solar power, and terraces or balconies right on the beach. Owners Bob Villier and Caroline Wexler encourage you to relax: it's a fine place for watching pelicans, but Bob is a dive master, and it's great for snorkeling and fishing too.
SEE ALSO DIVING, SNORKELING, AND WATERSPORTS, P.55
Sin Duda Villas
Beach road, 10.9km north of Xcalak; tel in US: (415) 868 9925; www.sindudavillas.com; $$–$$$; Map p.139 D2
A personal creation of archi-

Price ranges, given as a guide only, are based on prices per night in US dollars for a standard double room, without breakfast unless stated, in the main winter-spring (but not the Christmas peak) season:
$$$$	over $200
$$$	$100–$200
$$	$50–$100
$	under $50

Above: another busy day at Casa Carolina, Xcalak.

tect Robert Schneider and Margo Vorheis. The house – combining Mexican colors, ecological principles, and inventive design – throws up surprises at every turn, and the six rooms are delightful.

FELIPE CARRILLO PUERTO
Casa Regina
Avenida Lázaro Cárdenas, corner of Calle 68; tel: (983) 267 1229; www.hotelcasaregina.com.mx; $; Map p.139 D4
Felipe Carrillo's best hotel has big rooms with all the basics – air-con, a boon in this hot spot – and extras such as free WiFi in some rooms.

RÍO BEC
Puerta Calakmul
Highway 186 km 98; tel: (998) 884 3278; www.puertacalakmul.com.mx; $$$; Map p.138 A2
It's hard to be closer to the Calakmul forest and still enjoy creature comforts like this. At the start of the Calakmul road off the highway (behind the wardens' huts), a 1km track leads to 15 amazingly well equipped jungle cabins (with solar power), and a restaurant. Prices are high, supposedly due to high costs. Extra bug repellent is a must-have.
Río Bec Dreams
Highway 186 km 142, 2km west of Chicanná; no phone; www.riobecdreams.com; $–$$; Map p.138 A2
The Río Bec's most welcoming hotel. Canadians Diane

Phone links to the Costa Maya and Río Bec are unreliable, so email is, even more than usual, the way to contact hotels, allowing time for replies to get through. There are no banks or ATMs either, so take cash for your stay, in **pesos**, or ask hotels to advise on longer stays.

Lalonde and Rick Bertram created this spot in the forest, building ample two-bedroom cabins with terraces (around $80) and 'jungalows' sharing bathrooms (about $40). They also have the best restaurant for miles. They have a huge knowledge of Mayan ruins, and can put guests or passers-by in touch with local guides.
SEE ALSO RESTAURANTS, CAFÉS, CANTINAS, P.113

Campeche
SEE ALSO HACIENDAS, P.73
Hacienda Puerta Campeche
Calle 59 no. 71, x 18; tel: (981) 816 7508; www.thehaciendas.com; $$$$; Map p.24
Not really a hacienda – but run by the same Plan group as several hacienda hotels, see p.72 – but a town mansion in old Campeche restored in similar style. Its 15 rooms, restaurant, and pool have an intimate, enclosed feel.
Hotel América
Calle 10 no. 252, x 59 & 61; tel: (981) 816 4588; www.hotelamericacampeche.com; $; Map p.24

A big tiled patio gives this veteran hotel off Campeche's main square a distinctive, airy feel. Rooms vary a lot: the best have loads of light, and nice views of the streets below.
Hotel Castelmar
Calle 61 no. 2, x 8 & 10; tel: (981) 811 1204; www.castelmarhotel.com; $$; Map p.24
Once decrepit, this colonial-style hotel has been attractively renovated, making the most of its colonnaded patios.

CAMPECHE STATE
Hotel Tucán Sihoplaya
Carretera Campeche–Champotón km 35; tel: (982) 823 1200; www.hotelestucan.com.mx; $$$; Map p.137 D4
One-on-its-own hotel on a crag above the Gulf of Mexico. The setting is fabulous, with a little beach, a great pool, and terraces from which to take in the magnificent sunsets.

Below: Río Bec Dreams.

Language

In Cancún and the Riviera Maya, as the phrase goes, 'broken English is spoken perfectly,' and many service staff, especially, talk to foreigners in English near-automatically. But, to get beyond this veneer, and deal with people outside these tourist zones, you have to try a little Spanish – which will get you a more personal response, too. Spanish makes things easy for beginners: pronunciation is clear in spelling, and meanings – such as questions – are often given by intonation, not word order. Plus, Mexicans (and above all Yucatecans) speak far more slowly than most other Spanish-speakers, giving visitors, and everyone else, time to think.

...ORTANTE

*...ad de contribuir a la
la zona arqueológica
...así como por su
...d, se le recomienda:*

*...e los senderos
...que pueden extraviarse.
...a los montículos y
...s edificios para evitar*

*...s muros ya que esto
...servación de los
...de estuco.
...ctar piedras, pedacería*

Pronunciation

Correct stress is essential to pronouncing Spanish words understandably, but this is clearly indicated by spelling and accents. Stress is usually on the last syllable in a word ending with a consonant, and the last but one in words ending in a vowel, an s or n; in exceptions the stressed syllable is shown with an accent, as in Mérida or Celestún.

MAYAN WORDS OR NAMES

In Mexican Spanish *x* usually indicates a guttural *h* sound, as in the Spanish pronunciation of *Mexico*, but in Mayan words it represents a soft *sh*, preceded by a slight vowel if before a consonant, so *Xcaret*, *Xcalak* are *Eesh-caret*, *Eesh-calak*, etc. Zs are very hard in Yucatec (especially in *dz* or *tz*), but other Mexicans often say them more like the *s* in *soft*.

Some Basics

yes *sí*; **no** *no*; **please** *por favor*; **thank you (very much)** *(muchas) gracias*
hello *hola*
goodbye *adios, hasta luego*
good morning *buenos días*

good afternoon *buenas tardes*; **good evening, good night** *buenas noches*
I am/my name is… *Soy/mi nombre es…*
what is your name? *¿cómo se llama?*
how are you? *¿cómo está?*
great, very well *muy bien*
you're welcome *de nada*
I'm sorry *lo siento*
sorry/excuse me *disculpe*
excuse me (to attract attention) *oiga, por favor*
I don't understand *no entiendo*; **do you speak English?** *¿habla inglés?*
what do you want?/what would you like? *¿qué quiere?/¿qué desea?*
I want… *quiero…*
I like… *me gusta…*
I don't like… *no me gusta…*
it doesn't matter *no importa*
I don't know *no sé*
what's this? *¿qué es esto?*
what? *¿qué?*; **who?** *¿quién?*
when? *¿cuándo?*
where? *¿dónde?*
where is…? *¿dónde está…?*
how? *¿cómo?*
how much? *¿cuánto/cuánta?*
how many? *¿cuántos/cuántos?*
with *con*; **without** *sin*

there is/there are *hay* (pronounced *ai*)
¿are there any…? *¿hay…?*
there aren't any *no hay*
here *aquí*; **there** *aquí, allá*
over there, that way *p'allá*
near/far *cerca, cercano/lejos*
left/right *izquierda/derecha*
straight on *todo recto*
entrance/exit *entrada/salida*
good *bueno*; **bad** *malo*
very *muy*
more/less *más/menos*
small *pequeño, chico*; **big** *grande*; **medium** *mediano*
hot (food or drink) *caliente*; **cold** *frío, fría*; **I am hot/cold** *tengo calor/frío*; **this doesn't work** *esto no funciona*
toilets, restrooms *servicios, lavabos, baños, el excusado*
men *señores, hombres, caballeros*
women *señoras, damas*

Yucatec Maya is the first language of many people across the region, especially in villages. Most Mayan-speakers expect to deal with foreigners in Spanish (if not English), but asking about the Mayan words for things – especially foods – makes a very good ice-breaker.

NA'AN A WOJÉETIK

al a wáantaj ti' u kaláanil le
yéetel u bak'pachile', yéetel
ma' u yúuchul tech mixba'al
ku k'áata'ab tech:

a jóok'ol ti' le bejo'obo' tumen
áajtal a sa'atal.
a na'akal ti' le múulo'obo' mix
óok'ol le najo'obo' utia'al ma' u
nelo'ob.
a' a jo'ochik le pak'o'obo' tumen
o' ku k'askúuntik le chichkuna'an
uk'o'.
Ma'a bisik le mejen káacho'obil k'at
éetel lako'obo'.
Ma' a wokol ichil le najo'obo'. U
...chil yéetel u jats'utsile'ku
...le k'iiwiko'obo'.

For the pur...
the conservati...
zone and its e...
your own safe...

☐ Not to lea...
one could...
☐ Not to cl...
of the bu...
their...
☐ Not to c...
perman...
finish.
☐ Not to...
cerami...
☐ Not to...
monu...
splen...
the p...

Left: Spanish, Yucatec Maya, and English at a Mayan site.

One shortcut: *OK* is now part of Mexican Spanish, understood even in remote villages.

Hotels

do you have a single/ double room? *¿tiene una habitación sencilla/doble?* **with twin beds** *con dos camas*; **with a double bed** *con una cama de matrimonio/ king size*; **with a shower/ bathroom** *con ducha/baño* **family room** *cuarto familiar* **can we see the room?** *¿podemos ver el cuarto?* **are there rooms with more light?** *¿hay cuartos con más luz?*; **with a balcony** *con balcón*; **with a sea view** *con vista al mar*; **air-conditioning** *clima, aire acondicionado*

Shopping

open/closed *abierto/cerrado* **free** *gratuito* **how much is it?** *¿cuánto es?/¿qué precio tiene?* **do you take credit cards?** *¿aceptan tarjetas de crédito?* **cheap** *económico, barato* **expensive** *caro* **too much** *demasiado*

Mexican Specifics

Some words and phrases are particular to Mexican Spanish. **ticket** (for a plane, bus, concert) *boleto*; **postage/mail stamp** *estampilla* **pull/push** *jale/empuje* **to chat, talk** *platicar* **to return** *regresar* **swimming pool** *alberca* (*piscina* is also understood) **car** *carro, auto, coche* **car park** *estacionamiento* **tyre** *llanta*; **tyre repair shop** *llantera, vulcanizadora*

For food and dining vocabuary, see *Food and Drink, p.71.*

Spanish has both familiar *(tú)* and polite *(usted)* ways of saying *you*. For convenience all verbs are given here in the more formal *usted* form.

Time

what time is it? *¿qué hora es?* **at what time?** *¿a qué hora?* **it's 3 o'clock** *son las tres*; **at 3** *a las tres*; **half past 3** *las tres y media*; **a quarter past 3** *las tres y cuarto*; **a quarter to 3** *un cuarto para las tres* **morning** *la mañana*; **midday** *mediodía*; **afternoon/evening** *la tarde*; **night** *noche* **1am–dawn** *la madrugada* **yesterday** *ayer*; **today** *hoy* **tomorrow** *mañana* **tomorrow morning** *mañana por la mañana* **now** *ahora, ahorita* **soon** *pronto, dentro de poco* **later** *más tarde, después* **never** *nunca* **early** *temprano*; **late** *tarde*

Arrival and Transport

airport *aeropuerto* **customs** *aduana* **how much is a taxi to...?** *¿cuánto es un taxi a...?*

bus station *estación de autobuses* **I want to go to..** *quiero ir a..* **when does the next bus leave for...?** *¿a qué hora sale el próximo autobus para...?* **what time does it arrive?** *¿a qué hora llega?* **car rental, hire** *renta de autos*; **I want to rent a car** *quiero rentar un carro* **driving license** *carnet de manejar/conducir* **bicycle** *bicicleta* **gasoline, petrol** *gasolina* **dirt road** *camino de terracería* **give way/yield** *ceda el paso* **stop** *alto*

Below: street signs in Izamal.

87

Mayan Ruins and Relics

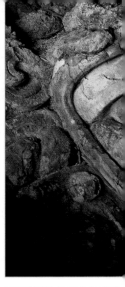

The Maya developed the most sophisticated civilization in pre-Conquest America, with ancient America's only true writing system. Its full complexity is a remarkably late discovery: more has been learned about the Maya in the last 30 years than at any time in history – including the deciphering of Mayan writing – and more finds are still being made. Don't only look at the obvious sites like Chichén Itzá or Tulum: lesser-known gems like Ek-Balam or Kohunlich throw up a fascinating picture of a very diverse, intricate world.

Cancún

El Meco

Punta Sam road, km 3; Map IBC
North of Cancún, El Meco was larger and older than El Rey on Cancún island, with structures dating back to AD 300, but it too enjoyed its greatest wealth in the Postclassic, after 1200. The main pyramid is imposing.

El Rey

Boulevard Kukulcán km 17.5; Map IBC
Cancún's main Mayan site, an engaging insight into the life of a small town in the last years of Mayan civilization.
SEE ALSO CANCÚN, P.6

The Islands

ISLA MUJERES

A small, much-battered temple survives at Isla's Punta Sur.

COZUMEL

San Gervasio

6km north of main island road, from turning 7.5km east of San Miguel; daily 7am–4pm; Map p.8
The largest, most complete of the Postclassic coastal cities, but less immediately impressive than Tulum. It was a major pilgrimage center at the time of the Conquest, and has large temples and a palace complex, the **Chichan Nah**.

Archeological sites in Mexico are run by the *Instituto Nacional de Antropología e Historia* (INAH), and are open daily 8am–5pm. All sites listed here keep to these times unless otherwise indicated (also, some smaller sites may 'unofficially' close early). The INAH also fixes entry charges (added to which, at a few sites, are extra charges levied by each state). Major sites (Chichén Itzá, Uxmal, Tulum) cost around $9; others are mostly $2.60–$5. Admission is free to everyone aged over 60 or under 13. Entry is free on Sundays only for Mexican citizens and residents.

Below: climbing the Nohoch Mul pyramid at Cobá.

Riviera Maya: South of Playa to Tulum

Cobá

45km north of Tulum on Valladolid road; Map p.135 C2
An entirely different site from Postclassic cities like El Rey or Tulum. Cobá was the largest city in northeast Yucatán from around AD 250 to 850, when it lost a titanic war with Chichén Itzá. It is still not fully excavated, and visible structures are widely dispersed around lakes, on paths through thick

Left: one of the enigmatic *Mascarones* of Kohunlich.

Above: on the streets of Tulum.

Mayan History, in Brief
Many people see only a small part of Mayan history – the tail end. The most visited Mayan sites, Chichén Itzá and Tulum, were at their peak in the later centuries of Mayan culture – Tulum at the very end. Yet Mayan culture first developed over 1,500 years earlier far to the south, near the Pacific coast of Guatemala and Chiapas, and moved northward.

In the **Classic Era** (*c.* AD 200–800), its great hubs were the Usumacinta valley of Chiapas, around **Palenque**, and the Petén from central Guatemala north into Yucatán, with the largest ever Mayan cities at **Tikal** and **Calakmul**. From about 500, cities expanded fast in the Río Bec and toward the Caribbean. In northern Yucatán, there were ancient cities such as **Cobá**, **Dzibilchaltún**, and **Acanceh**, but the region grew most spectacularly in the late or even 'Terminal' Classic, from 700–950, before succumbing to the great 'Mayan Collapse' that had already claimed the cities to the south. Then, from about 1200, Mayan culture revived in the north in the **Postclassic Era**, with the growth of **Mayapán** and small trading cities on the coast like **El Rey** (Cancún) and **Tulum**. *See also History, p.74.*

Tulum
Highway 307, 2km north of Tulum town; Map p.135 D2
Tulum's extraordinary setting, as the only Mayan site on a crag above a beach, and Riviera location have boosted visitor numbers and its prominence in Mayan history. The walled city began life around AD 500, but its wealth peaked in the century before the Spaniards arrived. As well as the famous **Castillo** pyramid on its rock, there are substantial structures such as the **House of Columns**, center of government, and carved and painted friezes, some showing a curious 'Diving God,' perhaps related to fishing. Tulum is often crowded, so unfortunately you're not allowed to get close to many buildings.

Xcaret (Polé)
Inside Xcaret eco-park; entrance charge to park; for details *see* Children, p.46.
Often unnoticed by the lagoon in Xcaret park are the remains of Polé, another small Postclassic Era trading town.
SEE ALSO CHILDREN, P.46

forest (the walk, and the number of birds, is one of Cobá's fascinations). They include two ball courts, remarkable carved stelae or standing stones, and the Yucatán's tallest pyramid, the huge **Nohoch Mul**, which, for once, you can climb.

Muyil
Highway 307, 25km south of Tulum; Map p.135 C1
Little-visited but intriguing: a tributary-city of Cobá from about AD 300, when its tall main pyramids were built, Muyil had a second life as a neighbor of Tulum from 1200.

Xel-Ha
Highway 307 km 245, opposite Xel-Ha snorkel park, 15km north of Tulum; Map p.135 D2
Also passed over by many visitors, especially to Xel-Ha snorkel park *(see Children, p.44)*, this is one of the most engaging Riviera sites, with some clear murals of parrots and birds that are among the oldest known Mayan paintings, from around AD 200.

Above: the astonishing sculptures of Ek-Balam.

Around Chichén Itzá
SEE ALSO CHICHÉN ITZÁ, P.14
Balankanché Caves
Highway 180, 5km east of
Chichén Itzá; museum daily
9am–5pm; guided tours daily in
English at 11am, 1pm, 3pm, in
Spanish at 9am, noon, 2pm, 4pm,
in French at 10am; Map p.134 B3
Like many Yucatán caves, this
vast cavern-complex is an
extraordinary natural phenom-
enon and a historic site: relics
found here date from around
AD 200 to the 1500s.
SEE ALSO CAVES AND CENOTES, P.41

Yucatán State
AROUND VALLADOLID
Ek-Balam
Ek-Balam village, off Highway
295 (Tizimín road), 18km north
of Valladolid; Map p.134 B3
Virtually ignored until excavations in 1998, Ek-Balam was

Below: dawn on the equinox
at Dzibilchaltún.

transformed by the uncovering
of its huge **Acropolis** temple,
with an extraordinary tomb
entrance in the shape of a
giant mouth from around 800,
called **El Trono** ('The Throne'),
that has some of the finest of
all Mayan carving, of monster
images, gods, and enigmatic
figures of kings. Also unique
are a four-sided arch, and a
strange spiral-shaped temple,
La Redonda.

IZAMAL AND AREA
Aké
Aké village, 35km east of Mérida,
via turn-off from Izamal–Mérida
road in Tixkokob; Map p.133 E3
One more demonstration of
Mayan variety: Ake's buildings
are unique in style, with
bizarrely massive columns.
Another attraction is the location: Aké village and hacienda
– which still worked henequen
until 2002 – were built on and
around the Mayan ruins.
Kinich Kakmó
Calle 27, opposite Calle 28,
Izamal; free; Map p.133 E3
When the Franciscans made
their base in Izamal, they took
over a Mayan town of 12 pyramids, which turn up all over
the town – some in back gardens. The largest, the Kinich
Kakmó, is a vast pyramid built
up over 1,000 years. Discover-
ing Izamal's other remains is a
lovely way to see the town.
SEE ALSO CHURCHES, P.48

AROUND MÉRIDA
Dzibilchaltún
Off Mérida–Progreso road at
km 12; from the turn it's about
5km to the ruins; Map p.133 D3
One of the most historic sites:
the oldest city in northern
Yucatán, occupied from c.300
BC to AD 1200 or later. Along a
white *sacbé* or Mayan road, it
has unusual structures such
as the **Temple of the Seven
Dolls**, through which the sun
pours at dawn on the equinox,

and a Spanish chapel from the
1590s. Dzibilchaltún also has a
dazzling cenote, **Xlacah**, and
one of the best site **museums**.
SEE ALSO CAVES AND CENOTES,
P.43; FESTIVALS, P.64
Xcambó
Dzemul road, off the Progreso–
Telchac coast road 36km east of
Progreso; from the turn it's 1.5km
to the ruins; Map p.133 E4
A tiny coastal town – possibly
once linked to Dzibilchaltún –
with a Catholic chapel built
onto one pyramid.

SOUTH
Acanceh
Off Highway 18, 26km
south of Mérida; Map p.133 D3
Another place, like Izamal,
where past and present are

intertwined: the worn pyramid on the village plaza is one of the Yucatán's oldest, begun before AD 300. This and two other Mayan structures at Acanceh all have well-preserved stucco friezes.

Mayapán
Off Highway 18, 56km south of Mérida; Map p.133 D2
By contrast, further south is 'the last great Mayan city.' Mayapán grew up around 1200, and in 1250–1440 was effective 'capital' of Postclassic Yucatán. It's like a small version of Chichén Itzá, with a **Castillo** pyramid very like that of the older city, and well-shaped plazas. There are also well-preserved painted panels.

Uxmal and the Puuc Cities

SEE ALSO UXMAL AND THE PUUC CITIES, P.20

Chacmultún
10km south of Tekax: take road to Kancab, then look for sign to Chacmultún; Map p.133 E2
A site for lovers of discovery, set apart on the very edge of the Puuc region. Built on the tops of unusually steep hills, Chacmultún has a building that has faint remains of large mural paintings.

Kabah
Highway 261, 24km south of Uxmal; Map p.133 D2

Above: the grand palacio at Sayil.

The **Codz-Poop** or 'Palace of Masks' at Kabah is one of the great demonstrations of Mayan skill and creativity, its façade covered top to bottom in extravagant carving, above all of the long-nosed rain god Chac. On the other side of the building there is more refined carving, with dramatic scenes of warriors subduing captives.

Labná
On Puuc Route road off Highway 261, 3km from Xlapak, 17km from Kabah; Map Map p.133 D2
The Puuc cities have the most refined Mayan architectural style, and there's no more elegant example than the **Arch of Labná**. It once connected two palace compounds, little of which remain. Labná also has a fine multilevel palace.

Loltún Caves
Junction of Puuc Route and Oxcutzcab–Xul road, 12km east of Labná; tours in English daily at 9.30am, 11am, 1pm, 3pm, in Spanish at 9am, 12.30pm, 2pm, 3pm, 4pm; Map p.133 D2
Some of the oldest human relics in the Yucatán have been found in these awesome caves, from around 5000 BC, yet there are also traces from every other age, from Classic Era carvings to defenses built in the 1840s Caste War.
Guides are unpaid, so tip well.

SEE ALSO CAVES AND CENOTES, P.43.

Oxkintok
Off Highway 180 Mérida–Campeche road: turn east north of Maxcanú to Calcehtok village, then follow signs for 2km to ruins; Map p.133 D2
Far less known than the main Puuc sites, but older than all of them, occupied from about 300 BC to the Postclassic. It's a beautifully peaceful site, and its many intriguing buildings include a strange labyrinth, the **Satunsat**.

Sayil
On Puuc Route road, 9km from Kabah; Map p.133 D2

Many artifacts from Mayan sites are in fine museums in Mérida and Campeche.
See Museums, p.97.

Below: fine carving from Kabah (left) and Labná.

Above: the vast Structure II pyramid at Calakmul, amid the forest rain.

The opulent life of the Maya elite is evidenced by Sayil's magnificent **Palacio**, which once had over 90 rooms. The spacious site also has a ball court, and a soaring small pyramid, the **Mirador**.

Xlapak
On Puuc Route road, 5km east of Sayil; Map p.133 D2
The smallest Puuc site, with just one **Palacio**, but wonderful for seeing birds.

Costa Maya and Río Bec

COSTA MAYA-CHETUMAL
Chacchobén
Near Lázaro Cárdenas, off Highway 293, 9km north of a turn off Highway 307 near Pedro Antonio de los Santos; Map p.139 D3
A small, recently excavated site, mostly from the Early Classic, before AD 600.

The Maya 'Long Count' Calendar is an extraordinary construction, of cycles within cycles and vast lengths of time. Virtually all known events fall within the current 'Great Cycle,' a period of about 5,200 years. This will end in December 2012. Speculation rages on what will happen next.

Dzibanché-Kinichná
Signposted off Highway 186, 55km west of Chetumal: follow road for 15km to ruins via village of Morocoy; Map p.138 C3
Two astonishing Classic Era sites (the same ticket admits to both) believed to have formed one city: Dzibanché, shrouded in forest, has some of the most theatrical of Mayan giant plazas; Kinichná consists of one, three-level pyramid, of phenomenal size.

Kohunlich
Signposted off Highway 186, 60km west of Chetumal: follow road 9km to ruins; Map p.138 C2
On every level one of the most enthralling Mayan sites: the jungle location alone, amid giant fan palms, is astonishing. It has remains of one of the largest Mayan palace complexes, but its great treasure is the **Pyramid of the Masks**, with six giant stucco *Mascarones* or heads staring silently from across history.

Oxtankah
14 km north of Chetumal, on road through Calderitas; Map p.139 D2

A very interesting Classic Era town that was taken over by the Spaniards in the 1530s.

Right: the walled city of Becán.

Above: Chenes-style monster-mouth temple at Chicanná.

RÍO BEC

An amazing density of ancient cities has been discovered here. For an update on access to other sites, ask at **Río Bec Dreams**, see Hotels, p.85.

Balamkú

Turning at Highway 186 km 96: then 2km to ruins; Map p.138 A2

Protected by a metal shed is a huge, intact Mayan stucco frieze, a weird vision of monkeys, toads, and creatures of this world and the underworld.

Becán

Highway 186 km 146, 7km west of Xpuhil; Map p.138 B2

One of the very special Mayan cities. Becán is ringed by a defensive wall, within which its many plazas have a peculiarly tight intimacy, combined with the exaggerated height typical of the Río Bec. Its complex palaces seem like mysterious mazes, and the quality of building, carving, and stucco work is exceptional.

Calakmul

Calakmul turn is at Highway 186 km 101: from there, it's 60km to the ruins: full distance from Xpuhil is 112km; Map p.138 A1

The greatest recent discovery in American archeology is this vast city, far from the main Río Bec within a rainforest reserve. It has been shown to have been perhaps the largest Mayan city, which for 400 years struggled with Tikal for dominance in the Petén. The

---

Ball Games

The ancient ball game of Mesoamerica is one of the oldest 'sports' on earth, traced back to 2000 BC. In Mayan mythology, the *Popol Vuh*, the 'Hero-Twins' Hunahpu and Xbalanqué, defy the Lords of Death by playing the game with them for days. It's not known exactly how it was played, but it seems that in small early Mayan courts it was played between two or four players, and that you scored by getting the ball past the opponent and out the far end of the court. In larger courts like the huge one at Chichén Itzá, games were probably played between teams of seven, and scoring required getting the ball through the rings on the side. In either style, players could not touch the ball with hands or feet, but only with head, shoulders and especially hips, protected by leather belts.

---

site is huge, centered on the largest of all Mayan pyramids, **Structure II**. Finds there have included jade funeral masks, now in Campeche's **Fuerte San Miguel** museum. Again, Calakmul's setting is fabulous. SEE ALSO MUSEUMS, P.98; TOURS AND GUIDES, P.121; WILDLIFE AND NATURE, P.129

Chicanná

Highway 186 km 144, 9km west of Xpuhil; Map p.138 A2

The Río Bec cities combined styles with the Chenes cities to the north, in their 'monster mouth' temples, representing the earth spirits. Chicanná has some of the most elaborate.

Xpuhil

Highway 186 km 153, west end of Xpuhil village; Map p.138 B2

A smaller Río Bec site, but with amazingly dramatic, ultra-steep temple platforms.

Campeche

SEE ALSO CAVES AND CENOTES, P.43

Edzná

55km from Campeche via Chiná, or Highway 261 to San Antonio Cayal, then south; Map p.137 D4

Another one-on-its-own city with a unique style, especially in its **Great Acropolis** and **Building of the Five Stories** palace and temple complex, aligned against one of the most rhythmic Mayan plazas.

Hochob

4km southwest of Dzibalchén, on Xpuhil road; Map p.137 E4

Three steep temples in the woods, typical of the Chenes.

Santa Rosa Xtampak

42km from Highway 261, via turn 5km north of Hopelchén; Map p.133 D1

Very remote (the terrible entry road deters most visitors), but the star of the Chenes region, a major Classic Era city that seems built on a bigger scale than most Mayan structures.

Below: the Building of the Five Stories dominates Edzná's plaza.

The Modern Maya

The Maya are not just an 'ancient' people, but still very much alive. They survived the Spanish Conquest and the famines and European diseases that followed more successfully and in greater numbers than any of Mexico's other indigenous peoples. In the small towns and villages of the Yucatán, above all, they make up around half or more of the population. Far from disappearing, Mayan identity, culture, manners, and idiosyncrasies have flowed into and given a distinctive color to the whole of Yucatecan life.

A Resilient Culture

The Maya are great survivors. Invaded nearly 500 years ago, they have kept their identity alive in part by being stubborn. At times they've been more belligerent – the Caste War of the 1840s remains the only Native American revolt where the Indians nearly won. More often, though, the Maya have kept going just by sticking to their ways and language, with a stony sense of pride in their own identity and culture.

Mayan pride and sense of belonging is a major element in community cohesion. Another is a strong sense of the right way to behave. This is a community that lays great importance on courtesy and respect, to a degree that can make the ways of more commercialized societies seem very coarse.

Today the Maya are under great pressures, of technology and economics. The brash Riviera seems to have little room for courtesy. The quiet, slow charm of Yucatán country people, though, is not a throwback to be laughed at: as one long-term resident has said, it's like gold dust.

Above: a local market in Oxcutzcab.

Village and Home

After centuries of intermingling, ethnic lines in Yucatán are not clear-cut, but in general the further you go down the line from city to small town to village, the higher will be the Mayan population.

Most Yucatán Maya still live in villages, and many still live in a *na*, the traditional palm-roofed wooden house, very like the ones in carvings at Uxmal, within its *jacal* or yard, which also contains other necessities like a washhouse, toilet area, and animal pens.

A *na* may appear primitive, but it's a resilient house for a tropical climate, which lets air circulate and is flexible enough to survive hurricanes. Inside, there are no beds, as it's almost part of Mayan identity to sleep in hammocks, tidied away each morning. There will be a cooking hearth of three big stones – another feature unchanged since ancient times – along with, increasingly, TVs and music systems.

Work

Most Mayan men are still mainly farmers, and work the *milpa*, the traditional slash-and-burn corn farm. At the start of the dry season, in

Left: varied styles on a Yucatecan street.

Religion

The Franciscans made all Maya Catholics – of a kind. Deciphering the 'syncretic religion' that resulted, which happily blends Catholic saints with ancient beliefs, is a favorite task for anthropologists. Since the 1960s the Maya have been heavily targeted by Protestant evangelical sects, and in any village you will see small chapels, including many of groups that are 'autonomous' of US-based churches.

The Yucatecan Mix

The special blending of the Mayan and *Mestizo* (mixed-race) and Spanish-speaking worlds in Yucatán is most prominent in everyday life. In food, *cocina yucateca* is at least half-Mayan, and many festivals have a strong Mayan content. Local Spanish is full of Mayan words. And Yucatecan country life goes at a very Mayan, courteous pace.

SEE ALSO FESTIVALS, 62–5; FOOD AND DRINK, P.67; LANGUAGE, P.86

Shamans and the *Ch'a Chaac*
Many – or maybe most – Mayan villages still have a local shaman, a healer and handler of supernatural forces. One of the main tasks they perform is the *Ch'a Chaac* ceremony, carried out by many farmers at the end of the dry season, when everyone is waiting for rain. *Chaac* is an old Mayan name for the rain gods and spirits: the shaman and his helpers build a wooden altar in the forest, and lay on it leaves in special patterns determined by Mayan numbers, with offerings of special sacred breads and *balché* or Mayan mead, before uttering a series of prayers for rain. Even many Protestants still practice the *Ch'a Chaac* when the time comes, but this is an intimate ceremony, so outsiders are rarely invited.

November, they mark out an area of forest, and cut down its trees. In May they set fire to the trees, which clears the *milpa* for planting and covers it with nutritious ash. Planting – of corn, beans, squash and chillis – begins with the first rains, and the harvest is ready by September. In a good year the *milpa* provides food for a family, and a bit over to sell. After two or three years a *milpa* is exhausted, and must be left to regenerate for at least 15 years. This has sustained the Maya for centuries, but population growth and the amount of land taken for other purposes has led to a shortage of land for new *milpas*.

Men and women have clear roles in traditional communities. Women tend the hearth, cook, make tortillas – fresh every day – tend the animals in the *jacal*, make hammocks, embroidery, and handicrafts, and take them to market. Hence many deal with the outside world more than men do.

Money is always short in Mayan villages, so men and women have not one job, but (like most Mexican country people) several. The *milpa* leaves many 'spare' periods, when men head for the Riviera to work in construction, or anything they can find. Many young girls go to work in hotels. Families also keep bees, to make honey to sell, and do all sorts of odd jobs.

For the most part the Maya had little say in the region's tourist boom, and their main role has been as maids or laborers. More traditional Mayan communities place great importance on respect; they dislike being treated as a tourist attraction and have often kept visitors at arm's length. However, recently there have been more projects in which village Maya themselves are in control. Villages are opening up their cenotes, as a source of income *(see Caves and Cenotes, p.40)*. Even some old 'rebel' villages in the Zona Maya of Quintana Roo have begun to welcome visitors – but only on trips run by local people. *See Tours and Guides, p.121.*

Museums

Treasures brought together from Mayan sites, together with the region's dramatic history and its richly colorful heritage of folk art, form the strong points of the Yucatán's museums. The range of Mayan artifacts, from giant sculpted panels to tiny, comical figurines and everyday objects like hair combs, brings alive the stones of the ruined cities. There are other departures, too, such as exciting contemporary art or a charming museum of Yucatecan song, and while Mérida and Campeche are the foremost museum centers, there are intriguing local museums in towns such as Cozumel, Valladolid or Izamal.

Above: Mayan ceramics from the Museo de San Roque.

Cancún

Cancún has a small **Museo de Arqueología**, with some outstanding Mayan relics from El Rey . It was housed in the Convention Center, but has been closed since Hurricane Wilma in 2005. It is due to reopen in a new location, but is still closed at time of writing.

La Casa del Arte Popular Mexicano
Boulevard Kukulcán km 4; tel: (998) 849 4332; www.museoarte popularmexicano.org; Mon–Fri 9am–9pm, Sat–Sun 11am–7pm; entrance charge; Map IBC
A colorful, slightly chaotic private collection with all kinds of folk art – toys, musical instruments – from across Mexico.

The Islands

COZUMEL
Museo de la Isla de Cozumel
Avenida Melgar, by Calle 6 Norte; tel: (987) 872 1475; www.cozumelparks.com; daily 10am–6pm; entrance charge; Map p.9
In a pretty building on the waterfront, Cozumel's museum has engaging displays (well labeled in English)

on ecology and history, from Mayan times to the chicle trade and recent hurricanes. The rooftop café is lovely.
SEE ALSO RESTAURANTS, CAFÉS, CANTINAS, P.106

Yucatán State

IZAMAL
Centro Cultural y Artesanal
On Parque Itzamná, Calle 31 no. 201, corner Calle 30; tel: (988) 954 1012; Mon–Wed, Fri 10am– 8pm, Thur, Sat 10am–10pm, Sun 10am–5pm; free; Map p.133 E3
The same foundation (linked to Banamex bank) that produced the Plan group, restorers of several haciendas, recently opened this lavish center on one of Izamal's main plazas. The permanent exhibit, of folk art by some of Mexico's finest craftspeople, is stunning, and there's a very attractive shop, part of a scheme to promote high-quality work by local artisans. Staff are charming, and at the back of the building there's a pretty restaurant on a patio beside a part of a Mayan pyramid, and even a small spa.
SEE ALSO SHOPPING, P.116

Museo Comunitario
Calle 31, corner of Calle 28; tel: (988) 954 0032; daily 8am–1pm, 6–9pm; free; Map p.133 E3
Izamal's old museum is a simpler affair than the Centro Cultural, a dusty but engaging run through local history.

VALLADOLID
Museo de San Roque
Calle 41, at Calle 38; no phone; daily 9am–9pm; free, donations requested; Map p.134 B3

Several haciendas have also been opened as museums of Yucatecan rural life. For these, see Haciendas, p.73.

Left: spectacular folk art in the Centro Cultural in Izamal.

tours, but erratically; contrary to some advertising, you must call ahead to book, preferably a few days in advance.

Museo de Antropología e Historia
Palacio Cantón, Paseo de Montejo, by Calle 43; tel: (999) 923 0557; www.inah.gob.mx; Tue–Sat 8am–8pm, Sun 8am–2pm; entrance charge; Map p.18
Mérida's foremost museum has one of the most important pre-Hispanic collections in Mexico, in the grandest of the Montejo mansions, the 1911 Palacio Cantón. Highlights include delicate ceramic faces from Mayapán, and a remarkable early carving of a hunting scene, with two men carrying a deer. The recently renovated museum covers every area of ancient Mayan life – trade, beliefs, cooking, the Maya's bizarre (to us) ideas of beauty. Oddly, while the new displays are translated in English, older ones are still Spanish-only.

Museo de Arte Contemporánea de Yucatán (MACAY)
Plaza Mayor, entrance in Pasaje de la Revolución; tel: (999) 928 3258; www.macay.org; Sun, Mon, Wed, Thur 10am–6pm, Fri, Sat 10am–8pm; free; Map p.18

There are also museums at **Chichén Itzá** and **Uxmal** with finds from these sites. The best archeological site museum, though, is at **Dzibilchaltún**, which also gives an overview of Mayan history. *See also Chichén Itzá, p.14; Uxmal and the Puuc Cities, p.20; Mayan Ruins and Relics, p.90.*

A very attractive museum in a disused church. Its great possessions are fine ceramics and other finds from Ek-Balam, but it also has fascinating displays (most Spanish-only) on topics like the Conquest, pirates, and Mayan folk traditions.

Mérida

Casa Frederick Catherwood
Calle 59 no. 573, x 72 & 74; www.casa-catherwood.com; daily 9am–2pm, 5–9pm; free; Map p.18
A labor of love, this fine early-1900s Mérida house has been beautifully restored to display a rare complete set of the original lithographs by Frederick Catherwood from 1844, reflecting his travels round the Yucatán and Mayan ruins with John Lloyd Stephens. It also has an original shop and café, and acts as a cultural center.

Casa-Museo Montes Molina
Paseo de Montejo 469, x 33 & 35; tel: (999) 925 5999; tours by appointment Mon–Fri 9am–5pm, Sat 9am–1pm; entrance charge; Map p.18
Of the sumptuous mansions built on Paseo de Montejo in the years before 1910, this is virtually the only one still owned by the family for whom it was created, and which still contains its original, luxurious furniture. They now open it to

Below: Tulum, one of the engravings in the Casa Catherwood.

Mérida's contemporary art museum (known as MACAY) has three permanent exhibits: works by Fernando Castro Pacheco, the same artist who did the murals in the nearby Governor's Palace, in a classic Mexican Revolutionary style; and dynamic abstracts by two living painters, Fernando García Ponce and Gabriel Ramírez Aznar. With plentiful space in its huge Plaza Mayor building, the MACAY also hosts lively temporary shows, and oversees a regularly changing exhibit of modern sculpture along **Paseo de Montejo**.

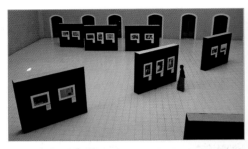

Above: contrasting shows at the MACAY.

Museo de Arte Popular de Yucatán

Parque de la Mejorada, Calle 50 no. 487, x 57 & 59; tel: (999) 930 4700; Tue–Sat 9.30am–4.30pm, Sun 9am–2pm; entrance charge, Sun free; Map p.18

Set up by the same foundation as the Centro Cultural y Artesanal in Izamal (see p.96), in an old Mérida mansion that has similarly been beautifully restored. The display of the finest Mexican folk art is fabulous, and there are informative videos and a charming shop.

Museo de la Canción Yucateca

Calle 57 no. 464, x 48 & 50; tel: (999) 923 7224; Tue–Fri 9am–5pm, Sat, Sun 9am–3pm; entrance charge; Map p.18

Yucatecans love their music of boleros and tríos, so it's fitting the 'Museum of Yucatecan Song' should recall, in detail and with great charm, the many composers and artists in the tradition since the 19th century. You can also listen to recordings, and the museum hosts regular concerts.

SEE ALSO MUSIC AND DANCE, P.100

Museo de la Ciudad

Calle 65, x 56 & 56A; tel: (999) 923 6869; Tue–Fri 8am–8pm, Sat, Sun 8am–2pm; free; Map p.18

Mérida's city history museum has recently relocated to the

Mérida has a fresh, innovative contemporary art scene. As well as exhibitions at the **MACAY** and **Museo de la Ciudad**, there's a varied mix of exhibits at **Centro Cultural Olimpo** on the Plaza Mayor. There are some lively independent galleries near Plaza Santa Ana, such as the **Casa de los Artistas**, Calle 60 no. 405, x 43 & 45, tel: (999) 928 6566, www.artistsinmexico.com, and **Galería La Luz**, Calle 60 no. 415A, x 45 & 47, tel: (999) 924 5952, www.laluzgaleria.com. Near Parque de Santiago there's **Galería Tataya**, Calle 72 no. 478, x 53 & 55, tel: (999) 928 2962, www.tataya.com.mx.

---

old post office in the market district, giving ample space to display a collection that's strongest on Mayan Ti'ho and the Colonial Era. A more exciting discovery can be the top floor, often used to host very original contemporary shows by young Yucatecan artists.

Costa Maya and Río Bec

Museo de la Cultura Maya

Avenida de los Héroes, corner of Avenida Gandhi, Chetumal; tel: (983) 832 6838; Tue–Thur, Sun 9am–7pm, Fri, Sat 9am–8pm; entrance charge; Map p.22

Unable to prize any major Mayan artifacts away from Mérida or Campeche, Chetumal's museum follows a different tack, seeking to explain Mayan ideas – the calendar, glyph writing – through imaginative, interactive displays.

Museo del Fuerte de Bacalar

Fuerte de San Felipe, Bacalar; no phone; Tue–Sun 11am–5pm, Fri; entrance charge; Map p.139 C2

Yucatán's only castle hosts an engaging little museum, mainly dealing with the town's tussles with Belize pirates.

Museo de la Guerra de las Castas

Off the village plaza, Tihosuco; no phone; Tue–Sun 10am–6pm; entrance charge; Map p.134 B2

Remote Tihosuco, between Valladolid and Felipe Carrillo Puerto and a flashpoint of the great Maya revolt and Caste War of the 1840s, is the location for the official museum of the war. The whole of Tihosuco is something of a museum, too, with a church burned in the Caste War that has never been fully restored.

Campeche

Centro Cultural Casa 6
Parque Principal, Calle 57, between Calles 8 and 10; tel: (981) 811 9229; daily 9am–9pm; free, charge for tours; Map p.24
A showpiece of Campeche, this lovely house on the main square has been painstakingly restored to reproduce a typical home of one of the city's wealthy merchant families in the 1830s. It also hosts an information center and shop, and weekly concerts.
SEE ALSO FESTIVALS, P.63

Museo de Armas y Marinería, Fuerte de San José el Alto
Calle F. Morazán, Colonia Bellavista; tel: (981) 816 2460; www.inah.gob.mx; Tue–Sun 9am–5pm; entrance charge; Map p.24
The most striking feature of Campeche's main museums is their location: in two massive Spanish forts from the 1780s, on hilltops either side of the city. San José, to the north, has the lesser collection, dedicated to post-Conquest history, especially Campeche's maritime traditions. If you don't have a car, take a taxi.

Museo Arqueológico de Campeche, Fuerte de San Miguel
Avenida Escénica; tel: (981) 821 0973; www.inah.gob.mx; Tue–Sun 9am–5.30pm; entrance charge; Map p.24
Fuerte de San Miguel to the south, in contrast, houses one of Mexico's most important pre-Hispanic collections: the Mérida museum is bigger, but Campeche has greater treasures, above all the superb jade funeral masks discovered in the 1990s in Calakmul – but they're often 'on tour' to other museums, so you can be disappointed. There is a wonderful array of ceramics, including many figurines made as tomb-offerings at nearby Isla Jaina, which show a more human side of the Maya than the large sculptures. Outside, from the ramparts, there's a fabulous view. Again, the best way there is by cab or car; buses stop on the coast road, from where there's a steep walk.

Museo de la Arquitectura Maya
Baluarte de la Soledad, Calle 8; tel: (981) 816 8179; www.inah.gob.mx; daily 8am–8pm; entrance charge; Map p.24
Housed in a bastion in the city wall, this museum's collection – despite the name – mainly consists of carved stelae (standing stones) or lintels from around Campeche State, especially Edzná and some of the more obscure sites.

Museo de la Ciudad
Baluarte de San Carlos, Calle 8; tel: (981) 811 3990; Tue–Fri 8am–8pm, Sat, Sun 8am–1pm; entrance charge; Map p.24
Another 'bastion museum,' going through Campeche's history in fair detail (in Spanish), from the pre-Conquest Maya through the Franciscans, pirates, and so on.

Museo de la Piratería
Puerta de Tierra, entrance on Calle 18, by corner of Calle 61; no phone; daily 9am–5pm; entrance charge; Map p.24
Maybe Campeche's most fun museum, which doesn't hide the fact that what most people want to know about pirates are tales of derring-do and bad behaviour. More expensive than others, as you have to pay for an audio guide.

Below: some of the extraordinary ceramics and Jaina figures in the Fuerte de San Miguel.

Music and Dance

Music is one of Mexico's great calling cards, a rich seam of tradition that can instantly identify the country throughout the world. Like its food, Mexican music is immensely varied, and the Yucatán, too, has its distinctive music and dances that are just as much a part of its own special color and flavor. Like the Yucatán as a whole, they are a kind of mid-point between central Mexico – the bouncy rhythms of *rancheras* and mariachis – and the more languid, sensual styles of Cuba and the Spanish Caribbean. This music is easy to enjoy, for, as in the whole of Mexico, music is everywhere here, in bars, in fiestas, and on the street.

Yucatecan Music

Local music and dances are a part of every fiesta, and also of weekly events in Mérida like Thursday's **Serenatas Yucatecas** or **Mérida en Domingo**. For all these:
SEE ALSO FESTIVALS, P.62

THE *JARANA*

The classic Yucatecan folk dance developed in *vaquerías* or country fiestas. Like many Mexican country dances it's flirtatious, but with a delicate grace rather than teasing. Men and women begin in separate ranks, divide into couples and reform, in many changing patterns. 'Prowess' dances are a tourist favorite, like the one in which dancers have trays and bottles on their heads.

Poise and gracefulness are central to the *jarana*, as are the outfits: all-white *guayabera* shirts and hats for men, and exquisite embroidered *terno* dresses, gold jewelry, and flowers in the hair for women, who naturally steal the show. Not forgetting the band, sweating away with lots of trombone and percussion, and special *jarana* rhythms.

> The essential place to find out more about Yucatecan music – especially trios – is Mérida's delightful **Museo de la Canción Yucateca**, with plenty to listen to as well as look at.
> *See Museums, p.98.*

TRÍOS AND BOLEROS

The other great Yucatecan musical style is defined most by the way it is played, in trios (nearly always male) with guitars, with one man as lead vocal and the others joining in on harmonies. It first appeared in the 1860s, influenced by Cuba and sensuous rhythms like the bolero. Since then a constant stream of musicians, together known as *la trova yucateca*, has produced hundreds of songs, all carefully recalled in the 'Museum of Yucatecan Song' *(see above)*.

Apart from the sinuous, very tropical sound, the other prime feature of *la trova* is that its lyrics are unashamedly, no-holding-back sentimental and romantic, in line with a widespread Mexican image of the Yucatecan character. Cynics, this may not be your music.

Below: mood music for a cantina, in Campeche's Rincón Colonial.

Left: tuning up for *jaranas* in Parque de Santa Lucía, Mérida.

The Modern Music Scene

Also full of energy: Mexico is just as much in love with salsa, cumbias, and other Latin dance styles as the rest of the Hispanic world, and local salsa bands also turn up in most fiestas. There are also stylish salsa venues, such as **Azúcar** in Cancún and the **Mambo Café** chain.

And while international pop and stars like Shakira are all present, Mexico always creates a huge range of music itself. *Norteño* bands with their accordions and chug-chug sound may seem to dominate radio play, but Mexico also produces very original performers such as Julieta Venegas, a huge hit across the Spanish-speaking world.
SEE ALSO BARS AND NIGHTLIFE, P.30

Classical Music

Traditionally a neglected field, but in the last few years the **Orquesta Sinfónica de Yucatán** has impressed international and (hugely enthusiastic) local audiences. It mainly plays in **Teatro Peón Contreras** in Mérida, and around the state in the **Otoño Cultural** in Oct–Nov. For programs, see www.osy.org.mx.
SEE ALSO FESTIVALS, P.62

Above: if it's Mexico, it must be mariachis.

Another side of trios is that they are part of Mexico's wandering minstrel tradition: on many nights you can see men with guitars around Mérida's Plaza Mayor, ready to be hired for a *serenata*. They also play in restaurants and cantinas, where, aided by a few beers, it's OK to sing along.

Music and Dances of the Rest of Mexico

Other Mexican traditional styles are also heard, especially in Cancún and the Riviera. Mariachis, most famous of all, play in many restaurants, and at the musicians' union on Avenida Yaxchilán in Cancún you can even hire one (or a trio) yourself. Mariachis also play in Mérida, in Saturday's **Noche Mexicana**, or **Mérida en Domingo**.

Colorful folk dances from across Mexico, with plenty of twirling skirts, are showcased on Fridays in Mérida, but the biggest displays are in the nightly show at **Xcaret** park, and at the Teatro de Cancún.
SEE ALSO CHILDREN, P.46; FESTIVALS, P.63

Teatro de Cancún
Boulevard Kukulcán km 4.5; tel: (998) 849 4848; shows Mon–Fri 7pm, 9pm; Map IBC
Two shows, *Voces y danzas de México* of Mexican folk styles, and the pan-Caribbean *Tradición del Caribe*.

Below: Julieta Venegas.

101

Pampering

The combination of lush tropical gardens, perfect warm sun, soft white beaches, gentle breezes, and the Yucatán's laid-back way of life is an automatic invitation to relax, so it's no surprise that this has also become one of the most popular locations for facilities that help you go a step further. Whether you want to smooth away every last knot of stress, re-encounter your inner self, get fit, tone up your looks, or just sink into some totally indulgent pleasure, you will find something to suit you in some of the world's most seductive spas – from treatments used by the ancient Maya to the latest therapy techniques.

Hotel Spas

Most of the Riviera's big hotels and resorts offer some kind of spa, but some – all in Cancún – stand out from the crowd. All are open to non-residents.

Dreams Cancún

Punta Cancún, off Boulevard Kukulcán at km 9; tel: (998) 848 7000; www.dreamsresorts.com/cancun; Map IBC
Sumptuous spa with superb sea view, and a choice of de-stress and beauty packages or an 'à la carte' spa menu.

Fiesta Americana Grand Coral Beach

Boulevard Kukulcán km 9.5; tel: (998) 881 0808: www.fiesta americana.com; Map IBC
This grand hotel offers a suitably opulent range of spa treatments, including massage by the beach.
SEE ALSO HOTELS, P.76

Kayantá Spa at the Ritz Carlton

Boulevard Kukulcán km 13.8; tel: (998) 881 3200: www.ritz carlton.com; Map IBC
Maybe the most luxurious of all the hotel spas, with exquisite treatment rooms and whirlpool baths with their own secluded terraces.

Above: a 'rain massage' table at the Tides Riviera Maya.

Haciendas

Some of the loveliest spas, in historic buildings amid gardens and highlighting Mayan treatments, are in Plan group hacienda hotels like **Temozón Sur**. **Hacienda Chichén** at Chichén Itzá also has a fine spa. All open to non-guests.
SEE ALSO HACIENDAS, P.73; HOTELS, P.82

Spa at Xcanatún

Hacienda Xcanatún, Carretera Mérida–Progreso km 12; tel: (999) 941 0213; www.xcanatun.com; Map p.133 D3
An especially lovely, tranquil spa, in the abundant gardens of Xcanatún. Mayan flower-

Mayan Treatments

Many Yucatán spas offer treatments claimed to be based in Mayan traditions (although just how 'historic' they are can be a little vague). The most common, and unquestionably traditional, is the **Temazcal** sweat lodge, found across Mesoamerica since ancient times. It works on a similar purification principle to a sauna or other sweat baths: in a small, enclosed space (often, a kind of clay igloo), red-hot volcanic stones are placed in the middle, while the participants sit around the sides. The distinctive feature – as well as a certain ritual – is in the woods and aromatic herbs thrown on the stones, which with the powerful heat create a specially intense atmosphere. Other techniques based on those of Mayan healers are flower, herb, and honey **massages**, and **cleansing** with herbs and mud.

and-honey massage is a specialty, but there's an ample range of treatments, and charming, expert staff.
SEE ALSO HACIENDAS, P.73; RESTAU-RANTS, CAFÉS, CANTINAS, P.111

Above: preparing for massage at the Maya Spa in Tulum.

Seductive Retreats

Several centers offer especially complete programs, rather than just as hotel options, for a total escape.

ISLA MUJERES
Spa Zenter at Casa de los Sueños
Carretera a Garrafón; tel: (998) 877 0651; www.casadelos suenosresort.com; $$$$; Map p.8
A very stylish spa in Isla's most secluded boutique hotel. Open to non-residents.
SEE ALSO HOTELS, P.77

RIVIERA MAYA: PLAYA DEL CARMEN
Maroma Resort and Spa
Off Highway 307 15km north of Playa del Carmen; tel: (998) 872 8200; www.maromahotel.com; $$$$; Map p.135 D3
With jungle and a huge beach to itself, this lush retreat invites you never to leave (if you can handle the price). The spa is dazzling, with a *temazcal* and every kind of treatment.
The Tides Riviera Maya
Playa Xcalacoco, off Highway 307 5km north of Playa del Carmen; tel: (984) 877 3000; www.tides rivieramaya.com; $$$$; Map p.135 D3
This intimate luxury resort, carefully pitched at couples (rooms have their own pools), has a suitably sexy spa, wonderfully located amid palms by the beach. Hard to resist.

RIVIERA MAYA: TULUM
Amansala – Bikini Boot Camp
Beach road, km 7.7; tel (998) 185 7430; www.amansala.com; $$–$$$; Map p.12
A big hit on Tulum beach, and it's easy to see why: one-week courses at Melissa Perlman's

'camp' are a well-honed mix of beauty treatments, fitness, pampering, and fun, plus, you stay in cabañas, the food's great, and it's on a perfect beach. It's mainly pitched at young women, but couples are welcome (men alone are not encouraged). Perlman also owns the **Casa Magna**.
SEE ALSO HOTELS, P.80
Maya Spa at Ecotulum
Beach road, km 3.3; for phones see website: www.ecotulum. com; $–$$$$; Map p.12
The three Ecotulum hotels (**Azulik**, **Cabañas Copal**, and **Zahra**) share this mellow spa, in a lovely location amid trees above the beach. Mayan treatments, and a temazcal, are a specialty. Also open as a day spa, with moderate prices.
SEE ALSO HOTELS, P.80
Maya Tulum
Beach road, km 6; tel in US: (770) 483 0238; www.mayatulum. com; $$$–$$$$; Map p.12
The Riviera's longest-running wellness center takes its role seriously, with a comprehensive 'Mind-Body-Spirit' program highlighting yoga. The lovely restaurant has excellent vegetarian food and seafood.

Smaller Venues

As well as larger hotels and specialist resorts, small hotels often provide massages, yoga, and so on. **CasaSandra** on Holbox, **Macan Ché** in Izamal and **Cascadas de Mérida** are examples, and it's always worth asking what is available.
SEE ALSO HOTELS, P.78

Price ranges for residential spas, based on prices per night in US dollars. Prices naturally vary by the treatments you take:	
$$$$	over $200
$$$	$100–$200
$$	$50–$100

Restaurants, Cafés, and Cantinas

You're never too far from somewhere to eat in the Yucatán – even leaving aside all the *taco*-stands and ice-cream stalls. There are restaurants in bougainvillea-shrouded gardens with graceful Mayan waitresses, chic modern places with designer furniture, or, at another point on the scale, village *loncherías* with plastic tables. You can find international fusion cuisine, or explore the wealth of Yucatecan cooking. Whichever you choose, you'll find plenty to enjoy, for eating well here is never simply a matter of price.

Cancún

HOTEL ZONE

Cancún island hosts an overwhelming number of restaurants, with several in each hotel and mall, and plenty that stand on their own. Their food can be of the enjoyable-but-nothing-special kind, but here are three worth a detour.

La Destilería
Boulevard Kukulcán km 12.5; tel: (998) 885 1086; $$$; daily 1pm–midnight; Map IBC
A homage to the Mexican heartland, with over 150 tequilas (in a tequila 'museum') and sophisticated cooking, including many rare traditional dishes. Service is smooth.

La Dolce Vita
Boulevard Kukulcán km 14.6; tel: (998) 885 0161; www.dolce vitacancun.com; $$$; daily noon–11.30pm; Map IBC
Cancún's premier Italian restaurant and one of its most stylish, with a terrace over-

looking Nichupté lagoon. The menu covers all the bases of refined Italian cuisine – with Caribbean touches – and the wine list, though expensive, is one of Cancún's best.

Laguna Grill
Boulevard Kukulcán km 16.5; tel: (998) 885 0267; $$$; daily 2pm–midnight; Map IBC
Out to impress, and doing so, in a lovely lagoon-side garden. The food is just as fashionable, a global-fusion mix of Asian and Mexican flavors.

CIUDAD CANCÚN

100% Natural
Avenida Sunyaxchén 62, corner Avenida Yaxchilán; tel: (998) 884 0102; www.100natural.com.mx; $$; daily 8am–11pm; Map IBC
This small wholefood chain and its imaginative, beautifully fresh salads, sandwiches, and more is much appreciated by anyone seeking a change from local fare, and a godsend to vegetarians, with lots of meat-and fish-free options. Fabulous juice combos are also a specialty. There are branches at Boulevard Kukulcán km 9.5, on Avenida 5 in Playa del Carmen, and in Tulum.

Los Arcos
Avenida Yaxchilán, corner of Calle Rosas; tel: (998) 887 6784; $$; daily 8am–5am; Map IBC
One of the most enjoyable of the many terrace restaurants on Avenida Yaxchilán. Service is friendly and not overbearing, and the classic Mexican meat and seafood dishes are subtly done as well as great value.

El Café de la Nader
Avenida Nader 5, behind City Hall; tel: (998) 884 1584; $$; daily 7am–11pm; Map IBC
A favorite with Cancún locals, this big terrace café by the city hall is great for

Below: in Parque de las Palapas.

Prices, roughly, for a three-course meal with beer or wine:	
$$$	over $25
$$	$15–$25
$	under $15

Left: La Casa Vieja, in Campeche's old city. *See p.113.*

For an introduction to Yucatecan and Mexican food, drink and dining customs, and the differences between restaurants, *loncherías*, cantinas and so on, *see Food and Drink, p.66.*

People who don't believe Cancún is a real city should try Pabilo, where some of the local intelligentsia gather at night. It's quite chic, with soft sofas, mellow jazz and eclectic art work. To eat there are ample salads and sandwiches, and the coffee is excellent.

Sanborn's
Avenida Uxmal, corner of Avenida Tulum; tel: (998) 884 0002; www.sanborns.com.mx; $$; daily 24 hours; Map IBC
A Mexican institution (despite being founded by a pair of gringos in Mexico City in 1903), Sanborn's has many attractions: it's always open, the classic Mexican food is delicious, and service leaves you feeling very well cared for.

The Islands
ISLA MUJERES
Casa O's
Carretera a Garrafón; tel: (998) 888 0170; www.casaos.com; $$$; daily 1–11pm; Map p.8

The best place in Cancún to find good restaurants with a more local flavor (and lower prices) is **Avenida Yaxchilán** in Ciudad Cancún, which has a line of busy restaurants like **Los Arcos** *(see left)*, bars, and clubs. Still more of a taste of Mexican life can be had at the bargain cafés on **Parque de las Palapas**, or the restaurant-court in **Mercado 28** market (not open at night).

classic Mexican breakfasts – with unusually good coffee – and has enjoyable larger dishes, too.

Labná
Calle Margaritas 29, by Parque de las Palapas; tel: (998) 884 3158; www.labna.com; $$$; daily noon–10pm; Map IBC
This charming, comfortable restaurant produces some of the most refined versions of classic Yucatecan dishes, with great fresh ingredients and intricate seasonings. Service is very attentive. The same owners also have **La Habichuela** nearby, with a pretty terrace.

El Pabilo
Avenida Yaxchilán 31, by Calle Gladiolas; tel: (998) 892 4553; $; Mon–Sat 5pm–1am; Map IBC

Below: 100% Natural is often a vegetarian's savior.

Above: typical of the island, Holbox's Isla del Colibrí.

Isla's prettiest restaurant, on a terrace beneath a palapa on the southwest shore, with a spectacular sunset view of Cancún. The menu is strong on seafood, and spiny lobster is a specialty.

Color de Verano
Avenida López Mateos, by corner of Avenida Rueda Medina; tel: (998) 877 1264; www.color deverano.com; $$; Mon–Sat 8am–noon, 4–11pm; Map p.8
A relaxing, stylish little French café and crêperie, with delicious wholefood breakfasts and baguette sandwiches.

French Bistro Français
Avenida Matamoros, between Avenidas Juárez and Rueda Medina; no phone; $$; Sun–Fri 8am–noon, 6–10pm; Sun 6–10pm; Map p.8
With its colorful dining room, this is an Isla institution. The mostly French dishes (onion soup, duck à l'orange) can be hit and miss, but the atmosphere makes up for it.

Zazil-Ha
Na Balam Hotel, Calle Zazil-Ha 118; tel: (998) 877 0279; www.nabalam.com; $$; daily 6am–11pm; Map p.8
Original, fresh vegetarian options are a highlight of this tranquil hotel restaurant.

COZUMEL
Café del Museo
Museo de la Isla de Cozumel, Avenida Melgar, corner of Calle 6 Norte; tel: (987) 872 1475; $; daily 8am–2pm; Map p.9
The roof terrace café above Cozumel's museum is one of the island's best spaces for taking time, with a great view. Good snacks and lunches, and you don't have to pay museum entrance to go up.
SEE ALSO MUSEUMS, P.96

Casa Denis
Calle 1 Sur, between Avenidas 5 and 10, off main plaza; tel: (987) 872 0067; www.casadenis.com; $$; daily 7.30am–11pm; Map p.9

Some of Cozumel's most enjoyable places to eat are over on the island's east coast, virtually deserted except for a few laidback bar-restaurants above the surf with great grilled fish. **Coconuts Bar & Grill**, near the **Ventanas del Mar** – the east side's only hotel – has a party atmosphere. A little south, the **Chen Río** sits on one of the east coast's best sheltered beaches, and offers wonderful fish platters that can easily feed four. Both restaurants close around 6pm. *See also Hotels, p.78.*

Cozumel's oldest restaurant is still in the same little wooden house as when it opened in 1945, while the plaza has grown up around it. With a shady outside terrace, it has lots of character, and the Mexican – good *arrachera* steaks – and Yucatecan dishes are reliably enjoyable.

Chi
Avenida Melgar, corner of Calle 3 Sur; tel: (987) 869 8156; http://chicozumel.com; $$$; daily noon–2am; Map p.9
An impressively sleek new arrival on Cozumel, on a terrace above the waterfront with great evening views. There's nothing very Mexican about it, as the menu is 'Pan-Asian' – covering Thai, Japanese, Chinese, and more. A very smart bar completes the picture, with a sybaritic cocktail list.

Cocos Cozumel Café
Avenida 5 Sur, between Calle 1 Sur and Calle A. Rosado Salas; tel: (987) 872 0241; $; Nov–Aug Tue–Sun 6am–noon; Map p.9
A time-honored spot for breakfast, friendly, cozy, and much loved by divers. You can choose between a Mexican or an American menu.

Las Palmeras
Avenida Melgar, corner of Avenida Juárez, opposite the ferry quay; tel: (987) 872 0532; $$; daily 8am–11pm; Map p.9
Food at this big, bright bar-restaurant – from burgers to classic *enchiladas* and great seafood grills – is a little expensive, but its location by the plaza and the ferry dock means it's always buzzing, and the margaritas and snacks go down fine.

HOLBOX
CasaSandra has an excellent restaurant: see Hotels, p.78.
La Isla del Colibrí
Avenida Tiburón Ballena, by the plaza; tel: (984) 875 2162; $; daily 7am–10pm; Map p.9

The essence of Holbox's no-shoes style, this amiable little wood-hut café answers many needs, with fresh breakfasts, salads, meat, or seafood grills, and addictive juice cocktails.

Pizzeria Edelyn

On the plaza; tel: (984) 875 2024; $$; daily noon–10pm; Map p.9
Holbox being a cranky little place, it no longer seems odd that its biggest restaurant is a pizzeria – although fresh-caught fish is also a specialty. The seafood pizzas, packed with fat shrimp, are delicious.

Riviera Maya: Cancún to Playa del Carmen

Towns listed north to south.

PUERTO MORELOS

Hola Asia

On the town plaza; tel: (998) 871 0679; www.holaasia.com; $$; Mon and Wed–Sat 3am–10pm, Sun 1–10pm; Map p.10
Liked by visitors with an itch for a change from Mexican fare, this laid-back restaurant offers an Asian mix (Chinese, Japanese, Thai). It's deceptively large, with a roof terrace that has great sea views.

John Gray's Kitchen

Avenida Niños Heroes; tel: (998) 871 0665; $$$; Mon–Sat 6–10pm; Map p.10
One of the Riviera's gourmet options, the showcase of US chef John Gray. His style mixes American, Mexican, and other touches, in dishes like crab cakes and chipotle may-onnaise. Other Gray restaurants are in Playa del Carmen and Cancún.

Los Pelícanos

Town plaza, by the beach; tel: (998) 871 0014; $$; daily 10am–11pm; Map p.10

Above: John Gray's Kitchen.

Leisurely sampling a *ceviche* of shrimp or conch here while watching the pelicans hang in the wind is one of the great Riviera experiences. This essential local institution was restored after a battering by Hurricane Wilma in 2005: the location is hard to beat, beneath a giant palm palapa above the beach, with tables inside or on a lovely terrace.

PLAYA DEL CARMEN

La Cueva del Chango

Calle 38 Norte, off Avenida 5; tel: (984) 876 2537; www.lacuevadel chango.com; $$; Mon–Sat 8am–11pm, Sun 8am–2pm; Map p.10
Some way from Playa's main drags near Shangri-La Caribe hotel, the 'monkey's cave' is worth finding, with some of the most imaginative Mexican food around – original twists

on standards like shrimp breaded in cinnamon and chili with apple compote, a lovely sweet-and-spice mix, or ultra-refreshing salads. Service is relaxed, prices exceptional.

The Glass Bar

Avenida 5, corner of Calle 12 Norte; tel: (984) 803 5805; www.theglassbar.com; $$$; daily 7am–1am; Map p.10
A very elegant spot on the corner that's the hub of Playa nightlife, with terrace tables ideal for dining while keeping up with the action. The menu is upscale Italian, with Mexican innovations, and there's a fine, if pricey, wine list.

Karen's Grill & Pizzas

Avenida 5, between Calle 2 and 4 Norte; tel: (984) 879 4064; $$; daily 8am–11.30pm; Map p.10
A long-running, cheap-and-cheerful standby on Quinta Avenida, with hefty seafood grills and enjoyable pizzas.

La Parrilla

Avenida 5, corner of Calle 8 Norte; tel: (984) 873 0687; www.laparrilla.com.mx; $$; daily noon–2am; Map p.10
La Parrilla is something of a phenomenon, with several branches in Cancún (one is on Avenida Yaxchilán), here in Playa and in Mérida and Campeche. The menu is a no-nonsense, meat-heavy Mexican mix of *fajitas*, *arracheras*,

Below: the irresistible view from Los Pelícanos.

Prices, roughly, for a three-course meal with beer or wine:	
$$$	over $25
$$	$15–$25
$	under $15

spicy *tacos*, and the like. Very popular, and don't try to eat here if you don't want to be interrupted by mariachis.

Restaurante-Coctelería Las Brisas

Calle 4 Norte, between Avenidas 5 and 10; no phone; $; daily noon–11pm; Map p.10

A good example of the Mexican rule that good restaurants don't need to be fancy or expensive: this big, no-frills terrace – one of a bunch on Calle 4 – has some of the best fresh seafood, delicious in *ceviches* and *cocteles*.

Ula Gula

Avenida 5, by corner of Calle 10 Norte; tel: (984) 879 3727; $$$; daily 5.30–11.30pm; Map p.10

A hip roof terrace above the Quinta Avenida that has many fans for its trendy style and fusion cuisine, mainly a mix of an Italian base with Mexican-Caribbean flavors.

Yaxche

Calle 8 Norte, between Avenidas 5 and 10; tel: (984) 873 2502; www.mayacuisine.com; $$$; daily noon–midnight; Map p.10

Playa's most renowned restaurant, where Alberto Lizaola has created original cuisine combining Mayan traditions with a sophisticated culinary training. Just reading the menu feels like an adventure, and the combinations of flavors of seafood, citrus and other fruits and subtle chilis are both endlessly surprising and richly enjoyable.

Riviera Maya: South of Playa to Tulum

Towns listed north to south.

AKUMAL

Imelda's Ecocina

Akumal village, next to Centro Ecológico; no phone; $; Mon–Sat 8am–3pm; Map p.135 D2

A favorite stop in Akumal for wholefood breakfasts, with larger dishes for lunch, one of which is always vegetarian.

Above: Yaxche in Playa del Carmen has imaginative, refined food

Qué Onda

Caleta Yal Ku, north of Akumal village; tel: (984) 875 9101; www.queondaakumal.com; $$; Wed–Mon 7.30–11am, noon–4pm, 5–10pm; Map p.135 D2

A very mellow little spot behind Media Luna bay, with a garden and superior Italian food and homemade pasta. They also have pretty rooms and suites, and a shaded pool.

PUNTA SOLIMÁN

Oscar y Lalo

Highway 307, km 238; tel: (984) 115 9965; $$; daily 11am–8pm; Map p.135 D2

A case of Mexican adaptability. This was one of the area's best beach restaurants, until hit by Hurricane Dean. It has relocated from Punta Solimán itself to a garden by the highway: not so magnetic a setting, but the Yucatecan food is fine.

TULUM

Don Cafeto

Avenida Tulum 64, between Calles Orion and Centauro; tel: (984) 871 2207; $$; daily 7.30am–11pm; Map p.12

A Tulum fixture, a big open terrace on the Pueblo's main street with satisfying breakfasts and classic Yucatecan and Mexican fare. Don Cafeto also has a terrace at **Mar Caribe** cabañas (Beach road, km 0.7), one of the best-value places to eat on Tulum beach.

El Pequeño Buenos Aires

Avenida Tulum, corner of Calle Beta; tel: (984) 871 2708; $$; daily 11am–11pm; Map p.12

Confirmed carnivores head for this friendly Argentinian steakhouse in the pueblo, with excellent barbecued steaks, pork and chicken in fresh marinades, and good wines.

Ph at Mezzanine

Beach road, km 1.5; tel: (998) 112 2845; www.mezzanine.com.mx; $$$; daily 8am–11pm; Map p.12

Tulum's trendiest boutique hotel naturally seeks to have its most chic restaurant, in a stylish terrace and enticingly comfortable dining room, with oriental fittings to match the global, Thai-oriented cuisine.

SEE ALSO BARS AND NIGHTLIFE, P.35; HOTELS, P.81

Prices, roughly, for a three-course meal with beer or wine:	
$$$	over $25
$$	$15–$25
$	under $15

based on traditional Mayan recipes.

¡Qué Fresco!
Zamas cabañas, Beach road, km 4; no phone; www.zamas.com; $$; daily 7.30am–10pm; Map p.12

A great outlook is one of the charms of this palapa-shaded terrace, on a crag above the sea. Others are unpushy service, and lively fish dishes, such as grouper (*mero*) in garlic and lime. One of Tulum's best beachside restaurants.

La Zebra
Beach road, km 8.5; tel (998) 112 3260; www.lazebra.com.mx; $$$; daily 8am–10pm; Map p.12

This cabaña hotel has a lot of style, and its 'beach cantina' is run with verve, with fresh seafood grills, *ceviches* and other food ideal for the beach. Top-rank margaritas, too.
SEE ALSO BARS AND NIGHTLIFE, P.35; HOTELS, P.81

Around Chichén Itzá

The **Hotel Dolores Alba** and hotels by the ruins all have restaurants, and there are plenty of places to eat in the neighboring town of **Pisté**.
SEE ALSO HOTELS, P.82

Las Mestizas
Calle 15, Pisté; no phone; $; daily 7.30am–10pm; Map p.134 B3

Some Pisté restaurants have blown up into giant venues for processing Cancún bus tours. Las Mestizas has grown, too, but has kept hold of its Yucatecan small-town charm. Local dishes like *sopa de lima* are nicely done, and its terrace is a great place to wind down after exploring Chichén.

Yucatán State

CELESTÚN
La Palapa
Calle 27 no. 299, x 28 & 30; tel: (988) 916 2063; $$; daily 9am–7pm; Map p.132 C3

As the name suggests, this bar-restaurant sits under a big palapa, by Celestún beach.

Many hacienda hotels also have restaurants that showcase high-quality Yucatecan cuisine, especially **Hacienda Temozón Sur**. See Haciendas, p.73.

Many tour groups call here after seeing the local flamingos, but the fish and seafood dishes are still good quality.

IZAMAL
Restaurante Kinich
Calle 12, corner of Calle 11; tel: (988) 954 0489; www.sabordeizamal.com; $$; daily noon–7pm; Map p.133 E3

In a leaf-shaded terrace a short walk from Kinich Kakmó pyramid, the Kinich is known as one of the Yucatán's best restaurants for complex traditional dishes like *queso relleno* (pork in melted cheese). Very popular with locals at weekends, so try to go in the week.

PROGRESO
Escaping up the road to Progreso for a seafood lunch by the beach is a vital part of Mérida life, so its beachfront **Malecón** is lined with great-value terrace restaurants.

Flamingos
Malecón, corner of Calle 72; tel: (969) 934 4050; $; daily 8am–10pm; Map p.133 D4

There is hot competition for the Yucatán's best *ceviche*,

Below: Tulum's Mezzanine, one of the Riviera's most stylish spots.

Prices, roughly, for a three-course meal with beer or wine:
$$$ over $25
$$ $15–$25
$ under $15

but Flamingos is certainly a candidate. A very friendly place to spend a few hours, watching the beachlife.

RÍO LAGARTOS
Restaurante Isla Contoy
Calle 19 no. 134; tel: (986) 862 0000; $; daily 7am–7pm; Map p.134 B4
This may look ramshackle under its palapa, but it serves superb cilantro-filled *ceviches* and seafood cocktails. Its owners the Núñez Martínez family are also among the best local tour and fishing guides.
SEE ALSO WILDLIFE AND NATURE, P.129

VALLADOLID
El Mesón del Marqués
Calle 39 no. 239, x 40 & 42; tel: (985) 856 2073; www.meson delmarques.com; $$; daily 7am–10pm; Map p.134 B3
The restaurant in Valladolid's most historic hotel occupies a beautiful old colonial patio, shaded by giant palms and fruit trees. Dishes to go for are local specialties, like *pollo oriental de Valladolid*. Service is very charming.

Above: a warm and wise welcome at Café Alameda.

Mérida
Amaro's
Calle 59 no. 507, x 60 & 62; tel: (999) 928 2451; $; daily 11am–2am; Map p.18
One of central Mérida's prettiest restaurants, with a patio dominated by a giant orchid tree. The menu is varied and original, with many vegetarian choices, especially crêpes made with the distinctive local vegetable *chaya*.

Café Alameda
Calle 58 no. 474, x 55 & 57; tel: (999) 928 3635; $; daily 7.30am–5pm; Map p.18
Diners take their time at this tranquil café, to chat over local news. Good breakfasts set you up for the day, and, since the owners are from Mérida's Lebanese community, the menu also has specialties like Arab breads and *kibis*, Lebanese meatballs.

Café-Club
Calle 55 no. 496A, x 58 & 60; tel: (999) 923 1592; $; Mon–Sat 7am–5pm; Map p.18
Another relaxing breakfast spot, opposite Santa Lucía church, with a varied mix of salads, sandwiches, and Mexican dishes later in the day. Plenty for vegetarians, too.

El Cangrejito
Calle 57 no. 523, x 64 & 66; tel: (999) 928 2781; $; Mon–Sat 11am–5pm; Map p.18
As said, you can never judge Yucatecan restaurants – above all in Mérida – by looks: this little *taco* restaurant can appear a tad chaotic (opening hours are erratic), but its fish and seafood *tacos* have an awesome reputation, and were even presented to Pope John Paul II.

La Casa de Frida
Calle 61 no. 526A, x 66 & 68; tel: (999) 928 2311; $$; Mon–Sat 6–11pm; Map p.18
Plenty of places in Mexico try use the Frida Kahlo color palette, but this one manages to avoid clichés in the bright tones of its comfortable old Mérida patio. Service is charming, and the menu features central Mexican rather than Yucatecan dishes, includ-

Below: the entertainment starts up at Eladio's.

Note that the best traditional Yucatecan restaurants do not open in the evenings.

ing a wonderfully subtle and smooth *chile en nogada* (large green chili stuffed with beef and herbs, with a walnut and pomegranate sauce).

Casa de Piedra
Hacienda Xcanatún, Carretera Mérida–Progreso km 12; tel: (999) 941 0273; www.xcanatun. com; $$$; Mon–Sat 8–11.30am, 1.30–11pm; Sun 8–11.30am, 1–6pm; Map p.18

Just outside Mérida, the restaurant in Hacienda Xcanatún is a place for a special meal: the setting is stunning, and the menu offers refined creations combining Yucatecan, Caribbean, and French traditions. The wine selection is superior as well.

SEE ALSO HACIENDAS, P.73; PAMPERING, P.102

Eladio's
Calle 59 no. 425, x Calle 44; tel: (999) 823 1087; www.eladios.com.mx; $; daily noon–8pm; Map p.18

Eladio's is a special kind of cantina-restaurant, and highly successful – there are five in Mérida and one in Progreso. Though they're very big, and very women- and family-friendly, they're run cantina-style, so you can order from a full menu or just order drinks, with the complimentary *botanas* – wonderfully tasty, and which will probably add up to more than a full meal. Live dance bands play on many afternoons, but there's also a separate area where you can actually talk. Hugely enjoyable, unbelievable value, and a really fun way to see local life.

El Lucero del Alba
Calle 56, x Calle 47, off Paseo Montejo; tel: (999) 924 8099; $; daily 11am–9pm; Map p.18

By contrast, this comfortable bar by Paseo de Montejo is a more upscale type of cantina, and the excellent *botanas* are skillfully prepared – but they still come free with each drink.

Market Restaurants
Mexican markets are always combined with plenty of places to eat, cheap *cocinas económicas* and lunch-stands, and Mérida's giant market naturally has a huge choice of them. The best are on the upper level, at the top of a ramp beside the craft market. You order at one of the stands – local specialties like *cochinita pibil*, fish *tacos* and the like – then sit at one of the long, tiled tables. They open early, but close with the market by mid-afternoon. There are maybe more tranquil budget restaurants around the smaller markets in **Parque de Santa Ana** and **Parque de Santiago**. And there are similar cheap-eats suppliers around every other market, such as in Campeche and Cancún.

Marlin Azul
Calle 62 no. 488, x 57 & 59; tel: (999) 928 1606; $; Mon–Sat 10am–10pm; Map p.18

Another Mérida surprise. This little place looks (and is) a simple, cheap, street-side bar, but its seafood, like fresh *ceviches* with lashings of good cilantro, is among the best in town.

Pizzeria Vito Corleone
Calle 59 no. 508, x 60 & 62; tel: (999) 923 6846; $; daily 11am–11.30pm; Map p.18

Loved for years by Mérida residents and visitors, this quirky little place has a genuine flame-fired oven to produce its high-quality pizzas, which run from Italian standards to inventions with a range of Mexican chilis.

Trotter's
Circuíto Colonias, by Calle 60; tel: (999) 927 2320; www.trotters merida.com; $$$; Mon–Sat 1pm–2am, Sun 1–6pm; Map p.18

Mérida's most spectacular restaurant, a gleaming dome-like space next to a gorgeous garden. The Trotter family – Canadians long established

Below: options: the Casa de Piedra (top) and El Cangrejito.

The Yucatán's fresh juice shops (*juguerías*) and ice-cream stands (*paleterías-neverías*) are irresistible and great for fending off the heat while sightseeing, with superb coolers like fresh-fruit *nieves* (water ices, *above*) in all kinds of flavors. Mérida has some of the best. **Dulcería Sorbetería Colón**, on the Plaza Mayor next to the Palacio del Gobernador, is the most refined, with only ice-cream and table service. Across the square next to the MACAY museum, **Jugos California** has every possible type of fruit, and one of the most enjoyable for every sort of juice is **La Michoacana**, on the corner of Calles 61 and 56. For a run-through of products sold at *juguerías* and ice-cream stands, *see Food and Drink, p.70*.

here – hit all the right notes with a clever mix of modern, international, and local dishes, and an excellent (and for once decently priced) wine list.

Uxmal and the Puuc Cities

Los Almendros
Calle 23 no. 207, corner of Calle 22, Ticul; tel: (997) 972 0021; $$; daily 11am–7pm; Map p.133 D2
Opened in 1963, and credited with being the first restaurant to present traditional Yucatecan food in a modern res-taurant setting. With success standards have slipped, but it's still an attractive place to visit, much more so than the bigger, newer branches in Mérida and Cancún.

Hacienda Ochil
Highway 261 km 176, 32km north of Uxmal; tel: (999) 910 6035; www.haciendaochil.com; $$$; daily 11am–7pm; Map p.133 D3
Part of the group that runs many hacienda hotels, Ochil has been restored only as a restaurant and museum. The restaurant, on a terrace by an exuberant garden, highlights refined Yucatecan dishes and inventive salads. A beautiful place for a relaxing lunch.
SEE ALSO HACIENDAS, P.73

The Pickled Onion
Highway 261 just south of Santa Elena, 16km from Uxmal; tel: (997) 111 7922; $; daily noon–9pm; Map p.133 D2
Puuc Route food options have been extended by Briton Valerie Pickles with this café outside Santa Elena. Menus mainly follow local tastes, with extras of her own like a *chaya* soufflé. She also offers sand-wiches and box lunches – very handy on the restaurant-free route. It's opposite Sacbé Bungalows (*see Hotels, p.84*).

El Príncipe Tutul-Xiu
Calle 26, x 25 & 27, Maní; tel: (997) 978 4086; $$; daily 11am–7pm; Map p.133 D2
Tucked away in Maní, this could be the best of all trad-itional Yucatecan restaurants: standards of ingredients and cooking are very high, and the *poc chuc* is superb. Service by local waitresses is utterly charming, and it has a special, wonderfully calm feel.

Above: Bacalar's *Balneario*.

Costa Maya and Río Bec

CHETUMAL AND BACALAR
Las Arracheras de Don José
Boulevard de la Bahía, corner of Avenida O.P. Blanco; tel: (983) 832 8895; $; daily 10am–1am; Map p.139 D2
Chetumal often swelters in the heat, so locals get down to the bay boulevard to catch the breeze. Don José's is one of the best places to join them, with generous fresh *fajitas* and *arrachera* steaks.

Balneario Bacalar Mágico
Costera Bacalar, at the bottom of Calle 36, Bacalar; no phone; $; daily noon–6pm; Map p.139 C2
At the *balnearios* by the lake in Bacalar you can swim between enjoying bargain *ceviches* and grilled fish.

Below: jungle refinements at Río Bec Dreams.

Prices, roughly, for a three-course meal with beer or wine:	
$$$	over $25
$$	$15–$25
$	under $15

For an explanation of cantinas and *botanas*, see Food and Drink, p.67.

Sergio's Pizzas

Avenida Obregón 182, corner of Avenida 5 de Mayo, Chetumal; tel: (983) 832 2355; $$; daily 7.30am–11pm; Map p.139 D2

Chetumal's best restaurant is eccentrically cozy (with great air-con): it does serve pizza, but the things to go for are more local, such as fish with tropical fruit sauces. Delightful for breakfast as well.

COSTA MAYA
The Leaky Palapa

Xcalak; tel: (983) 838 0431; $$; usually Nov–July Sat–Sun from 6pm; Map p.139 D2

Every season for the last few years two Canadian women have come down to Xcalak and turned this little hut into a great, original restaurant, to the gratitude of other Xcalakers. Timings vary, so ask.

FELIPE CARRILLO PUERTO
Hotel-Restaurante El Faisán y el Venado

Avenida Juárez 781; tel: (983) 834 0702; $; daily 7am–10pm; Map p.139 D4

Best by far in Felipe Carrillo, with a likeable, small-town feel. Breakfasts are generous.

RÍO BEC
Río Bec Dreams

Highway 186 km 142, 2km west of Chicanná; no phone; www.riobecdreams.com; $$; daily 8.30am–10pm; Map p.138 A2

As well as high-standard cabañas, the owners have created a restaurant that's amazingly comfortable for this remote spot. Their menu is an original for a Mexican rainforest, with pastas, salads, English dishes, curries, and more. The best for miles, and miles.

SEE ALSO HOTELS, P.85

Above: La Parroquia, Campeche.

Campeche
La Casa Vieja

Calle 10 no. 319 (on Parque Principal); tel: (981) 811 8016; $$; daily 9am–12.30am; Map p.24

Its location is the great draw of this charming restaurant, in the colonnade looking over the Parque Principal, but its food, with *campechano* fish dishes, is always enjoyable.

Chac-Pel

Avenida Lázaro Cárdenas 8, Valle del Sol; tel: (981) 813 1071; $$$; daily 11am–7pm; Map p.24

Out of the way south of the old city (take a taxi), but this buzzy restaurant is an unassuming showcase for Campeche cuisine. The daily fish specials are fabulous (and huge). In line with tradition, it's only open during the day, but plan to give it a whole afternoon.

La Parroquia

Calle 55 no.8, x 10 & 12; tel: (981) 816 2530; $; daily 24hrs; Map p.24

Whirring roof fans set the tone at this Campeche institution. Open all hours, it just seems to invite people to come and go. Perfect for breakfast, it has some good *campechano* dishes and Mexican standards for later in the day.

Rincón Colonial

Calle 59, x Calle 18, by Puerta de Tierra; no phone; $; daily approx. 9am–8.30pm; Map p.24

A remarkable survivor, this venerable, wooden-doored cantina is a very atmospheric relic of old Mexico. The regulars (who nowadays include women) have no problem with outside visitors, who can take a spot at the bar to enjoy the generous stream of *botanas*, and listen to the trio performing at the back.

Below: in the Rincón Colonial.

Campeche is very proud of its distinctive cuisine, based on fish and seafood. *Pan de cazón* (young hammerhead shark, finely chopped and cooked in a tomato sauce between tortillas) is the most famous *campechano* dish, but there are many more, often featuring delicious combinations of sea flavors and fruit, as in *camarón al coco* (shrimp in a tangy coconut sauce).

113

Shopping

Shoppers have two extremes to chose between in the Yucatán: the shiny, familiar, sized-and-packaged world of Cancún's giant malls, or the market districts of old cities like Mérida and Campeche, where crowds rub elbows, country people come to sell their produce, and shops and stalls jostle with each other to satisfy every imaginable human need, including some you may never have thought of. Between these opposites, you can browse through souvenir bazaars or charming small shops to find the region's signature products – ceramics, embroidery, hammocks, panama hats – as well as some very attractive surprises.

Cancún

One of the Caribbean's biggest shopping hubs, with every kind of international brand. Handicrafts here tend to be production-line, and relatively expensive: the wacky T-shirt is a more 'traditional' Cancún product.

MALLS

The Hotel Zone's giant malls are its foremost landmarks, spread along the Boulevard south from the bend in the '7.'

Flamingo Plaza
Boulevard Kukulcán km 11.5; tel: (998) 883 2855; www.flamingo.com.mx; daily 10am–10pm; Map IBC
An older mall with a fairly middle-of-the-road choice of stores and food outlets.

La Isla Shopping Village
Boulevard Kukulcán km 12.5; tel: (998) 883 5025; daily, hours vary by shop; Map IBC
Currently the biggest draw, not so much a mall as an area of pedestrian 'streets' open to the skies except for giant canopies, and ringed by an artificial river – so it doesn't feel claustrophobic, and you can walk out to see the lagoon

Above: the canopies of La Isla.

as a break from store-gazing. The store range covers every angle, with plenty of upmarket brands, and there are lively waterside restaurants.

Kukulcán Plaza
Boulevard Kukulcán km 13; tel: (998) 885 2200; www.kukulcan plaza.com; daily 10am–10pm; Map IBC
The biggest of the malls has recently added a 'Luxury Avenue' with names such as Cartier and Louis Vuitton to up its appeal. In the rest of the mall there are plenty of chic swimwear stores, and some quality handicraft dealers.

Plaza Caracol
Boulevard Kukulcán km 8.5; tel: (998) 883 4759; www.caracol plaza.com; daily 10am–10pm; Map IBC
A smallish, quieter mall with a good range of jewelry, and cigar stores for havana fans.

MARKETS

Mercado 28
Avenida Xel-Ha, at junction of Avenidas Sunyaxchén and Tankah, Ciudad Cancún; most stalls daily 8am–6pm; Map IBC
Cancún's main market fulfills all the basic functions of a Mexican market – fresh fruit stalls, cheap restaurants – but also has plenty aimed at tourists, in lanes of tiny souvenir and jewelry shops of unpredictable quality. Be ready to haggle.

Plaza La Fiesta
Boulevard Kukulcán km 9; tel: (998) 883 2116; daily 9am–7/8pm; Map IBC
A huge, flea market-like handicrafts mall. A lot of the stuff on show is colorful junk, but you can also find very attractive pieces of Mexicana. Now has branches in Playa del Carmen, Cozumel, and other locations.

Things to Buy

For traditional handicrafts, the best place to look is Mérida, especially the market district.

Clothing and embroidery: women all over the Yucatán make traditional embroidery – bright white, with patches of vibrant flowers – as *huípil* dresses, blouses, or decorative cloths. Many shops also sell textiles from other parts of Mexico, with a broader color range. For men the traditional garment is the *guayabera*, the shirt-jacket used as Caribbean formal wear.

Panama hats: traditionally made in northern Campeche, but now sold everywhere. For the best range of sizes, try the Mérida market district.

Hammocks: street hammock-sellers are everywhere, but quality is very variable: the best are at specialist hammock shops.

Ceramics and carved wood: vastly varied – every kind of pot, plus painted animals, parrots, and complete original objects.

Jewelry: international styles and silverware from Taxco in central Mexico are favorite buys, but in smaller shops you can also find beautiful local work.

The Islands

ISLA MUJERES

Scores of souvenir and beachwear shops line the streets of Isla town, but with little that's outstanding. Hippyish handicrafts are a local trademark.

COZUMEL

The hundreds of cruise passengers that land daily on Cozumel have helped fill San Miguel with stores offering handicrafts, jewelry, and luxury goods. These are tax-free for tourists on Cozumel, but the price advantages can be less than you expect.

Below: Mexican colors can be relied on to stand out.

Los Cinco Soles

Avenida Melgar, corner of Calle 8 Norte; tel: (987) 872 0132; www.loscincosoles.com; daily 9am–9pm; Map p.9

An attractive, uncluttered store with a much better than average display of Mexican handicrafts: fine hand-blown glass, Talavera pottery, lacquered boxes, and much more.

Punta Langosta

Avenida Melgar, between Calles 7 and 11 Sur; no phone; daily 10am–10pm; Map p.9

Cozumel's main mall, right opposite one of the cruise terminals; several floors of shops and restaurants, with familiar brands.

Unicornio

Avenida 5, between Calle 1 Sur and Calle A. Rosado Salas; tel: (987) 872 0933; daily 9am–7pm; Map p.9

You must watch your elbows as you squeeze between the racks in this packed handicrafts store, but in among a lot that's plain tacky you can discover very pretty ornaments, lamps, ceramics and so on.

HOLBOX

Noa

Calle Damero, off the plaza; tel: (984) 875 2362; email: noanoa@aol.com; Thur–Mon 6–10pm; Map p.9

Holbox isn't associated with shopping, but in this little workshop American Noa Watson and her associates make elegant, original jewelry.

Riviera Maya: Cancún to Playa del Carmen

PLAYA DEL CARMEN

A different experience from shopping in Cancún, as instead of going from mall to mall you stroll along the Quinta Avenida, with souvenir and fashion stores (chic, sexy beachwear, a specialty) that seem to grow in size each month. Major brands have now replaced many of the smaller shops, but you can discover some nice surprises.

Wayan Natural Wear

Avenida 5, between Calle 18 and Avenida Constituyentes; tel: (984) 803 3543; www.wayan.com.mx; daily 9am–10pm; Map p.10
Local company with cool lines of beach and casual wear with multi-ethnic designs, made from natural fibers.

PUERTO MORELOS
Alma Libre Bookstore

On the town plaza; tel: (998) 871 0713; www.almalibrebooks.com; Nov–May Tue–Sat 10am–3pm, 6–9pm; Map p.10
The Riviera's best English-language bookshop.

Riviera Maya: Tulum
Artesanías Mikix

Avenida Tulum, between Calles Alfa and Jupiter; no phone; Mon–Sat 9am–9pm; Map p.12
Tulum's best handicrafts shop, small, laid-back and with a bright, varied stock. They also have a small branch on the beach, near Piedra Escondida hotel.

Yucatán State

Traditional craftwork (*artesanía*) is made all over the state, but only in a few cases are local makers in direct contact

with the public, and the best place to find the best work is, as usual, Mérida.

IZAMAL
Centro Cultural y Artesanal

On Parque Itzamná, Calle 31 no. 201, corner Calle 30; tel: (988) 954 1012; Mon–Wed, Fri 10am–8pm, Thur, Sat 10am–10pm, Sun 10am–5pm; Map p.133 E3
The shop in this impressive cultural center has beautiful work by local craftspeople, especially stunning jewelry, in silver and rarer materials.
SEE ALSO MUSEUMS, P.96

Hecho a Mano

Calle 31 no. 323, between Calles 30 and 32 (by town hall); tel: (988) 926 0002; www.joeking.com/emano; Mon–Sat 10am–2pm, 4–7pm; Map p.133 E3
Treasure-trove of a shop inseparable from its founder, Texan-Yucatecan Hector Garza, who scoured Mexico for original, often quirky, craftwork. Sadly, he died suddenly in 2007, but his partner now carries it on in the same spirit.

VALLADOLID

The town and nearby villages are famed for producing some of the best Yucatecan embroidery, which is always on sale in the Parque Principal square.

Yalat Arte Mexicano

Calle 39, corner of Calle 40 (on the Parque Principal); tel: (985) 856 1969; daily 9am–8pm;

Map p.134 B3
Also on Valladolid's main square is this charming little shop, with an exceptional display of handicrafts and folk art from all over Mexico: jewelry, Day of the Dead memorabilia, superb ceramics. The same owners also have another shop on the square, **Maruja** (Calle 41, corner of Calle 40), with coffee, organic jams, and natural clothing from local producers.

Mérida

Markets are among the oldest institutions in Mesoamerica, and for many country people Mérida's main function is as a giant market, a place for the whole state to buy and sell. Hence the best local products – of all kinds – end up here.

Traditional markets naturally hold the most fascination, but there's a modern side to Mérida too, with several malls, mostly around Prolongación de Montejo. As well as the main market there are also smaller markets that are more tranquil. **Parque de Santa Ana** has one of the best.

THE MARKET

Mercado Luis de Gálvez and Mercado San Benito, between Calles 65, 71, 54, and 58; Mon–Sat 7/8am–5/6pm; Map p.18

Below: embroidery is one of the Yucatán's brightest symbols.

Mérida's market officially consists of two huge buildings, but it really sprawls over several blocks all around them, a vast, permanently crowded bazaar. The new building, **San Benito**, opened in 2006, but market traders did not leave the older **Mercado Luís de Gálvez**, parts of which date from 1790, so instead of being relocated the market simply got bigger. A handicrafts section, the **Bazar de Artesanías**, is up a ramp at the junction of Calles 67 and 56. The best cheap market restaurants are on the adjacent floor, too.

Even if you're not going to buy piles of every kind of chili, fabulously fresh fruit, or a machete, a walk around the market is endlessly fascinating. Among the more intriguing stalls are the ones selling religious images, or magic spells; more practical might be the stacks of panama hats.

SEE ALSO RESTAURANTS, CAFÉS, CANTINAS, P.111

SHOPS AROUND THE MARKET DISTRICT

The streets around the market are also the place to find Mérida's best specialist shops.

Guayaberas Jack
Calle 59 no. 507, x 60 & 62; tel: (999) 928 6002; Mon–Sat 9am–1pm, 4–7pm; Map p.18
Superb-quality *guayaberas* made to measure.

La Poblana
Calle 65 no. 492, x 58 & 60; tel: (999) 927 9896; Mon–Sat 9am–2pm, 4–7pm; Map p.18
Hammocks of all sizes and materials, of the very best quality, and bluff but very helpful, and very honest, service.

El Sombrero Popular
Calle 65 Departamento 18, x 58 & 60; no phone; Mon–Sat 9am–2pm, 4–7pm; Map p.18
Tiny, friendly little shop, with panama and other sunhats for every size of head.

Above: market life.

ELSEWHERE IN MÉRIDA

Amate Books
Calle 60 no. 453A, x 49 & 51; tel: (999) 924 2222; www.amate books.com; Tue–Sun 10.30am–1.30pm, 3.30–8.30pm; Map p.18
Attractive shop with books in English and Spanish on Mexican art, life, and history.

Casa de las Artesanías
Calle 63 no. 503, x 64 & 66; tel: (999) 928 6676; Mon–Sat 8am–8pm, Sun 9am–1pm; Map p.18
The official state handicrafts store is a bit of a mixture, but as well as production-line work there are usable bags, textiles, and other pieces.

Ki-Xocolatl
Calle 55 no. 513, x 60 & 62; tel: (999) 920 5869; www.ki-xocolatl.com; Mon–Sat 9am–10.30pm, Sun 10am–6pm; Map p.18
The project of a Belgian chocolate-maker, who makes delectable chocolates using Mexican organic cacao.

Mexicanísimo
Calle 60 no. 496, x 59 & 61; tel: (999) 924 7622; Mon–Sat 10am–9pm, Sun 10am–2pm; Map p.18
Original, elegant clothing for men and women in beautiful, lightweight Mexican cottons.

Uxmal and the Puuc Cities

Arte Maya
Calle 23 no. 301, Ticul (Highway 184, Mérida road, towards west side of town); tel: (997) 972 1669; www.artemaya.com.mx; daily 9am–7pm; Map p.133 D2
Ticul is known for ceramics, of all sorts. This workshop produces very fine quality work, including reproductions of ancient Mayan ceramics.

Taller de Artesanía Los Ceibos
Calle 13 no. 201, Muna (off old road through town); tel: (997) 971 0036; daily 9am–6pm; Map p.133 D2
The Martín Morales family have spent years studying and reproducing Mayan ceramics, using ancient techniques.

Campeche

Casa de Artesanías Tukulná
Calle 10 no. 333, x 59 & 61; tel: (981) 816 9088; www.tukulna.com; Mon–Sat 9am–8pm; Map p.24
Campeche's handicrafts showcase is much better than the one in Mérida: an airy, comfortable shop with beautiful ceramics, embroidery, and basketwork, and many other things to catch the eye. **117**

Sports

Heat, and that ever-seductive combo of palm trees, sea, and sand – maybe with a cocktail on the side – mean that many people don't feel like being too active when they get to the Yucatán. When they do, diving, fishing, or otherwise getting close to the water are naturally the biggest draws. But there are active ways of enjoying the Yucatán on land too, by bike or on horseback, as well as a growing string of golf courses. If you want to see some competition, get in touch with one of the Yucatán's passions – baseball – or check out Cancún's new soccer team. For all watersports, *see Diving, Snorkeling, and Watersports, p.52.*

Cycling

Bikes and *triciclos* (tricycle carts) are everywhere in the Yucatán – but not, usually, ridden by foreigners. However, many small Riviera hotels have bikes available for guests' use, especially in **Puerto Morelos** and **Tulum**, which also has a few bike-rental shops. The islands **Isla Mujeres**, **Holbox**, and (to a lesser extent) **Cozumel** are ideal for getting around by bike, and the same island shops that rent out golf carts also have bikes. Many are pretty worn out, though, so check when renting.

A bike track runs beside Boulevard Kukulcán all the way down **Cancún** island: there are very few places to rent a bike, but hotels often have bikes for guests. There's also a handy bike track from **Valladolid** out to the cenotes at Dzitnup. And, of course, the flatness of the Yucatán makes the whole place very easy to cycle.

Antonio 'Negro' Aguilar
Calle 44 no. 195, x 39 & 41, Valladolid; tel: (985) 856 2125; Mon–Sat 9am–1pm, 3–7pm; Map p.134 B3

One of the real characters of Valladolid, former baseball pro El Negro rents out decent bikes at low rates, ideal for a day trip out to Dzitnup.

Bike Mexico
347 Wycliffe Avenue, Woodbridge, Ontario L4L 3N8; tel: (1-416) 848 0265; www.bikemexico.com
Canada-based outfit that offers a range of small-group tours by bike in various parts of Mexico, including 'Yucatán Backroads.'

Ecoturismo Yucatán
Calle 3 no. 235, x 32A and 34, Colonia Pensiones, Mérida; tel: (999) 920 2772; www.ecoyuc. com; daily 9am–5pm

A fun one-day bike tour to Mayapán and a cenote, and also mountain bikes to rent. SEE ALSO TOURS AND GUIDES, P.121

Golf

Golf is booming on the Riviera, with nine courses open and more being built. For a full list, see www.golfinmexico.net. For some considerations on the effects of golf here, *see Environment, p.57.*

El Camaleón Golf Club, Maya Koba
Highway 307 km 298, 8km north of Playa del Carmen; tel: (984) 206 3088; www.maya kobagolf.com; Map p.135 D3

Below: the Hilton Cancún's greens, by Laguna Nichupté.

Left: the Leones de Yucatán in to bat.

Rancho Loma Bonita
Highway 307 km 315, 5km south of Puerto Morelos; tel: (998) 887 5465; www.rancholoma bonita.com; daily 10am–7pm; entrance charge; Map p.135 D3
Jungle and beach riding tours, with the chance to 'swim with your horse' in the waves. Also ATVs, and wave-runners.
SEE ALSO CHILDREN, P.46

Skydiving
Sky Dive Playa
Plaza Marina (entrance to Playa-car), Playa del Carmen; tel: (984) 873 0192; www.skydive.com.mx; Mon–Sat 9am–5pm; Map p.10
First-timers make a 'tandem' jump on an instructor's back.

Spectator Sports
BASEBALL
One trait of the Yucatán is that its favorite game is not soccer, but baseball. The main season runs from March to August.
Leones de Yucatán
Parque Kukulcán, Circuíto Colonias, corner of Calle 28, Mérida; tel: (999) 926 3022; www.leones deyucatan.com.mx
One of the best teams in the Mexican League – champions in 2006, and finalists in 2007.

FOOTBALL (SOCCER)
One more sign of Cancún taking shape is that in 2007 it acquired a soccer team, by the very Cancún method of buying one – Atlante, a historic Mexico City team founded in 1916, and so 55 years older than the city it now represents.
CF Atlante
Estadio Andrés Quintana Roo, Avenida Kabah, Cancún; tel: freephone 1-800 702 8000; www.club-atlante.com; Map IBC
To widespread amazement, in its first season in Cancún Atlante won Mexican soccer's winter tournament.

Above: San Antonio Chalanté.

The most lavish of the Riviera courses, and the one most carefully designed by Greg Norman to respect the local ecology. It's also due to host Mexico's first PGA tour event.
SEE ALSO ALL-INCLUSIVES, P.29
Hilton Cancún Golf Club
Boulevard Kukulcán km 17, Cancún; tel: (998) 881 8000; www.hiltoncancun.com; Map IBC
Popular, well-landscaped course with holes divided by channels off Nichupté lagoon.

Horseback Riding
Riding facilities are not well developed here, though on some Riviera beaches you can find horses to rent.

A popular marathon, the **Maratón de la Marina**, is run between Mérida and Progreso each year in early June (with the start at 6am, to avoid the heat). Details and information on how to register are posted a few weeks earlier on the Yucatán state sports website, www.idey.gob.mx, but there's no facility for registering online.

Hacienda San Antonio Chalanté
2.7km east of Sudzal village, 8km south of Izamal; tel: via Mérida: (999) 132 7411; www.hacienda chalante.com; Map p.133 E3
Riding is a specialty at this beautifully tranquil hacienda near Izamal. Guided horseback tours are an ideal way to experience the real peace of the Yucatecan countryside.
SEE ALSO HACIENDAS, P.72

Rancho Buenavista
Carretera Perimetral km 32.5, Cozumel; tel: (987) 872 1537; www.buenavistaranch.com; daily 9am–7pm; entrance charge; Map p.9
Big, popular center offering a variety of guided horseback tours around Cozumel.

119

Tours and Guides

Many of the Yucatán's most special places and experiences do not leap out at you from the roadside – remote lagoons with rare wildlife, the most exquisite forest cenotes. To find them, you need the aid of some local knowledge. All kinds of tours are on offer to the visitor here: some are anonymous operations where the main concern is to get the bus-load to a souvenir-mart as fast as possible. The best, in contrast, lead you to places with a beauty you'll remember forever, or give real contact with local people, in a way that you would never be able to do on your own. Below is a choice of memorable possibilities.

Whale Shark-Watching on Holbox

The gathering of whale sharks at Cabo Catoche near Holbox between June and September was only discovered around 2001, but the number of trips offering the chance to snorkel alongside these huge (but harmless) fish has grown at an amazing pace. Operators on Holbox all have to observe strict conservation guidelines: there is a maximum of six people plus guides in each boat, and only two snorkelers can be in the water at a time.

Operators on Isla Mujeres now offer Holbox trips that do not keep to these rules, sometimes encouraging people to 'ride' on sharks. These tours are to be avoided (they also require a long boat ride). Riviera operators also offer one-day tours in association with Holbox guides. It's far more relaxing to stay on Holbox and arrange a tour directly there.

Posada Mawimbi
Calle Damero, by the beach; tel: (984) 875 2003; www.mawimbi.net; Map p.9
Some of the best whale-shark trips, with expert guides, for

For more on the Yucatán's nature reserves and natural attractions, *see Wildlife and Nature, p.126*.

around $90 per head. In other months there are great lagoon and birdwatching trips.
SEE ALSO HOTELS, P.78

Around Tulum and Sian Ka'an

As well as its deepest caves, the Tulum area has some of the Yucatán's densest forest. To the south, boat tours into the vast Sian Ka'an reserve are a true 'must see.'

Alltournative
Main offices: Avenida 5, by Calle 2 Norte, Playa del Carmen; and Avenida Tulum, on corner of Cobá road, Tulum; tel: (984) 803 9999; www.alltournative.com; office daily 9am–7pm; Map p.12
No Sian Ka'an trips, but an energetic company that combines high-fun-factor day trips around Tulum with concern for ecology and relationships with local communities. Visits to Mayan villages combined with cenote snorkeling and zip-line rides at treetop height in the forest are popular options.

Above: exploring Sian Ka'an.

CESiak – Centro Ecológico Sian Ka'an

On Highway 307, by old entrance to Tulum ruins, Tulum; tel: (984) 104 0522; www.cesiak.org; office daily 9am–5pm; Map p.12
Excellent Sian Ka'an tours with friendly, well-informed guides. Small boats take you through mangroves and fresh-water lagoons, with a chance to float on an amazing current between two lagoons. Other options include trips at sunset, when birds are more active, a kayak tour, and fly-fishing. CESiak has a superb place to stay in the reserve as well, at **Boca Paila Camp**.
SEE ALSO HOTELS, P.81

Left: Alex, of Posada Mawimbi, looking out for whale sharks.

guests. Within the day 'tour' is a swim in a local lagoon, visits to old men of the village to hear stories (translated) of the Caste War and local customs, and a superb meal. The best way to contact them is via this agency:

Xiimbal
Inside Balam Na Computación, Calle 65 (on town plaza), Felipe Carrillo Puerto; tel: (983) 834 1073; www.xiimbal.com; daily 9am–5pm; Map p.139 D4
A friendly young team dedicated to developing sustainable tourism in the area.

Calakmul
The rainforest reserve around the ruins is vast, and a guide is essential to see its wildlife.

Servidores Turísticos de Calakmul
Tourist information hut, Avenida Calakmul, by Calles Okolhuitz and Payán, Xpuhil; tel: (983) 871 6064; email: servidoresturisticos @yahoo.com; Map p.138 B2
Fernando Sastre and Lety Santiago run the best local guide group (who speak basic English), based at this little information hut. They also run the only authorized **campsite** at Calakmul. Get in contact at least two weeks before you arrive in the area.

Ecotours and Cenotes in Yucatán State

Ecoturismo Yucatán
Calle 3 no. 235, x 32A and 34, Colonia Pensiones, Mérida; tel: (999) 920 2772; www.eco yuc.com; daily 9am–5pm
Real experts in the field who offer a huge range of tours, but birdwatching and creating 'made-to-measure' itineraries of all kinds are specialties.
SEE ALSO SPORTS, P.118

Mayan Ecotours
Calle 80 no. 56, x 13, Colonia Pensiones, Mérida; tel: (999) 987 3710; ww.mayanecotours.com; office daily 9am–5pm
Connie Leal and her team provide great-value day tours to snorkel in two cenotes in the woods south of Mérida, Yaax-Ha and Kankirixche, followed by a fine meal in the home of Doña Adela, a Mayan grandma. Other routes can also be arranged.

Many of the most rewarding, individual tours are run by small operations, who organize tours according to demand. Hence, when arranging a tour, get in touch with time to spare.

Yucatecan Culture

Iluminado Tours
Calle 66 no. 588, x 73 and 75, Mérida; tel: (999) 924 3176; www.iluminadotours.com
Very original tours that take you close to many aspects of local life: Mayan beliefs, food, traditions, and more.

Visiting a Mayan Village
The once rebel Mayan villages north of Felipe Carrillo Puerto long resisted attempts to involve them in impersonal, commercial tourism, but one, **Señor**, has begun to invite small groups of visitors – on the basis that you are their

Below: exploring Kankirixche cenote with Mayan Ecotours.

Transportation

The Yucatán is easy to get to, and to get around. There are abundant international flights into Cancún and other cities, and an extensive domestic flight network for fast hops within Mexico. Once on the ground, Mexico's fantastic bus system in all its many forms – first-class, second-class, *combis*, *colectivos* – can get you even to the remotest village, while taxis will carry you any distance, for the right price. Frequent ferries link the mainland with the Yucatán's three islands. If you really want to explore, a car will be a great asset, but this is no problem, as driving and car rental here are equally easy to handle.

Getting There

FROM NORTH AMERICA

Frequent flights, scheduled and charter, run to **Cancún** from every part of the US and Canada. There are also scheduled flights to **Mérida** from Miami, Houston, and Atlanta, and to **Cozumel** from Houston. Both airports also have charter services.

Driving is an option for longer stays: allow for a 4–5-day drive from the Texas border. For the papers you will need, see www.mexonline.com. A ferry service from Florida to Progreso that began in 2002 is not currently in operation.

FROM THE UK AND EUROPE

The main direct service to Cancún from Europe is with Iberia from Madrid, but there are many charter flights. The most common way to get there by scheduled flight is via a change in the US, usually in Miami or Houston.

AIRLINES
Aeroméxico
www.aeromexico.com
American Airlines
www.aa.com

Above: Mayab buses connect up the Riviera.

British Airways
www.britishairways.com
Continental
www.continental.com
Delta Airlines
www.delta.com
Iberia
www.iberia.com
KLM
www.klm.com
Mexicana
www.mexicana.com
Northwest
www.nwa.com
United Airlines
www.united.com
US Airways
www.usairways.com
Virgin Atlantic
www.virgin-atlantic.com

Arrival

CANCÚN AIRPORT

The flight hub for all southern Mexico, 15km south of Ciudad Cancún. Since 2007 it has two main terminals: the distribution of airlines is complicated – so always check – but in general, most US and European airlines now use **Terminal 3**; Mexican airlines, Air Canada, and many charters use the older **Terminal 2** (Terminal 1 is only used for private flights).

Arriving in Cancún has long been notorious for its irritation factor. After you come through international arrivals, in either terminal, the only form of

Left: one budget option – the *tricitaxi*.

Getting Around

DOMESTIC FLIGHTS

The arrival of low-cost airlines has cut prices on Mexico's internal network, but also led to a narrower range of services. Cancún and every state capital have direct flights to Mexico City, but there are relatively few local connections.

AIRLINES
Aeroméxico
tel: (01 800) 021 4010;
www.aeromexico.com
Alma de México
tel: (01 800) 800 2562;
www.alma.com.mx
Aviacsa
tel: (01 800) 284 2272;
www.aviacsa.com
Click Mexicana
tel: (01 800) 122 5425;
www.click.com.mx
Mexicana
tel: (01 800) 801 2010;
www.mexicana.com

BUSES

The bus is a basic Mexican institution: every village has a bus or *combi* service of some sort, so there really is nowhere that cannot be reached by public transportation. Unless

transport initially offered is the *colectivo* vans, which take you direct to your hotel in Cancún for about $8 per person. However, they only leave when they have at least eight passengers, and if you are staying in Ciudad Cancún you first have to go through the Hotel Zone, so the journey can take over an hour. A **taxi** to Cancún will cost about $33, to Playa del Carmen $62.

There is also a Riviera **airport bus** service, every 30 mins to the bus station in Ciudad Cancún ($3.20), and every hour to Puerto Morelos and Playa del Carmen ($7.30), but this leaves from outside the Domestic Arrivals hall in Terminal 2. From Terminal 3, there is a free shuttle bus to Terminal 2; from International Arrivals in Terminal 2, turn right out the door, and walk the length of the building to find the bus. *Colectivos* to Playa also run from the same place.

A hassle-free alternative is to book your own transfer with a service like Cancún Valet:
Cancún Valet
tel: (998) 848 3634;
www.cancunvalet.com

Mexipass
Visitors who may take several flights within Mexico should check out the Mexipass, which gives discounts of up to 50 percent on Mexicana and Aeroméxico domestic flights. You can enter Mexico with any airline, but must buy the Mexipass in advance outside the country, and take at least three internal flights per person on the trip (two, if traveling from Europe). For details, in the **US and Canada** call tel: 1 800 531 7921, in the **UK** tel: 0870 890 0040.

A reliable company offering pick-ups and transfers to Cancún for $40 one-way, Playa del Carmen for $65, and a range of other services.

OTHER AIRPORTS
Other airports are less stressful to use. **Cozumel** airport is just north of San Miguel, and *colectivos* ($5–$8 per person) and taxis (from $22) are the means of getting into town.

Mérida's tranquil airport is south of the city: *colectivos* into town are about $5 per person, a whole taxi from $12.

Below: Cancún bus station.

you hire a car, buses will be your main way to get around.

Buses come in different kinds. **First-class buses** are air-conditioned, modern, and very comfortable, and run between cities and towns with only a few stops. All luggage is checked in, and buses are pretty punctual. The main first-class company in Yucatán is ADO; there are also two extra-luxury services, with more legroom, ADO-GL and UNO.

Second-class buses provide local services and follow many of the same routes as first-class, but stop frequently. They are cheaper, less comfortable (though many now have air-conditioning) and naturally slower than first-class.

There are also **intermedio** services, which stop often but have first-class comfort. The most important are the **Riviera** shuttle buses that run every 15 mins between Cancún and Playa del Carmen, and **Mayab** buses (one or more each hour) along the length of the Riviera between Cancún and Tulum.

In many cities first and second-class buses have their own stations, but in smaller places they usually share. A sample fare for first-class is $22, Mérida–Cancún one-way. As well as at the stations, first-class tickets can be bought at **Ticketbus** shops in many cities, and sometimes online.

Main Bus Stations
Cancún: at the junction of Avenidas Tulum and Uxmal
Conveniently, there is only one station for all services.
Playa del Carmen: Avenida Juárez, corner of Avenida 5, on main plaza
For all Riviera local services, and airport buses.
Avenida 20, between Calles 12 and 14 Norte
For long-distance buses.
Mérida: CAME, Calle 70, x 69 & 71
For first-class services.

Above: a fast Ultramar ferry to Cozumel.

Terminal de Autobuses, Calle 69, x 68 & 70
Second-class, including a daily 'Puuc Route' tour bus.
Campeche: Avenida Patricio Trueba, corner of Avenida Casa de Justicia
All first-class and many second-class routes; a taxi-ride away from the center.
Ticketbus
www.ticketbus.com.mx
Has a list of Ticketbus offices.

COMBIS/COLECTIVOS

Two words for the same thing, small minivans or *combis* that fill in all gaps left by first- and second-class buses. They may shadow the same routes, but stop wherever they're asked to, and serve places too small to have a full bus service. Using *colectivos* often requires being prepared to ask where they're going, but they're a very cheap, friendly, adaptable way of traveling.

CITY BUSES

Most cities have local buses. Cancún's are particularly useful, as they have route numbers: route **R-1** runs up and down 24 hours daily from Ciudad Cancún all the way down the Hotel Zone. In Mérida, destinations are written on bus windscreens, so using buses is more complicated.

TAXIS

Everywhere in Mexico has some taxis, which in villages blend into *colectivos*. Most Mexican taxis do not have meters, but instead there are fixed rates for each area, which are posted up at taxi stands (and listed in local English-language magazines).

This system usually works well, with the big exceptions of Cancún and the Riviera, where (some) taxi drivers have a reputation for playing rook-the-tourist. Also, Cancún has a confusing system whereby taxi rates are higher in the Hotel Zone than in the city. The general rules are, get an idea of what the correct rates should be, and always agree a fare **before** getting into a cab.

Below: grabbing a cab on the Cancún strip.

Mérida now has meters in many cabs. Older cabs still stick to fixed rates: metered companies like Econotaxi or Taximetro are cheaper.

Taxis will often take you long distances, so long as you agree a price beforehand.

Taxi Phone Numbers
Cancún: tel: (998) 840 0651
Mérida: Econotaxi, tel: (999) 945 0000; Taximetro, tel: (999) 928 3031
Campeche: tel: (981) 816 1113

FERRIES TO THE ISLANDS
Isla Mujeres
There are passenger ferries from **Puerto Juárez**, north of Cancún, run by the Magaña and Ultramar companies. Both sail every 30 mins about 6am to midnight, with the same fare, $3.20. Buses R-1 and R-13 run to Puerto Juárez. Car ferries run from **Punta Sam**, five times each way daily.
Cozumel
Passenger ferries run from **Playa del Carmen**. The two companies, Mexico and Ultramar, have ferries every 1–2 hours daily, 6am–11pm. Single fare is about $10. Car ferries run from **Puerto Calica**, south of Playa, 4–5 times daily.
Holbox
The ferry port is tiny **Chiquilá**, a 2–3-hour drive from Cancún.

Island Runabouts
On **Isla Mujeres** and **Holbox**, since they're so small, the favorite way to get around is by **golf cart**. There are plenty of rental shops on each island, and rates are around $40 a day on both, even though on Holbox there are fewer places to get to. On Isla the same shops usually rent **motor scooters** (from around $18), and on both islands you can also rent **bikes** for a quieter ride. **Cozumel** is that much bigger, so rental cars or scooters are popular.

Above: *topes* – do not ignore this sign.

Boats cross over every 1–2 hours, 5am–6pm; the fare is $3.60. Second-class buses run to Chiquilá and back from Cancún and Mérida.

Driving in the Yucatán

There are no special terrors to driving in Mexico: main roads are generally quite well maintained, although on back roads you may find potholes and stretches of dirt track.

There are a few quirks about driving here, chief of which is the *tope*, the Mexican speed bump. Vehicles do not have automatic priority on Mexican country roads, and this is enforced by the placing of frequent *topes*. They are usually announced by *tope* signs, but it's near-inevitable to come on a few unawares.

For most of its route the Highway 180 Cancún–Mérida road is flanked by a fast **toll highway** (*cuota*), which cuts

journey times. However, it's little-used due to the high toll (about $28 for the whole trip).

If you have a car problem, there is a free highway assistance service, the **Angeles Verdes** or 'Green Angels.' They can be contacted on tel: (01 55) 5250 8221.

Parking is restricted in city centers, if the curb is painted yellow. If possible, find a hotel with parking, or use a car park (*estacionamiento público*).

GAS/PETROL
Gasolineras, all run by the state company Pemex, are easy to find in cities, but scarce in some areas, such as southern Quintana Roo. Plain unleaded gas is called *magna*.

CAR RENTAL
In general you get better deals here from small local agencies than the big international names. To rent a car you need to be over 21 and show your passport, driving license and a credit card for a deposit (but many agencies will give discounts if you pay in cash). For bike rental.
Cancún
Easyway, tel: (998) 886 2464; www.easywayrentacar.com Enterprising company with good weekly offers. Also in Playa del Carmen and Mérida.
Mérida
Mexico Rentacar, Calle 57A, x 58 & 60 (Callejón del Congreso); tel: (999) 923 3637; email: mexico rentacar@hotmail.com; Map p.18 An exceptional, family-run company, with bargain rates, well-kept vehicles, and very attentive service: rent a car, and you make a friend.
Veloz Rentacar, Calle 60 no. 486, x 55 & 57; tel: (999) 928 0373; www.velozrentacar.com.mx; Map p.18 More conventional, but another reliable local agency, with a branch in Cancún.

125

Wildlife and Nature

The Spanish friar Diego de Landa was the first outsider to marvel at the unique mix that is the natural world in the Yucatán: thin limestone soil, the elusive jaguars and rodents of the woods, the turtles of the beaches, an astonishing range of birdlife. He did not even go on to see all the undersea life just offshore, or the dense rainforest to the south. Nature is never far away here, for even in the most hectic tourist area you will hear the morning whistle of the *zanate* bird, or see stone-like iguanas by the roadside.

Cancún

Visitors sometimes scoff at suggestions that Laguna Nichupté, the broad stretch of water between Cancún island and the mainland, can have much natural life left in it. Waste from the city and over-use by tourist trips have caused deterioration, especially at the northern end, but further south and east the lagoon and its mangroves can be surprisingly alive, and there are still plenty of birds. Rumors of crocodile sightings have not been confirmed.

The Islands

ISLA MUJERES

As well as its reefs, Isla has the **Tortugranja** turtle farm (*see Children, p.45*), and is the start-point for visits to Mexico's main seabird reserve.

Isla Contoy

30km north of Isla Mujeres; information via Amigos de Isla Contoy, tel in Cancún: (998) 884 7483; www.islacontoy.org; Map p.8
Contoy, an uninhabited mangrove island north of Isla, is home to turtles and huge colonies of **sea birds** – cormorants, boobies, and more.

There's also a coral lagoon. Many tours are run from Isla Mujeres (about $40 per head), but note that Isla's operators have been notorious for running badly managed trips with no ecological awareness, so for anyone who actually wants to see birds they can be a big disappointment. Check the website of the Amigos de Isla Contoy group, which seeks to raise standards and has a list of approved boat operators.

COZUMEL

Compared to its reefs, Cozumel on-land is relatively plain, but still full of birds.
Parque Punta Sur
Carretera Costera Sur km 27; tel: (987) 872 0914; www.cozumelparks.com; admissions daily 9am–3pm; entrance charge, children under 8 free; Map p.9
Extending round Cozumel's southern tip, this reserve has large expanses of bird-rich forest and lagoons, including one with wild crocodiles.
SEE ALSO CHILDREN, P.45

Below: whale sharks, the most mysterious visitors to Holbox.

For dolphin enclosures and shows, *see Children*, p.46.

Left: pelicans are ever-present around the Yucatán coast.

Riviera Maya: Cancún to Playa del Carmen

PLAYA DEL CARMEN

Aviario Xaman-Ha

Paseo Xaman-Ha, Playacar; tel: (984) 873 0318; daily 9am–5pm; entrance charge; Map p.10
Booming Playa doesn't exactly seem at one with nature, but half-hidden in the Playacar development is this lovely garden-aviary, with parrots, toucans, and more native birds amid explosive greenery.

PUERTO MORELOS

The woods round Puerto Morelos have been hit hard by hurricanes, but still have plenty of attractions – as well as the Riviera's best-protected stretch of reef. A popular attraction is **Crococún** zoo SEE ALSO CHILDREN, P.46

Yaax Che-Jardín Botánico Dr Alfredo Barrera

Highway 307 km 320, 1km south of Puerto Morelos; tel: (998) 206 9233; Nov–Apr daily 8am–4pm, May–Oct Mon–Sat 9am–5pm; entrance charge; Map p.135 E3
Amazingly lush, just a short way from Highway 307, this compact garden gives a beautiful introduction to Yucatán plant life, especially palms, bromeliads, and cacti. On the nature trail you can also see birds, monkeys (sometimes) and a tiny Mayan ruin.

Riviera Maya: South of Playa to Tulum

AKUMAL

The most important breeding beaches for giant **sea turtles** in the Yucatán are around Akumal, a name that means 'place of the turtle' in Maya. Tourist development has led to a massive drop in turtle numbers, and Akumal is now the center of several turtle conservation programs.

Above: iguanas (top) are everywhere; turtles are now more rare.

HOLBOX

Laguna Yalahao, between Holbox and the mainland, is essentially part of the sea, but is also fed by underground freshwater currents. This creates a special mix of plant and animal life, especially birds such as **flamingos** or herons, while **turtles** breed on the ocean side of Holbox. There are fabulous places to snorkel around the lagoon, which is also one of the best places to see **dolphins** in the wild.

It would, of course, be ideal to see the region's most exotic wildlife – jaguars and other cats, toucans – in the wild, but this can take a lot of time and resources, so for most visitors the best chance of seeing them is in animal collections. The best is in **Xcaret** ecopark, which has jaguars, pumas, turtles and many other creatures, all native to the Yucatán. **Crococún** at Puerto Morelos is also a charming, low-key local zoo. For both parks, see Children, p.46.

Holbox is now most known for **whale sharks**. Only in 2001–2 was it discovered that large numbers of the world's largest fish were gathering to feed off Cabo Catoche each year, between about June and September. It's still not clear quite why, since whale sharks are usually solitary. Trips to snorkel alongside these harmless, silent giants are run from Holbox; assuming that people who want to see whale sharks don't want to harm them, avoid the badly run trips offered from Isla Mujeres.
SEE ALSO TOURS AND GUIDES, P.120

Right: flamingos in the Río Lagartos lagoon.

Centro Ecológico Akumal
Akumal; tel: (984) 875 9095; www.ceakumal.org; Mon 2–6pm, Tue–Fri 8am–2pm, 4–6pm, Sat 10am–2pm; Map p.135 D2
Turtle protection is one of the main roles of this organization. Visitors can join carefully run night-time 'turtle walks' along the beaches in the May–Oct breeding season. Volunteers who wish to help the work of the CEA can also stay for a month or so at low cost.

PUNTA LAGUNA
Around Cobá the Yucatán forest becomes denser, providing a home for spider monkeys.
Punta Laguna Spider Monkey Reserve
On road between Cobá and Nuevo Xcan, 17km north of Cobá; no phone; charge for guides and canoe hire; Map p.135 C3
The lake (a big cenote) that gives this village its name attracts monkeys each day. Mayan guides lead tours, and they also have a campsite and rent canoes. The best times to see monkeys are early in the morning or late afternoon.
SEE ALSO CHILDREN, P.46

Many Mayan sites, since they are protected areas of forest, are also excellent places to see birds and, with luck, animals. Along the forest paths at **Cobá** you can see all kinds of birds, especially orioles and cardinals. Quieter Puuc sites like **Labná** or **Xlapak** are also rich in birds, and **Dzibanché-Kinichná, Kohunlich** and the Río Bec sites are some of the places where you have most chance of catching a glimpse of more exotic birds like toucans. Keep an eye (and an ear) out, too, for bush-pig-like rodents such as the *tepezcuintle* (paca, in English).

SIAN KA'AN
The Riviera Maya is sharply closed off to the south by this 530,000-hectare biosphere reserve around Ascension Bay. There are a few tiny villages such as **Punta Allen**, which existed before the reserve, and a few (controversial) building plots. Otherwise, Sian Ka'an is a vast, uninhabited expanse of mangrove, reefs, salt- and freshwater lakes, savanna, and tropical forest. Somewhere inside is every kind of Yucatán wildlife – jaguars, tapirs, crocodiles. Easier to see are the millions of wetland and forest birds. Tours, run from Tulum by **CESiak** and other organizations, are among the Riviera's most satisfying experiences. You can also stay in the reserve, at **Boca Paila** or **Punta Allen**, beloved of fly-fishermen.
SEE ALSO DIVING, SNORKELING, AND WATERSPORTS, P. 55; HOTELS, P.81; TOURS AND GUIDES, P.120

Yucatán State
The state has two special landscapes: the *selva baja* or 'low jungle' that covers most of it inland, and the kilometer on kilometer of mangrove and lagoon between the main land mass and the sandbars that line the northwest Yucatán coast. These wetlands shelter over 500 bird species, residents and winter migrants from North America: flamingos are only the most famous. A 'birdwatching festival,' the **Festival de Aves Toh**, is held each November, a magnet for birders from around the world.

RÍO LAGARTOS
One of two famous places to see **flamingos** in the Yucatán, at the end of a long road from Valladolid. It's the more enjoyable, as it gets little traffic, and guides are friendly and careful about what they do. Since it is remote, the best way to visit

The Yucatán is home to many different kinds of big cat – not just jaguars and pumas but also smaller lynx, jaguarundis (*leoncillo* in Spanish), and margays (*tigrillos*). However, it's very hard to see any in the wild. Jaguars especially wander over huge distances, and are even spotted in the woods inland from Playa del Carmen, but they bolt at the first sign of humans.

is to get there the day before, stay in one of the small local hotels, and arrange a tour for early the next morning, from Río Lagartos or **San Felipe**, 12km west. Boatmen take you along the long lagoon to the east, for trips of 2 (around $45 per boat) to 4 hours. Flamingos are most numerous in July–August; you can also see ibis, herons, egrets, eagles, and much more.
SEE ALSO BEACHES, P.39

Río Lagartos Expeditions
Restaurante Isla Contoy, Calle 19 no. 134; tel: (986) 862 0000; www.riolagartos expeditions.com; Map p.134 B4
The family that runs Río Lagartos's most fun restaurant are also very professional, reliable tour and fishing guides.
SEE ALSO RESTAURANTS, CAFÉS, CANTINAS, P.110

Below: blue herons are common in the Yucatán's lagoons.

UAYMITÚN
Progreso–Telchac road, 15km east of Progreso; tower daily 8am–6pm; free; Map p.133 D4
At an empty spot on the coast east of Progreso, an observation tower allows you to scan the wetlands. A warden lends you binoculars (leave a tip).

CELESTÚN
96km west of Mérida; Map p.132 C3
The most popular place to see **flamingos**, due to its closeness to Mérida, but a more 'processed' experience than Río Lagartos. Celestún lagoon is home to pink sheets of flamingos from November to May, and many other birds. Boats set off from an **embarcadero** outside the village; the fixed charge is around $54 for four people (boats take up to six, but charges don't vary much). Tour routes are also set, and take one or two hours.

Celestún boatmen are criticized for going too fast and harassing flamingos, but they usually only do so because they've been asked to by passengers. Celestún is also a placid beach village, and you can see a different side of the area at the 'ecohotel' at **Xixim**.
SEE ALSO BEACHES, P.39; HOTELS, P.83

Above, from top: vulture; bird of paradise; morpho butterfly.

Costa Maya and Río Bec
CALAKMUL
Entry at Highway 186 km 101, 52km west of Xpuhil; cars admitted daily 7am–6pm; entrance charge; Map p.138 A1–B4
The largest of all Mexico's forest reserves, running from 'low jungle' in the north to real rainforest in the south. All the most spectacular plants and wildlife in the Yucatán are here – its largest jaguar population, ocellated turkeys, 85 orchid varieties – as well as the **Calakmul** ruins. Some birds and animals, such as yellow-headed parrots and even margays (*see box above*) are so common they're quite easy to spot (in the early morning). Because it is so vast, though, others are hard to find, so it's well worth going with a guide.
SEE ALSO MAYA RUINS AND RELICS, P.93; TOURS AND GUIDES, P.121

Atlas

The maps of the Yucatán that follow
will make it easy to find places and
attractions listed in our A–Z section.
An index to towns, villages and sights
will help you find other locations
throughout the region .

Map Legend

══	Freeway	🚌	Bus station
═══	Divided highway	✈	Airport
⊏⊐	Highway	✈	Regional airport
═══	Minor road	ℹ	Tourist information
───	Track	★	Sight of interest
─ ─ ─	Ferry	⊞	Cathedral / church
wwww	Coral reef	🏰	Castle / fort
▪ ▪ ▪	International boundary	Λ	Statue / monument
─ ─ ─	Province boundary	∴	Ruin
───	National park	Ω	Cenote / cave
▭	Park	🗼	Lighthouse
▭	Urban	☇	Beach
▭	Swamp	☼	Viewpoint

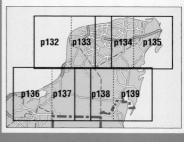

p132 p133 p134 p135

p136 p137 p138 p139

p132   p133   p134   p135

p136   p137   p138   p139

G U L F   O F

4

3

Reserva de
Biósfera
Ría Celest

Xixim

Celestún

Punta Nimún   Este
Céle

Isla
Arena

Punta Ixpuc   San Ar
de Car

2

B a h í a   d e
C a m p e c h e

Isla
Jainá

24

1

Campeche

Fuerte de San Miguel
Lerma

China

180

Poxyaxum

Punta Morro
Seybaplaya

Uayamón

0   5   10   15   20   25km

0   5   10   15   20   25miles

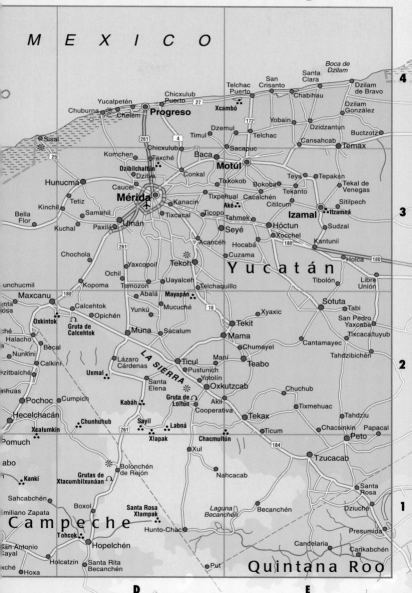

MEXICO

Boca de
Dzilam

Chuburna Yucalpetén Chicxulub Puerto
Chelém Progreso
Xcambó
Telchac Puerto San Crisanto Santa Clara Dzilam de Bravo
Chabihau Dzilam Bravo
Sisal
Dzemul Yobain Dzilam González
Timul Telchac Dzidzantun Buctzotz
Sacapuc Cansahcab Temax
Komchen Baca
Taxché Conkal Motúl
Dzibilchaltún Tixkokob Bokoba Teya Tepakán
Hunucmá Caucel Cacalchén Tekanto Tekal de Venegas
Komchen Citilcum Sitilpech
Mérida Kanacin Tixpehual Izamal Itzamná
Tetiz Samahil Tixcacal Ticopo Tahmek Hóctun Sudzal
Bella Flor Kinchil UMÁN Paxilá Seyé Xocchel
Kuchal Acancéh Hocabá Kantunil
Chocholá Cuzama
Yaxcopoil Tekoh Yucatán Holca
Ochil Uayalceh Tibolón
unchucmil Kopoma Tamozon Telchaquillo Libre Unión
Maxcanu Abalá Mayapán
osa Calcehtok Yunkú Mucuché Xyaxic Sotuta
Oxkintok Opichén Tabi
Halacho Gruta de Calcehtok Muna Sácalum Tekit San Pedro Yaxcabá
Nunkiní Becal Mama Tixcacaltuyub
zitbalché Calkiní Lázaro Cárdenas Ticul Chumayel Cantamayec Tahdzibichén
nhuas Uxmal Maní
Pochoc Cumpich Santa Elena Pustunich Teabo
Hecelchacán Kabáh Yotolín Chuchub
Xcalumkin Chunhuhub Sayil Gruta de Loltún Oxkutzcab Tixmehuac Tahdziu
Labná Cooperativa
Pomuch Xlapak Tekax Chacsinkín Papacal
Xul Chacmultún Ticum Peto
abo Tzucab
Kankí Grutas de Xtacumbilxunáan Bolònchén de Rejón Nahcacab
Sahcabchén Santa Rosa
Emiliano Zapata Boxol Dziuché
Campeche Santa Rosa Xtampak Becanchén Laguna Becanchén
Tohcok Hunto-Chàc Presumida
San Antonio Cayal Hopelchén Candelaria Cankabchén
Holcatzin Santa Rita Becanchén Put Quintana Roo
Hoxa

133

0　5　10　15　20　25km

0　5　10　15　20　25miles

Punta Holchit　Río　Las Colo
Lagartos　(Yulu
Punta Yalkubul　San Felipe　Reserva de la Bi
Boca del Isolete　Reserva Ecológica
Bocas de Dzilam
Boca Dzilam
Yálsihon　Loché　Yoac
4　Telchac　San　Santa　Dzilam de Bravo　Da
Puerto　Crisanto　Clara　Carre
Chabihau　Panabá　Xcala
Xcambo　Yobain　Dzilam González
Dzemul　Dzidzantun　Buctzotz　295
Telchac　Cansahcab　176　Sucila　Kikil　Buenav
Sacapuc　Temax　Santo　Sucopo
Motúl　Domingo　**Tizimín**
Teya　Tepakán　Tixbacab
Bokobá　Tekal de　Espita　Tahcabo　Ti
Cacalchén　Tekanto　Venegas　Calotmul
Aké　Citilcum　Sitilpech　J. Cenotillo　**Ek-Balám**
3　Tahmek　**Izamal**　**Itzamná**　Xuilub　Hunuku
Seyé　**Hóctun**　Sudzal　Tunkas　Quintana　Temozón　Santa
Xocchel　Roo　Rita
Hocabá　Kantunil　Y u c a t á n　Dzitas
Cuzama　180　Tinum　Uaymá　Popola
Holca　Yokdzonot　Gruta de　Ebtun　**Valladolid**　X-C
Tibolón　Libre　Pisté　Balankanché　Kunkunul　Dzitnup　Ch
Unión　**Chichén Itzá**　Kaua　Chichimila
Xyaxic　Sotuta　Tabi　Xcalacoop　**Cenote Dzitnup**
Tekit　San Pedro　Tekom
Mama　Yaxcaba　Chankom　Tixcacalcupul　X-Uil
Chumayel　Cantamayec　Kancabdzonot　**Yaxuná**　Chamul　Hono
2　Teabo　Tixcacaltuyub
Tahdzibichén　Xuxcab
Akil　Chuchub
Chikindzonot
Tekax　Tixmehuac　Tahdziu　Tepich
Ticum　Chacsinkin　Tihosuco　**Quintan**
Chacmultún　**Peto**　Papacal　Ichmul　X-Cabil
184　Calotomul　San José　San Ramón
Tzucacab　X-Querol　Felipe
Zacalaca　Berriozabal
Sabán　295　Melchor
Santa Rosa　Ocampo
1　Becanchén　Tabasco　Dzoyolá
Dziuché　Rojo Gómez　Tusik
Laguna de　Filomeno
Chicnancanab　Mata　Señor
Presumida　Laguna　Yaxley
Esmeralda　José M.P
Candelaria　José María　Suárez
Morelos
Cankabchén　Xiatil　X-Pichil

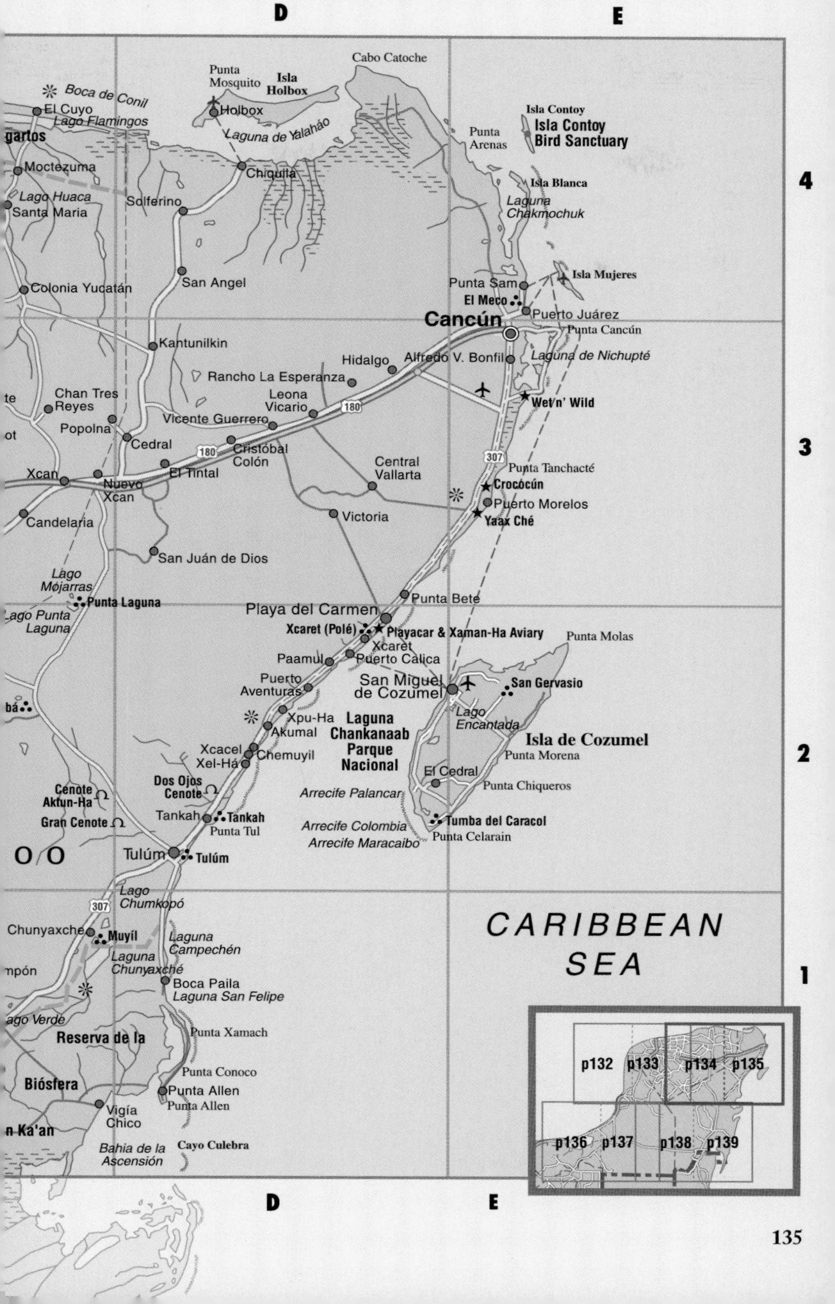

Punta Mosquito
Isla Holbox
Cabo Catoche
Boca de Conil
El Cuyo
Lago Flamingos
gartos
Holbox
Laguna de Yalaháo
Isla Contoy
Isla Contoy Bird Sanctuary
Moctezuma
Chiquilá
Punta Arenas
Lago Huaca
Santa María
Solferino
Isla Blanca
Laguna Chakmochuk

4

Colonia Yucatán
San Angel
Punta Sam
El Meco
Isla Mujeres
Puerto Juárez
Cancún
Punta Cancún
Kantunilkin
Hidalgo
Alfredo V. Bonfil
Laguna de Nichupté

te
Chan Tres Reyes
Rancho La Esperanza
Leona Vicario
180
Wet'n' Wild
Popolna
Vicente Guerrero
ot
Cedral
180
Cristóbal Colón
Central Vallarta
307
Xcan
El Tintal
Punta Tanchacté
Crococún
Nuevo Xcan
Puerto Morelos
Candelaria
Victoria
Yaax Ché

3

San Juán de Dios
Lago Mejarras
Punta Laguna
ago Punta Laguna
Punta Beté
Playa del Carmen
bá
Xcaret (Polé)
Playacar & Xaman-Ha Aviary
Xcaret
Punta Molas
Paamul
Puerto Calica
Puerto Aventuras
San Miguel de Cozumel
San Gervasio
Xpu-Ha
Akumal
Laguna Chankanaab Parque Nacional
Lago Encantada
Xcacel
Xel-Há
Chemuyil
Isla de Cozumel
Punta Morena
Cenote Aktun-Ha
Dos Ojos Cenote
El Cedral
Punta Chiqueros
Gran Cenote
Tankah
Tankah
Arrecife Palancar
O O
Punta Tul
Tulúm
Tulúm
Arrecife Colombia
Tumba del Caracol
Arrecife Maracaibo
Punta Celarain

2

Lago Chumkopó
307
Chunyaxché
Muyil
Laguna Campechén
mpón
Laguna Chunyaxché
Boca Paila
Laguna San Felipe
ago Verde

1

CARIBBEAN SEA

Reserva de la
Punta Xamach
Biósfera
Punta Conoco
Punta Allen
n Ka'an
Vigía Chico
Punta Allen
Bahía de la Ascensión
Cayo Culebra

p132 p133 p134 p135

p136 p137 p138 p139

0 5 10 15 20 25km

0 5 10 15 20 25miles

B a h í a   d e

C a m p e c h e

Huay
Estero Saba

Sabancuy

**Península
El Palmar**

San B

Puerto Real

**Isla
Cañon**

Punta
de Piedra

La Cri

Punta
Xicalango

**Ciudad del
Carmen**

180

Cerillos

Xicalango

Isla del
Carmen

Nuevo
Campechito

Puerto
Rico

Zacafal

Laguna de Términos

*Laguna
San Carlos*

*Lago
Chocajito*

Franc

Boca Palizada Vieja

Boca Chica

*Boca
Balchacah*

Lago Sitio Viejo

Pit

**Pantanos
de Centla
Biosphere
Reserve**

*Laguna
del Este*

Marentes

Balchacah

Coyoc

El C

*Laguna
El Vapor*

Buenavista

San Miguel

Palizada

Mameyal

Conquista
Campesina

Santa Elena

Jonuta

El Zapote

El Aguacatel

Paraíso Nu

La Florida

T a b a s c o

*Lago
Playa Larga*

186

La Hulería

Cuauh

Miguel
Hidalgo

Playa Larga

San
Elpidio

Villa El Triunfo

Cuidad
Pemex

Chable

La Pita

La Cucl

Tecolpan

Santa Rosa

Balancán

Moral

San

Guyo
Obregón

**Emiliano
Zapata**

Ti

Playas de
Catazajá

Netzahualcoyotl

C h i a p a s

Cacao

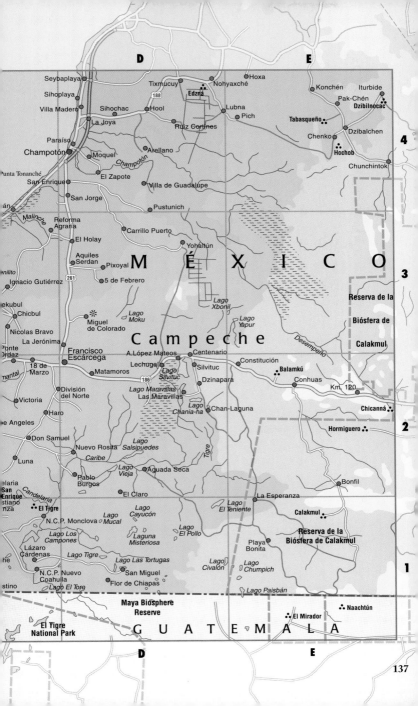

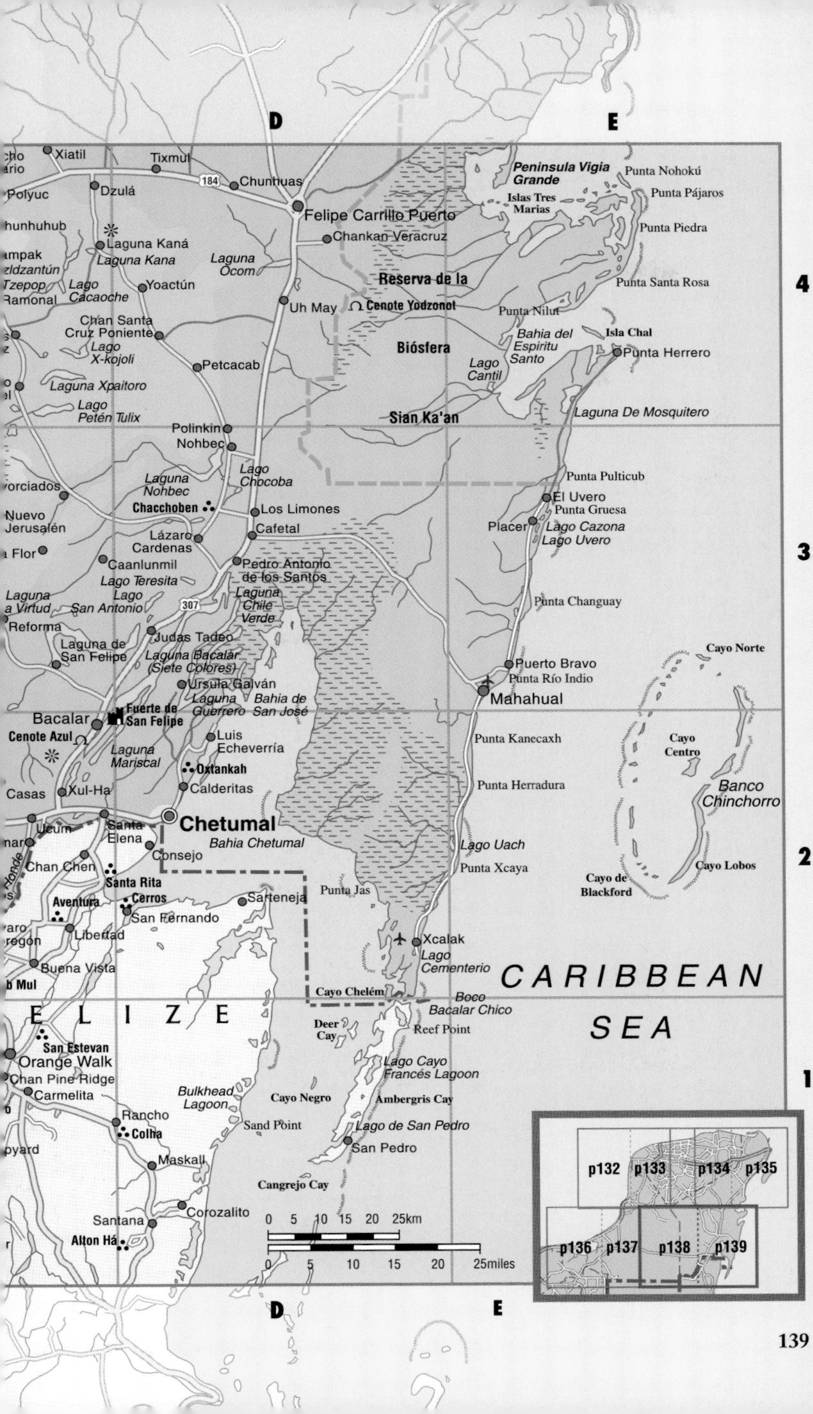
D
E
Xiatil
Tixmul
184
Chunhuas
Dzulá
Polyuc
Felipe Carrillo Puerto
Chankan Veracruz
Laguna Kaná
Laguna Kana
Laguna Ocom
Lago Cacaoche
Yoactún
Reserva de la
Uh May
Cenote Yodzonot
Biósfera
Chan Santa Cruz Poniente
Lago X-kojoli
Petcacab
Laguna Xpaitoro
Lago Petén Tulix
Sian Ka'an
Peninsula Vigia Grande
Islas Tres Marias
Punta Nohokú
Punta Pájaros
Punta Piedra
Punta Santa Rosa
Punta Nilut
Bahia del Espiritu Santo
Isla Chal
Punta Herrero
Lago Cantil
Laguna De Mosquitero
4
Polinkin
Nohbec
Lago Chocoba
Laguna Nohbec
Chacchoben
Los Limones
Nuevo Jerusalén
Lázaro Cardenas
Cafetal
Caanlunmil
Pedro Antonio de los Santos
Lago Teresita
Lago San Antonio
Laguna Chile Verde
307
Reforma
Judas Tadeo
Laguna de San Felipe
Laguna Bacalar (Siete Colores)
Ursula Galván
Punta Pulticub
El Uvero
Punta Gruesa
Placer
Lago Cazona
Lago Uvero
3
Punta Changuay
Puerto Bravo
Punta Río Indio
Mahahual
Cayo Norte
Bacalar
Fuerte de San Felipe
Laguna Guerrero
Bahia de San José
Cenote Azul
Luis Echeverría
Laguna Mariscal
Oxtankah
Calderitas
Casas
Xul-Ha
Ucum
Santa Elena
Chetumal
Bahia Chetumal
Consejo
Chan Chen
Santa Rita
Aventura
Cerros
Sarteneja
San Fernando
Libertad
Buena Vista
Punta Kanecaxh
Punta Herradura
Cayo Centro
Banco Chinchorro
Lago Uach
Punta Xcaya
Cayo Lobos
Cayo de Blackford
Punta Jas
2
Xcalak
Lago Cementerio
CARIBBEAN SEA
Cayo Chelém
Boco Bacalar Chico
Deer Cay
Reef Point
BELIZE
San Estevan
Orange Walk
Chan Pine Ridge
Carmelita
Lago Cayo Francés Lagoon
Bulkhead Lagoon
Cayo Negro
Ambergris Cay
1
Rancho
Colha
Sand Point
Lago de San Pedro
San Pedro
Maskall
Cangrejo Cay
Corozalito
Santana
Alton Há
0 5 10 15 20 25km
0 5 10 15 20 25miles
p132
p133
p134
p135
p136
p137
p138
p139

141

Index

Insight Smart Guide:
Cancún and the Yucatán

Written by: Nick Rider
Edited by: Jason Mitchell
Proofread and indexed by: Neil Titman
Photography by: Alex Havret, except
Nick Rider 3, 13B, 16, 22B, 37B, 55T,
78B, 83B/T, 85T, 96/97; Getty Images
21, 44/45, 65BC, 65BL, 65BR, 65T,
101B; Alamy 17B, 41B, 41C, 98C, 98T;
Secretaría de Turismo de Yucatán 5TR,
17T, 19BL, 21T, 43T, 48C, 68B, 71B,
72/73, 90B, 90T, 111C, 128T; Bridge-
man 20, 43B, 74B, 97B; La Zebra 5MR,
35T, 36/37, 81B; Superstock 29BL,
29BM, 29BR; Coco Bongo 30/31; Blue
Parrot 33; Photolibrary.com 40/41; Lat-
inphoto 118/119
Picture Manager: Steven Lawrence
Maps: David Priestley

Series Editor: Jason Mitchell
First Edition 2008

© 2008 Apa Publications GmbH & Co. Ver-
lag KG Singapore Branch, Singapore.
Printed in Singapore by Insight Print
Services (Pte) Ltd
Worldwide distribution enquiries:
Apa Publications GmbH & Co. Verlag KG
(Singapore Branch) 38 Joo Koon Road,
Singapore 628990; tel: (65) 6865 1600;
fax: (65) 6861 6438
Distributed in the UK and Ireland by:
GeoCenter International Ltd
Meridian House, Churchill Way West,
Basingstoke, Hampshire RG21 6YR; tel: (44
1256) 817 987; fax: (44 1256) 817 988
Distributed in the United States by:
Langenscheidt Publishers, Inc.
36–36 33rd Street 4th Floor, Long Island
City, New York 11106;

tel: (1 718) 784 0055; fax: (1 718) 784
0640l

Contacting the Editors
We would appreciate it if readers would alert
us to outdated information by writing to:
Apa Publications, PO Box 7910, London
SE1 1WE, UK; fax: (44 20) 7403 0290;
e-mail: insight@apaguide.co.uk
No part of this book may be reproduced,
stored in a retrieval system or transmitted in
any form or by any means (electronic,
mechanical, photocopying, recording or otherwise), without prior written permission of
Apa Publications. Brief text quotations with
use of photographs are exempted for book
review purposes only. Information has been
obtained from sources believed to be reliable, but its accuracy and completeness,
and the opinions based thereon, are not
guaranteed.

OVER 250 DESTINATIONS IN 14 LANGUAGES

Let us be your guide

Your first visit – or a familiar destination? A short stay – or an extended exploration? Whatever your needs, there's an Insight Guide in a format to suit you. From Alaska to Zanzibar, we'll help you discover your world with great pictures, insightful text, easy-to-use maps, and invaluable advice.

www.insightguides.com

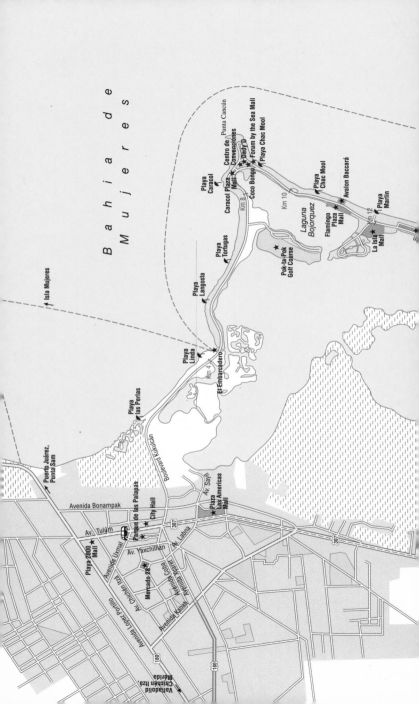